WRITING THE WAR ON TERRORISM

MANCHESTER
1824

Manchester University Press

New Approaches to
Conflict Analysis

Series editor: Peter Lawler, Senior Lecturer in
International Relations, Department of Government,
University of Manchester

Until recently, the study of conflict and conflict resolution remained comparatively immune to broad developments in social and political theory. When the changing nature and locus of large-scale conflict in the post-Cold War era is also taken into account, the case for a reconsideration of the fundamentals of conflict analysis and conflict resolution becomes all the more stark.

New Approaches to Conflict Analysis promotes the development of new theoretical insights and their application to concrete cases of large-scale conflict, broadly defined. The series intends not to ignore established approaches to conflict analysis and conflict resolution, but to contribute to the reconstruction of the field through a dialogue between orthodoxy and its contemporary critics. Equally, the series reflects the contemporary porosity of intellectual borderlines rather than simply perpetuating rigid boundaries around the study of conflict and peace. *New Approaches to Conflict Analysis* seeks to uphold the normative commitment of the field's founders yet also recognises that the moral impulse to research is properly part of its subject matter. To these ends, the series is comprised of the highest quality work of scholars drawn from throughout the international academic community, and from a wide range of disciplines within the social sciences.

PUBLISHED

Eşref Aksu
The United Nations, intra-state peacekeeping and normative change

M. Anne Brown
Human rights and the borders of suffering:
the promotion of human rights in international politics

Lorraine Elliott and Grame Cheeseman (eds)
Forces for good:
Cosmopolitan militaries in the twenty-first century

Tami Amanda Jacoby and Brent Sasley (eds)
Redefining security in the Middle East

Jan Koehler and Christoph Zürcher (eds)
Potentials of disorder

Helena Lindholm Schulz
Reconstruction of Palestinian nationalism:
between revolution and statehood

David Bruce MacDonald
Balkan holocausts?
Serbian and Croatian victim-centred propaganda and the war in Yugoslavia

Jennifer Milliken
The social construction of the Korean War

Ami Pedahzur
The Israeli response to Jewish extremism and violence:
defending democracy

Tarja Väyrynen
Culture and international conflict resolution:
a critical analysis of the work of John Burton

Writing the war
on terrorism

Language, politics
and counter-terrorism

RICHARD JACKSON

Manchester University Press

MANCHESTER AND NEW YORK

distributed exclusively in the USA
by Palgrave

Published by Manchester University Press
Oxford Road, Manchester M13 9NR, UK
and Room 400, 175 Fifth Avenue, New York, NY 10010, USA
www.manchesteruniversitypress.co.uk

Distributed exclusively in the USA by
Palgrave, 175 Fifth Avenue, New York,
NY 10010, USA

Distributed exclusively in Canada by
UBC Press, University of British Columbia, 2029 West Mall,
Vancouver, BC, Canada V6T 1Z2

British Library Cataloguing-in-Publication Data
A catalogue record for this book is available from the British Library

Library of Congress Cataloging-in-Publication Data applied for

ISBN	0 7190 7120 8	*hardback*
EAN	978 0 7190 7120 1	
ISBN	0 7190 7121 6	*paperback*
EAN	978 0 7190 7121 8	

First published 2005

14 13 12 11 10 09 08 07 06 05   10 9 8 7 6 5 4 3 2 1

Typeset
by Helen Skelton, Brighton, UK
Printed in Great Britain
by CPI, Bath

Contents

Acknowledgements

There are several reasons why I wanted to write this book. As a scholar, I was anxious to understand the momentous events that were transpiring around me. In particular, I was curious about the kinds of language and knowledge that necessarily underpin such a massive amount of political and military activity; at the very least, going to war requires a major degree of social and political consensus – which is only possible through the deployment of language. It was a disappointment to find that apart from one or two notable exceptions little attention had been paid to the role of language and discourse in the construction of the 'war on terrorism'. I therefore felt it incumbent to embark upon my own study. As a teacher, I wanted to write a book that my students and my friends could understand. Too often, books about the role of language are written from a deeply theoretical perspective and employ a level of specialised jargon that makes their important message inaccessible to the majority of readers. I did not want to write about the language of the 'war on terrorism' solely for other specialists in the field – the subject matter is far too important to be confined to the ivory towers. Finally, as a citizen and concerned individual I wanted to contribute to the crucial debate about how society should respond to political violence and whether even greater counter-violence is a sufficient answer. If nothing else, my hope is that this book will in some way help to stimulate genuinely substantive discussions, dissent, arguments, questioning and controversy – the stuff of real politics and something all too rare these days. It is never too late to reclaim the political space for genuine dialogue, even that which has been lost to the suffocating atmosphere of anxiety and acquiescence engendered by myopic leaders and a subservient press. It only requires that we rigorously interrogate every word spoken in public, we learn to abhor hypocrisy, we open our ears to alternative voices and stories and we adopt an attitude of principled scepticism to authority.

Writing a book, like raising a child or building a house, requires a community, and I would not have been able to complete this book without the assistance and comradeship of the following people. Inderjeet Parmar, a friend and colleague at the Centre for International Politics at the University of Manchester, not only showed me what a real scholar should be – meticulous, intellectually honest and politically responsible – he also took the time to read drafts of my chapters and offer excellent suggestions for improvements. Jan Hancock and Randal Hall also proved to be true friends by reading a draft of the book and offering their considered insights. The departmental Research Colloquium, organised by Stuart Shields, provided a forum where I first presented my ideas; its able members offered real encouragement and constructive criticism. I am extremely grateful to Stuart Shields, Ilan Danjoux, Sophie Hague, Lucy Ferguson, Helen Dexter, Jonathan Gilmour, Simona Rentea and Greig Charnock. The students in my graduate course 'The Discourses of Terrorism' also taught and inspired me with their enthusiasm for the subject.

Other members of the Department of Government at the University of Manchester gave me advice and encouragement when I needed it. Peter Lawler, executive series editor, first suggested that I submit my proposal to Manchester University Press and then took the time to read a draft of the manuscript; his mentoring, encouragement and advocacy on my behalf have been indispensable to my first years in the department. I am also indebted to Simon Bulmer, David Farrell, Paul Cammack, Rorden Wilkinson and Adrian Jarvis for advice and assistance in matters relating to my research programme. Victoria Rees and Karen Charters were instrumental in giving me time to complete the manuscript by dealing with numerous administrative chores.

I also want to express my appreciation to those critical voices among the intellectual community and the wider global civil society that have grasped the nettle and demonstrated the courage to question accepted wisdom and challenge the discourses of the powerful. They are true examples of the role that intellectuals should play in society. Joseba Zulaika and William Douglass's work remains, in my mind, the defining text on the discourses of terrorism (Zulaika and Douglass 1996). It was their book that most influenced my thinking on the subject and in an ideal world it would be required reading for every class on terrorism and political violence. Other contemporary writers who have inspired and influenced me and whose works deserve to be widely read include: David Campbell; Rahul Mahajan; Noam Chomsky; Paul Rogers; Ziauddin Sardar; James Der Derian; John Pilger; Robert Fisk; Arundhati Roy; Howard Zinn; John Gray; David Cole; and Michael Moore. Of course, these are only some of the most well-known authors in this great band of political critics; sagacious voices are all around, even if they are less well known.

Finally, I must thank the members of my whanau, the community of friends, family and colleagues who have stood with me in good times and bad; it is the company of a supportive whanau that gives life its vibrant colours and deep joys. My parents, David and Kathryn Wells, first taught me to pursue wisdom and seek knowledge; this lesson has led me down one of life's greatest pathways and I am eternally grateful. The other members of this extended family to whom I owe a debt of gratitude include: the Allans, the Gilmours, the Redpaths, the Painters, the Thompsons, Paul and Coral Bramley, Rachel, Fiona, Alan, Wendy and Bruce Jackson, Robert Jarvis, Mary Hay, Sophie Broad, Stephen and Feni Hamlin and my brothers Steven Wells and D. J. Wells and their families, Jacob Bercovitch, Robert Patman, and Chris and Manami Rudd. Special mention must go to Martin Taylor, a true friend, a great fishing companion and the most loyal opposition a man could ask for.

My deepest thanks however, go to my wife Michelle, who first suggested that I study terrorism, and who motivated me to write more like an ordinary person and less like an academic. Her enthusiasm to learn about contemporary political issues is a real inspiration. She also put up with prolonged periods of inattention while I was writing and applied her unrivalled editorial skills to the final manuscript, going well beyond the call of duty and making suggestions that vastly improved the final text. More importantly, she has supported me like no other throughout my career and I would not be where I am today without her. In large part, I wrote this book for her.

As usual, all mistakes, misconceptions, omissions and opinions expressed in this work are solely my own, and I apologise to anyone I may have forgotten to thank.

Hohou rongo.

Introduction:
language and politics

In private I observed that once in every generation, without fail, there is an episode of hysteria about the barbarians. (J.M. Coetzee, *Waiting for the Barbarians*)

THIS BOOK IS ABOUT the public language of the 'war on terrorism' and the way in which language has been deployed to justify and normalise a global campaign of counter-terrorism. The enactment of any large-scale project of political violence – such as war or counter-terrorism – requires a significant degree of political and social consensus and consensus is not possible without language. For a government to commit enormous amounts of public resources and risk the lives of its citizens in a military conflict, it has to persuade society that such an undertaking is necessary, desirable and achievable. In addition, governments have to regularise and institutionalise the practice of war, especially when it appears likely to last for many years. The authorities have to make it seem reasonable and unquestionable because once public consensus begins to break down and large sectors of society start to doubt the necessity or rightness of the conflict, as occurred during the latter stages of the Vietnam War, it becomes extremely difficult to sustain. The process of inducing consent – of normalising the practice of the war – therefore requires more than just propaganda or 'public diplomacy'; it actually requires the construction of a whole new language, or a kind of public narrative, that manufactures approval while simultaneously suppressing individual doubts and wider political protest. It requires the remaking of the world and the creation of a new and unquestioned reality in which the application of state violence appears normal and reasonable.

In this book I explain how the public language of the American administration has been used to construct a whole new world for its citizens. Through a carefully constructed public discourse, officials have created a new social reality where terrorism threatens to destroy everything that ordinary people hold dear – their lives, their democracy, their freedom, their way of life,

1

their civilisation. In this new reality, diabolical and insane terrorists plot to rain down weapons of mass destruction across western cities, while heroic warriors of freedom risk their lives in foreign lands to save innocent and decent folk back home; good battles evil and civilisation itself stands against the dark forces of barbarism. Within the confines of this rhetorically constructed reality, or discourse, the 'war on terrorism' appears as a rational and reasonable response; more importantly, to many people it feels like the right thing to do. In this way, the *language* of the 'war on terrorism' normalises and reifies the *practice* of the 'war on terrorism'; it comes to be accepted as part of the way things naturally are and should be. Language and practice, in other words, reinforce each either – they co-constitute the reality of counter-terrorism.

This book has two primary goals. First, it seeks to explore the nature of the overarching narrative or story of the 'war on terrorism': its main themes and appeals, its forms and expressions and the kinds of cultural and political myths that it encompasses. It examines the language that officials in the Bush administration have used to explain to the American (and global) public why the war was necessary in the first place, who the enemy is, what kind of threat they pose and why the war will succeed. Second, it explains how the language of the 'war on terrorism' has become the dominant political paradigm in American foreign policy since September 11, 2001, and the different kinds of reality-making affects that the adoption of this language has. It describes how the official language of counter-terrorism has been reproduced and amplified across society, and the impact this has had on American political life.

The overall argument is fairly simple: the language of the 'war on terrorism' is not simply an objective or neutral reflection of reality; nor is it merely accidental or incidental. It is not the only way to talk and think about counter-terrorism. Rather, it is a deliberately and meticulously composed set of words, assumptions, metaphors, grammatical forms, myths and forms of knowledge – it is a carefully constructed *discourse* – that is designed to achieve a number of key political goals: to normalise and legitimise the current counter-terrorist approach; to empower the authorities and shield them from criticism; to discipline domestic society by marginalising dissent or protest; and to enforce national unity by reifying a narrow conception of national identity. The discourse of the 'war on terrorism' has a clear *political* purpose; it works for someone and for something; it is an exercise of power.

This book also argues that to a great extent, this project of rhetorically constructing a massive counter-terrorism campaign has been highly successful; the 'war on terrorism' is now the dominant political narrative in America, enjoying widespread bipartisan and public support. Individuals and social actors from across the spectrum now speak the language of the 'war on terrorism' and accept its assumptions, its forms of knowledge and its policy prescriptions; and those who oppose it are largely ignored, silenced and excluded from the policy debate. Even more critically, the 'war on terrorism' is embedded into the institutions and practice of national security and law enforcement, the legal system, the legislative and executive processes and increasingly, the wider political culture; it is now fully institutionalised and normalised. From this perspective, the outcome of the American presidential race in November 2004 was inconsequential; the 'war on terrorism' has taken on a life of its own and any administration would find it extremely difficult to unmake or alter to any significant degree, even if they wanted to. In either case, it is fairly clear that the Democrats are just as eager to pursue and expand the 'war on terrorism' as the Republicans, if not more so. John Kerry, for example, stated in 2004 that the 'war on terrorism' needed to be refocused on other terror-supporting states and reoriented to include greater international cooperation, not that it should be completely reformulated. Thus it is highly unlikely that the troops in Afghanistan and Iraq will be brought home any time soon, or the defence budget slashed, or the USA Patriot Act repealed or the Department of Homeland Security disbanded. The architecture of the campaign is firmly established; although it has taken a relatively short time to construct, the 'war on terrorism' is going to be with us for a long time to come.

There are therefore, a number of reasons why this is a critical subject for inquiry. In the first instance, the 'war on terrorism' is more than just a passing phase of American foreign policy; it is actually the most profound conflict since the cold war and it has already made an indelible mark on both international relations and the domestic politics of most countries. Its effects are horizontal and vertical, penetrating outwards towards other states and inwards into the belly of domestic politics. Its impacts can be clearly seen in security, policing, foreign policy, the legislative process, immigration, banking, travel, the media, race relations, popular culture, education, health and sport – to name just a few. Clearly, no country or people can remain immune from its effects. It is vitally important that we understand such a profound transformation of global interactions, if for no other reason than so we can retain some control over its potential outcomes.

Second, and of greater consequence, the deployment of language by politicians is an exercise of power and without rigorous public interrogation and critical examination, unchecked power inevitably becomes abusive. This is never more true than during times of national crisis when the authorities assume enhanced powers to deal with perceived threats; unfortunately, the abuse of state power under the banner of the 'war on terrorism' is already well advanced – from the unconstitutional powers to try 'enemy combatants' in secret courts to the manipulation of intelligence information about Iraq and the unconstitutional violation of civil liberties in America and elsewhere. The systematic and institutionalised abuse of Iraqi prisoners first exposed in April 2004 is a direct consequence of the language used by senior administration officials: conceiving of terrorist suspects as 'evil', 'inhuman' and 'faceless enemies of freedom' (and with hoods on they really are faceless) creates the atmosphere where abuses become normalised and tolerated. There is therefore, an urgent need to cross-examine and scrutinise the language of political leaders, to challenge what they say, rather than just passively and uncritically absorb it.

In a related sense, this is a critical subject for inquiry because the threat of political violence in all its forms – terrorism, counter-terrorism, war, insurgency, revolution, ethnic cleansing – is real and pervasive and we need to discover genuine solutions that go beyond the reflexive application of massive counter-violence. Unless we acquire a proper understanding of the nature of terrorism, the reasons why people are willing to kill themselves and others in pursuit of political goals, and the dangers and consequences of violent forms of counter-terrorism (such as the moral hazard of becoming terrorists ourselves through the abuse of suspects and prisoners), there is a genuine risk that we will end up worse off than when we started; that through misplaced and misguided policies we will make the world a more violent and unjust place, instead of making it safer and more stable. Terrorism is a complex problem; it will require a complex solution based on clear thinking, informed analysis and realistic assessment.

One of my key concerns in writing this book is that the language of the 'war on terrorism' actually *prevents* rather than facilitates the search for solutions to political violence; that it actually encourages terrorism and increases the risk to vulnerable populations; that it is entrenching cycles of global violence which will be extremely difficult to break; and that it misunderstands and misinterprets the nature of terrorist violence thereby handicapping the counter-terrorist campaign before it has even started. My purpose is not to engage in a critique of American foreign policy or simply to blame America for its own problems; rather, it is to assist the search for genuine and lasting solutions to the problem of political violence. I believe that it is only through a careful and systematic interrogation of the discourse that we can go back to 'ground zero' as it were – the beginning – and start to think clearly about the problem. And it is only by finding a new language of counter-terrorism – one that illuminates rather than obfuscates – that we can imagine (and perhaps build) a better world than this.

Overview of the chapters

In Chapter 1, 'Analysing the language of counter-terrorism', I begin by providing a brief overview of the practice of the 'war on terrorism' – its military, legal, intelligence and diplomatic dimensions. I then set the scene for the book's central analysis by explaining why the language of politics is so important – why words matter – and the main methodological approach that I have employed for analysing the language of counter-terrorism, namely, critical discourse analysis. The core of the book however, lies in Chapters 2 through 5 where I examine in

4

some detail the actual words used by senior administration officials to describe the purpose and progress of the 'war on terrorism'.

Chapter 2, 'Writing September 11, 2001', starts by examining the language employed to describe and explain the terrorist attacks. I argue that the words chosen to describe these events were not simply a neutral reflection of what had happened, but actually worked to enforce a particular interpretation and meaning, most significantly that they were an 'act of war'. This politically constructed understanding of the events normalised the administration's response; because it was an 'act of war', a 'war on terrorism' appeared reasonable and logical. This war-based approach was reinforced by embedding the narrative of September 11, 2001 within larger meta-narratives about Pearl Harbor and World War II, the cold war, civilisation versus barbarism and the advance of globalisation. In large part, the purpose of the language was to prevent any interpretation that implicated American foreign policy.

Chapter 3, 'Writing identity: evil terrorists and good Americans', focuses on the way in which language was deployed to construct the main identities of the protagonists; how the terrorists – 'enemy aliens' – were created as evildoers, savages and barbarians, cruel and inhuman, while Americans were constructed as innocent, decent, kind, loving, peaceful, united and heroic. The function of this language is to establish clear boundary markers between 'them' and 'us' – between citizens and aliens, foreign and domestic, inside and outside. Simultaneously, it functions to demonise and dehumanise the enemy to such an extent that any counter-violence towards them appears acceptable and proportionate. This language is the real origin of the prisoner abuse scandal that engulfed the administration in April 2004; encouraging soldiers and prison guards to speak and think of their enemies as 'evil', 'savages' and 'animals' led directly to the kinds of institutionalised mistreatment displayed in the Abu Ghraib photos.

Chapter 4, 'Writing threat and danger', demonstrates how terrorism is rhetorically constructed as posing a catastrophic threat to the American 'way of life' – to freedom, liberty and democracy and even to civilisation itself. It explores how the terrorists are made out to be incredibly sophisticated, ruthless and numerous; how they hide in communities – the perennial 'enemy within' – where they plot evil; and how so-called 'rogue states' want to provide terrorists with weapons of mass destruction so that they can kill millions of Americans. When the 'reality' of such a massive threat becomes widely accepted as true, a defensive war seems like a purely rational and reasonable response. The truth is for the last thirty-five years terrorism has resulted in no more than about 7,000 fatalities per year for the entire world, even including the year 2001. This is a fraction of the deaths caused by 'ordinary' crime (there are 10,000 gun murders per year in America alone), which in turn, is dwarfed by the fatalities attributed to automobile accidents, disease, natural disasters and even suicide. This chapter examines how such a minor form of criminal activity which poses a miniscule risk to personal safety – statistically, there is a greater chance of choking to death on one's lunch than of dying in a terrorist attack – has come to be accepted as the single greatest threat to western societies.

In Chapter 5, 'Writing the good (new) war on terrorism', I analyse how the administration's counter-terrorism campaign has been rhetorically constructed as an essentially 'good' and 'just war', similar to America's role in World War II. Administration officials have argued that it fits all of the criteria of a just war: it has a just cause, it is purely defensive, it is a last resort, it is conducted with due care for innocent civilians and it is clearly winnable. Meanwhile, to avoid creating the impression that terrorists are like all other enemy soldiers, officials have had to remake the 'war on terrorism' as a 'new' and 'different' kind of war. This designation allows them to ignore the Geneva Conventions and preventively detain them as 'enemy combatants' instead.

In Chapter 6, 'Language and power: reproducing the discourse', I survey some of the overall features of the language of the 'war on terrorism' – its strategies, its continuities with previous wars against terrorism by presidents Reagan and Clinton, its use of popular myths, its gendered language and its success within society. I also examine the ways in which the language has been reproduced and augmented across American politics and society. I argue that other important social actors such as the media, academic institutions, think-tanks and religious leaders have been instrumental in amplifying the official language, with the result that the 'war on terrorism' is now the pre-eminent foreign policy paradigm in American politics; even the opposition Democrats have adopted its language and assumptions.

Finally, in the Conclusion, 'Politics, violence and resistance', I explore the dangers of the 'war on terrorism', particularly the manner in which it destabilises the moral community – by making violence, torture and human rights abuses acceptable and 'normal' – the means by which it damages the functioning of democratic politics – by imposing unity and demonising dissent – and the ways in which it is making global terrorism worse. I conclude that responsible citizens have a moral duty to oppose and resist the official language of counter-terrorism, not least because it prevents the possibility of finding alternative counter-terrorism policies that are likely to be more effective and which do not involve simply applying greater counter-violence. Throughout the book, my aim is ultimately to advance the search for genuine, long-lasting solutions to the problem of political violence.

A note on transcription conventions

For the sake of clarity, some words in the texts of official speeches have been emboldened to indicate the basis of claims and analyses. I have also made no attempt to correct the primary texts of any errors, preferring instead to present the language as it was actually used. In popular usage, the attacks of September 11, 2001 have been shortened to 'September 11' or even to '9-11'. Such practices are neither natural nor without consequences; rather, the effect is to erase the history and context of the events and turn their representation into a cultural-political icon where the meaning of the date becomes both assumed and open to manipulation (see Chapter 2). In this book I deliberately resist this mythologising practice and use the full date as often as possible to maintain a sense of concrete history. Also, the 'war on terrorism' is often used interchangeably with the 'war on terror' or the 'war against terror/terrorism' by officials and commentators. I have preferred to use the former term in this book; in any case, these expressions all refer to the foreign and domestic efforts by America and its allies to fight terrorism around the world, as well as to the corpus of official language about terrorism and counter-terrorism. Quotation marks around the designation 'war on terrorism' have been employed throughout the book to indicate its special and artificial quality; I did not want to contribute to its normalisation by leaving it undistinguished in the text.

In the Appendix I have reproduced a number of key speeches and interviews so that readers can examine for themselves a few of the most important official texts of the 'war on terrorism' in their entirety. This allows for a first-hand observation of how the discourse is constructed in individual speech acts, how different discursive strategies are employed in the same text and how different narratives are woven together to create powerful hybrid rhetorical constructions. Additionally, the reader will be able to see how the rhetorical themes and strategies are maintained and sustained across different speakers and speeches. It should be noted that the examples of the language used by officials in the following chapters represent only a small illustrative sample of literally hundreds of identical cases. The speeches in the Appendix are therefore, a substitute for the marshalling of large amounts of evidence.

1

Analysing the language of counter-terrorism

T HE 'WAR ON TERRORISM' is the most extensive counter-terrorist campaign in history and the most important conflict since the fall of the Berlin Wall. Its scope and expenditure of resources are so great that in a few years it could soon rival the cold war. In trying to make sense of this new historical era, there is a temptation to focus solely on its most visible aspects: the wars in Afghanistan and Iraq; the strategic dimensions of American oil policy; the operation and organisation of terrorist cells around the world; international security cooperation between nations; the fate of prisoners at Guantanamo Bay; the legal dimensions of counter-terrorism; new homeland security measures such as law-enforcement cooperation and immigration control; and the Bush administration's 'public diplomacy' initiative in the Middle East. What many observers fail to appreciate is that the construction of a military and political project on this scale – one that simultaneously extends externally over the entire globe and at the same time penetrates inwardly into almost every aspect of domestic life – could not be initiated or sustained without widespread public consent or at least acquiescence. Nor would it be achievable without an overarching rationale or a set of guiding assumptions, beliefs and forms of knowledge about the nature of terrorism and counter-terrorism. Ultimately, all this activity would not be possible without the deployment of language; at the very least, the institutions which put government policies into practice, and to a lesser degree the wider society, have to be convinced both of its necessity and its likelihood of success.

The 'war on terrorism' therefore, is simultaneously a set of actual practices – wars, covert operations, agencies and institutions – and an accompanying series of assumptions, beliefs, justifications and narratives – it is an entire language or discourse. At the most basic level, the *practice* of counter-terrorism is predicated on and determined by the *language* of counter-terrorism. The language of counter-terrorism incorporates a series of assumptions, beliefs and knowledge about the nature of terrorism and terrorists. These beliefs then determine what

8

kinds of counter-terrorism practices are reasonable or unreasonable, appropriate or inappropriate: if terrorists are assumed to be inherently evil, for example, then eradicating them appears apposite while negotiating with them appears absurd. The actual practice of counter-terrorism gives concrete expression to the language of counter-terrorism – in effect, it turns the initial words into reality. Language and practice, in other words, are inextricably linked; they mutually reinforce each other; together they co-constitute social and political reality. For this reason, understanding the language of counter-terrorism is essential for a fully informed understanding of the 'war on terrorism'. Unfortunately, apart from some notable exceptions (see Collins and Glover 2002; Murphy 2003; Silberstein 2002; Zulaika and Douglass 1996), studies on the language of counter-terrorism are few and far between. This book seeks to fill this gap through a systematic and critical analysis of the main features and aspects of the language of the 'war on terrorism'.

In this chapter, I establish the foundation for the overall study by first of all providing a brief overview of the primary concrete or tangible dimensions of the 'war on terrorism' – how it has been practiced and institutionalised in international relations and American domestic life – , as well as its main rhetorical or linguistic components. Second, and more critically, I explain why the analysis of language is so crucial to the understanding of political events – or, why words matter in political analysis. Finally, I explain the main method or approach that I have applied in the study and what I hope to achieve in the rest of the book.

The practice of the 'war on terrorism'

The most visible (and controversial) practice of the 'war on terrorism' has been its military dimension, namely, the construction of a global military campaign involving two major wars, covert assassinations, foreign military assistance programmes and the expansion of America's military presence into new regions. As one American military official put it: 'There should be no doubt, we are at war, and it is **a world war**. There is simply no other name for it' (Melshen, 27 June, 2003). This global military campaign or 'world war' began in the first hours after the September 11, 2001 attacks when President George W. Bush declared on prime-time television that America was launching a 'war against terrorism' (Bush, 11 September, 2001b). The military was put on full alert and just a few weeks later on October 7, 2001 Afghanistan was attacked; the campaign was called 'Operation Enduring Freedom'. In the following nine weeks, 14,000 tons of bombs were dropped on Afghanistan; the most conservative estimates suggest that between 2,969 and 3,413 civilians were killed, and 4,000 to 6,000 Taliban and Arab soldiers died (Herold 2002: 216, 226, 228; see also Hiro 2002). Other observers believe the figures could be much higher. American and British forces

9

lost more than a dozen soldiers in the initial ground invasion, but more than two-and-a-half years later Coalition troops continued to be killed regularly in renewed attacks and counter-terrorism operations. As of September 2004, more than 130 American soldiers had died in Operation Enduring Freedom (see www.Antiwar.com). As usual, many times these numbers of civilians and Afghan soldiers were maimed and injured over this period. At the time of writing, Afghan civilians and government soldiers continue to be killed by unexploded ordinance, in fighting between warlords, in renewed insurgency by remnants of the Taliban, in terrorist attacks and in general lawlessness and criminal activity. It is clear that the Afghanistan conflict is far from over and a long counter-insurgency campaign is only just beginning. Explaining this action, President Bush said that 'Afghanistan is the first overseas front in this war against terror' (Bush, 29 November, 2001).

In March 2003, a second and much larger military front in the 'war against terrorism' – code-named 'Operation Iraqi Freedom' – was launched with a massive aerial bombing campaign on Iraq; soon after, nearly 300,000 mainly American and British ground troops invaded from Kuwait. The Second Gulf War (an earlier war against Iraq having taken place in 1991) resulted in the deaths of more than 10,000 civilians, and perhaps as many as 15,000 Iraqi military personnel; America and Britain lost more than 100 soldiers in the initial assault. Since the toppling of the regime and the announcement of the end of major combat operations in May 2003 however, the occupation of Iraq has turned into a brutal and widespread guerrilla war. In late 2004, Iraq was the central military focus of the 'war on terrorism' with Coalition forces coming under attack twenty to thirty times per day across the country. Roadside ambushes, suicide car bombings and guerrilla-style attacks on the occupying Coalition forces continued to kill and injure dozens of soldiers every week throughout 2004. As of September 2004, the casualty figures for Coalition forces were over 1,000 killed, most of them American, and as many as 12,000 injured (Iraq Coalition Casualty Count; see also www.antiwar.com). In addition, nearly 1,000 Iraqi civilians were being killed every week in civil disturbances and rioting, accidental shootings by Coalition forces, assaults on insurgent forces, suicide bombings and attacks on Iraqis who cooperated with the Coalition forces, criminal activity and the effects of unexploded ordinance. It is estimated that by late 2004 anywhere up to 55,000 Iraqis had died in the conflict (Pilger 2004). Meanwhile, given the military situation in the country, the unwillingness of other countries to get involved and failure to achieve any of the key political objectives behind the invasion (such as establishing a free, democratic and effective government) the conflict seems likely to continue for several more years.

In addition to these two major wars, America has also attacked and killed terrorist suspects in a number of covert military operations, such as the operation that took place in Yemen in 2002 where an unmanned aerial vehicle destroyed a car carrying an al Qaeda suspect and four companions. Direct military operations in pursuit of militants and terrorist suspects by Special Forces have also been conducted in Pakistan, Georgia and the Philippines. Another aspect of the military dimensions of the 'war on terrorism' has been the reinvigoration of large foreign military assistance programmes to partner states deemed to be fighting their own wars on terrorism or who directly assist America's war – such as Indonesia, Colombia, the Philippines, Uzbekistan and Pakistan. In fact, the level of cooperation with America's 'war on terrorism' has now become the main criteria for determining overseas aid packages. America has also used the 'war on terrorism' to further expand its global military presence, particularly in strategic regions such as the Middle East and Central Asia. Apart from its ongoing occupations of Afghanistan and Iraq, the Pentagon has revealed that since September 11, 2001 military tent cities have sprung up at thirteen locations in nine countries neighbouring Afghanistan; more than 60,000 US military personnel now live and work at these forward bases (Mahajan 2002: 62–3).

The military dimension of the 'war on terrorism' is predicated on a new approach to security called the 'Bush Doctrine' in which America reserves for itself the right to attack any country that it believes to be supporting terrorists who might threaten American interests (see Callinicos 2003; Mahajan 2003). This is known as 'pre-emptive self-defence' and it involves a profound rewriting of the internationally accepted laws of war. Whereas in the past states were bound only to attack other states when they were directly threatened and in immediate danger, this new doctrine purports to allow countries to attack each other if they suspect that future terrorist attacks are being planned or even if terrorists are simply being given sanctuary. Critics argue that in practice, this new doctrine amounts to 'preventive' rather than 'pre-emptive' war. The distinction is crucial because pre-emptive strikes are legal under international law, whereas preventive attacks are a recognised war crime. In any case, the potential for the further destabilisation of the international system is obvious, especially given the large number of insurgencies and terrorist campaigns presently under way around the globe. For instance, it is not inconceivable that using this same doctrine, Russia could attack Georgia or other former Soviet Republics for allowing Chechen 'terrorists' to operate from their territory; India and Pakistan could attack each other for aiding Kashmiri militants; Rwanda could attack any number of its neighbours for harbouring Hutu militiamen; and Turkey could attack bordering states like Syria and Iran in its war against Kurdish insurgents.

Less public, but no less important, the 'war on terrorism' also has a major security dimension involving a worldwide intelligence-gathering exercise; increased cooperation with foreign security agencies; presidential authorisation to employ any means necessary including deadly force, breaking into facilities to obtain information and robust interrogation (torture); the launch of psychological operations (psych-ops); major increases in the budgets and

11

personnel of the security services; and a massive rendition programme – the capturing or snatching of terrorist suspects on foreign soil. This is the CIA's 'secret global war on terror' (see Woodward 2002: 74–8). As a result, and in cooperation with law-enforcement agencies in dozens of countries, the United States arrested as many as 3,000 terrorist suspects in a series of operations across more than forty countries from America to Afghanistan and Pakistan to The Gambia. By late 2004 around 600 detainees were being held prisoner at American military facilities in Guantanamo Bay, Cuba; others were incarcerated at military bases in Afghanistan and Iraq, in foreign countries and in America itself. This programme resulted – at least in the short term – in a significant increase in America's ability to collect information, as key intelligence agencies in the Middle East and elsewhere were effectively 'bought' through the provision of training, new equipment and money.

At the same time, George Tenet, the former CIA chief, admitted that the CIA was working closely with services who have dreadful human rights records and regularly employ torture to gain confessions (Woodward 2002: 76–7). Of course, both the American military and intelligence services have also directly employed torture and abusive interrogation methods against suspected terrorists and militants in Iraq, Afghanistan, Cuba and elsewhere. It is alleged that Secretary of Defense Donald Rumsfeld officially sanctioned a secret programme of global intelligence gathering that was to include torture and 'any means necessary'. This is perhaps why it took until April 2004 and the release of damaging photographs of prisoner abuse by US soldiers for President Bush to publicly condemn the torture and mistreatment of detainees as un-American; the president of Amnesty International had previously called on the president to renounce the use of torture as a method of interrogation in early 2002. Another unsavoury feature of the security dimension of the campaign was the use of American intelligence to spy on UN Secretary General Kofi Annan in the lead up to the Gulf War – as revealed by an MI6 whistleblower. The 'secret war on terrorism' is a no-holds-barred affair.

The diplomatic dimension of the 'war on terrorism' includes the effort to build a worldwide coalition against terror, attempts to force the United Nations to authorise the use of force against Iraq (sometimes using outright bribery or subtle coercion to force members of the Security Council to vote in support of American plans), the use of foreign aid programmes to enlist the support of poor countries, increased funding for the National Endowment for Democracy to promote American values in the Middle East and most importantly, a major 'public diplomacy' initiative. Under the *Freedom Promotion Act of 2002*, the Secretary of State was instructed to 'make public diplomacy an integral component in the planning and execution of United States foreign policy' (quoted in Rampton and Stauber 2003: 10). With a budget running into hundreds of millions of dollars and under the direction of a top advertising executive, this 'public diplomacy' exercise involved broadcasting pro-American television and radio programmes into the Middle East, massive advertising campaigns, travelling exhibitions, cultural exchanges, training programmes for foreign journalists, websites and new communications offices around the world where senior officials monitor and respond to local media stories (see Van Ham 2003). The aim was to try to improve the negative public image of America and undercut anti-Americanism, particularly in the Middle East.

The ripple effects of this global military and diplomatic offensive have been felt in nearly every country in the world. Since September 11, 2001, most countries have introduced new legislation to combat terrorism, and have allocated greatly increased resources to agencies tasked with security – the military, police, intelligence and prison services. In almost every case, these new laws greatly increase the powers of the security agencies, allow for the detention of suspects without trial and widen the definition of the kinds of activities that fall under the rubric of terrorism. Some countries have adopted the language of the 'war on terrorism' to describe their own fight against internal insurgents and dissidents, notably Russia, India, China, Zimbabwe, the Philippines, Colombia and Israel. Linking rebels and dissidents at home to the global 'war on terrorism' gives these governments both the freedom to crack down on them without fear of international condemnation, and in some cases, direct military assistance from America. A number of human rights organisations have noted an increase in human rights violations under the new legislation; Amnesty International has concluded that the 'war on terrorism' has actually made the world more dangerous by curbing human rights, undermining international law and shielding governments from scrutiny (Amnesty International 2004). All over the globe, but most notably in Europe and North America, there has also been an increase in violence and ill-treatment towards asylum seekers and immigrants, many of whom also face harsher treatment from officials and more stringent rules of entry.

In addition to these international dimensions, the 'war on terrorism' has had an equally important domestic front. This domestic campaign against terrorism has also involved a massive investment of resources and personnel – new legislation has been enacted, new departments and agencies have been created, new national strategies have been developed and new federal and local programmes have been initiated. Within a few months of September 11, 2001, the activity of these new laws, agencies and programmes had already culminated in the arrest and preventive detention of more than 1,200 mainly Muslim suspects across America. Here, I briefly explain some of the most important domestic dimensions of the counter-terrorism campaign.

A few weeks after the September 11, 2001 attacks and in record time, the American government passed the *Uniting and Strengthening of America to Provide Appropriate Tools Required to Intercept and Obstruct Terrorism Act of 2001 – The USA*

Patriot Act. This major piece of legislation amounts to 342 pages and covers 350 subject areas. It also encompasses forty federal agencies and carries twenty-one legal amendments (see Thomas 2002: 94). Apart from its name being deliberately designed to insinuate that anyone who opposes it must be unpatriotic, its most important provisions include: (1) increased powers for government surveillance, including federal law-enforcement access to private medical, financial, educational and business records; (2) the enhancement of electronic surveillance authority, such as tapping into e-mail, electronic address books and computers; (3) the use of 'roving wiretaps' by investigators which permit the surveillance of an individual's telephone conversations on any phone anywhere in the country; (4) the use of nationwide (instead of local) search warrants; (5) powers to view bank records; (6) the detention of immigrants without charge for up to one week on suspicion of supporting terrorism; (7) the deportation of immigrants who raise money for designated or suspected terrorist organisations; and (8) the Secretary of State is empowered to designate any group, foreign or domestic, as 'terrorist', and this decision is not subject to review. The Act also creates a new crime, 'domestic terrorism', which includes 'activities that involve acts dangerous to human life that are a violation of the criminal law, if it appears to be intended (i) to intimidate or coerce a civilian population; (ii) to influence the policy of government by intimidation or coercion; or (iii) to affect the conduct of government by mass destruction, assassination or kidnapping' (Thomas 2002: 95–6). Obviously, these provisions have major implications for national law enforcement, the legal system and civil liberties; this Act is the most extensive overhaul of American law enforcement since the McCarthy years (see Cole 2003).

While the USA Patriot Act is the most important new anti-terrorism law, other important legislative measures include: the *Mobilization Against Terrorism Act* which gives greater powers to detain suspected terrorists; new legal powers given to the FBI, Immigration and Naturalization Services and federal prosecutors to spy on, apprehend and interrogate terrorist suspects; the Military Order signed by President Bush on November 13, 2001 which allows for non-US citizens suspected of involvement in 'international terrorism' to be tried by special military commissions instead of the normal courts of law; and the *Department of Homeland Security Act of 2002*, which created a powerful new Cabinet-level department.

Another important feature of the domestic 'war on terrorism' has been the creation of several new departments and agencies. The Department of Homeland Security is the most well-known and most important of these new bodies. A conceptual and organisational expansion of the existing Office of Homeland Security, the new department absorbs the functions of several federal agencies: the Immigration and Naturalization Service, the Coast Guard, the Customs Service, the Federal Emergency Management Agency and many other smaller bureaus (see Martin 2003: 408–9). The central purpose behind this reorganisation is to bring about central operational coordination and to put an end to overlapping duties. After the Department of Veterans Affairs and the Department of Defense, the Department of Homeland Security is now the third largest federal agency with over 40,000 employees. Its main functions are to ensure border and transportation security, and coordinate national emergency preparedness and response to terrorist incidents. Supporting the new department, a wide range of other national-level agencies have been created or reinvigorated: The Terrorist Threat Integration Centre, The Foreign Terrorist Tracking Task Force, The Joint Interagency Task Force for Counter-Terrorism, The Counter-Terrorism Campaign Support Group, FBI counter-terrorism units, CIA counter-terrorism units and a vast range of local-level joint terrorism task forces.

To guide these new agencies the administration has developed a whole series of special national strategies which outline the operational goals and functions of national counter-terrorism. For example, there is the National Security Strategy, the National Strategy for Homeland Security, the National Strategy for Combating Terrorism, the National Strategy to Combat Weapons of Mass Destruction, the National Strategy to Secure Cyberspace, the National Strategy for the Physical Protection of Critical Infrastructure and Key Assets, the US VISIT system, the Proliferation Security Initiative and many more. The authorities have also inaugurated a number of domestic campaigns and programmes aimed at preparing the public for terrorist incidents, eliciting public support in information gathering and protecting airline security. For example, among others there is the Ready Campaign, the Responsible Cooperators Program, the Terrorism Information and Prevention System Program (TIPS), the Federal Air Marshal Program and the terrorist identification system.

In addition to the hundreds of thousands of people newly assigned to the counter-terrorism effort, America has also spent vast sums on its prosecution. The total cost of the 'war on terrorism' was well over $100 billion dollars in the first two years: immediately following the September 11, 2001 attacks Congress approved $40 billion in an Emergency Response Fund for the anti-terrorism effort; by mid-2004 the war in Afghanistan had cost more than $20 billion; over $20 billion was allocated to homeland defence and the new Department of Homeland Security; the war against Iraq could add up to more than $100 billion – at the time of writing, ongoing military operations were costing the United States government $4.7 billion per month; several billion dollars was also provided in military assistance to other countries cooperating in the war on terrorism, such as Pakistan, Colombia, Indonesia and the Philippines; and the budget for the American military increased by more than $50 billion following September 11, 2001 (Hartung 2003). These costs will undoubtedly continue to rise: the White House military budget request for the 2004 fiscal year was $399.1 billion, an increase of nearly $20 billion from 2003 (Mahajan 2003: 59). As a special report commissioned by the Fourth Freedom Forum noted, the 'war on terrorism' has the potential to rival the costs of the cold war:

> Given the Bush administration's expansive military strategy, the costs of war could become the biggest 'wild card' in the federal budget over the next decade. In less than one and one-half years, the Bush administration's objectives have expanded from a post-9/11 pledge to act against the 'terror network of global reach,' to a threat to use force to disarm and displace regional tyrants like Saddam Hussein, to a commitment to use American military might to promote 'democracy and free markets' throughout the world. This open-ended definition of U.S. strategic priorities goes far beyond anything the United States committed itself to during the Cold War, when the stated mission was containing the Soviet Union. (Hartung 2003)

In reality, these figures are only the initial direct costs and do not include the flow-on and indirect costs of the humanitarian and nation-building expenditures in Iraq and Afghanistan, the effects on markets (financial markets and the oil market in particular) and the macroeconomic impacts on tax policies, employment, veterans benefits, investment, consumer confidence, deferred welfare assistance and the like. Nor do they include the expenditures by American allies, particularly Britain, who has also spent billions of dollars fighting the wars in Afghanistan and Iraq, improving national security, expanding intelligence-gathering capabilities and providing its own foreign assistance to other states.

As this brief survey demonstrates, the practice of the 'war on terrorism' involves a truly staggering amount of activity and an immense commitment of resources. One of its most remarkable features is that this massive global campaign was fashioned and enacted in little over two years. My argument in this book is simply that this amount of activity did not just occur spontaneously or naturally; nor was it necessarily an inevitable consequence of the events of September 11, 2001. As later chapters will demonstrate, there are a myriad of possible responses to terrorist attacks; the 1988 Lockerbie bombing, the 1995 Oklahoma bombing and the 1998 African embassy bombings each elicited a different kind of approach from the authorities. The fact is that large-scale counter-terrorism responses are not possible without a significant degree of social and political consensus, or a clear belief about what caused terrorism and how best to fight it; in turn, consensus and knowledge require the deployment and manipulation of language.

The language of the 'war on terrorism'

As I have stated, the 'war on terrorism' is both a set of institutional practices and an accompanying set of assumptions, beliefs, forms of knowledge and political and cultural narratives. It is an entire language contained in a truly voluminous store of 'texts' – any act of written or spoken speech, from speeches to interviews to postings on websites to e-mails between officials. In the first instance, the language of the 'war on terrorism' consists of the whole corpus of official speeches, media interviews, press releases, radio and television addresses and articles written by leading figures in the administration. This first layer of text is the most important component of the language of the 'war on terrorism' because it sets out the parameters of official thinking and forms the basis of policy and action; it establishes the core principles, assumptions and knowledge of the counter-terrorism approach, implies the kinds of actions that will be undertaken and provides the overall story or narrative for public understanding of the issues. In this case, the US Department of State website shows that there were over 6,000 speeches, interviews and press releases by senior administration officials related to the 'war on terrorism' in the first two years since September 11, 2001. Some of them, such as the President's Address to Congress and the American People on September 20, 2001 were watched by upwards of 80 million people; strikingly, national sporting events were interrupted to allow the fans to watch the speech (see Woodward 2002: 108).

A second layer of language flows directly from the first. As a consequence of articulating the broad policy goals and intentions of the government's new counter-terrorism campaign, new laws are written and passed by legislators, policy documents and national strategy statements are carefully drawn up by advisers and official reports are researched and presented to Congress or other government bodies. All of these texts are based on the parameters and assumptions set by senior officials, and they reproduce and amplify the first layer of language. Put another way, the words of figures like President Bush or Secretary of State Colin Powell – and the assumptions, beliefs and knowledge contained in that language – find their way into all the documents produced by the next level of officials. Again, this is a truly voluminous set of words: apart from the hundreds of reports and policy and strategy documents drawn up since September 11, 2001, the USA Patriot Act alone consists of over 340 pages.

A third and by far the largest layer of the language of the 'war on terrorism' includes all the briefing papers, internal reports and documents, official websites, interdepartmental memos, e-mails, letters, operations manuals, rules and standard operating procedures of all the agencies and institutions involved in the counter-terrorism effort, of which there are now hundreds. That is, the language of the 'war on terrorism' includes all the paperwork and all the spoken words produced by the Department of Homeland Security, the FBI, the CIA, the Pentagon, and all the other agencies (federal and local) that relate to the counter-terrorism effort. As before, these literally millions of texts are in turn based on, and reproduce, the language and assumptions of the first two layers.

A final component of the language of the 'war on terrorism' consists of all the symbolic and emblematic representations of the counter-terrorist campaign.

After all, symbols are a powerful form of communication that contain both obvious and covert meanings and messages. If we think of words as vestibules of meaning, then symbols are also words of a sort as they too contain social and cultural meanings; society is made up of literally millions of symbols that communicate messages and meanings, from traffic signs to product logos to national flags. The symbols of the 'war on terrorism' include all the seals, flags, emblems, insignia, logos, letterheads, colour-coded warnings on websites, iconic images from 'ground zero' and Iraq, memorials and any other visual representation of the campaign. All these symbols form part of the overall language and they reproduce and amplify the central meanings, assumptions and knowledge of the counter-terrorism campaign.

The discourse of counter-terrorism

In addition to all the concrete and tangible activity, the 'war on terrorism' consists of literally millions of pages of text, words and symbols that form the basis and rationale for the actions of officials. Collectively, all these words and symbols constitute what we call a *discourse* – the discourse of the 'war on terrorism'. A discourse is a particular way of talking about and understanding the world that involves a limited number of statements and words, or a 'way of speaking which gives meaning to experiences from a particular perspective' (Jorgensen and Phillips 2002: 157). Another way to think about discourse is as 'the kind of language used within a specific field' (Jorgensen and Phillips 2002: 66). For example, there are many different kinds of discourses in society: medical, scientific, media, educational, academic, religious, corporate, cultural and political discourses – to name a few. Each has its own terminology and specialised jargon, its own unique ways of expressing ideas and its own kinds of logic, assumptions and reasoning.

Discourses are composed of (and also create) what we call *discursive formations* or *constructions* – groups of related statements about a subject that determine its meaning, characteristics and relationship to other discursive formations. For example, the notion of 'evil terrorists' so often referred to by President Bush is discursively constructed through a set of related statements which define who they are, what their essential nature is and how they are to be viewed and treated; 'evil terrorist' is a specific discursive construction. Moreover, within the discourse, the 'evil terrorist' construction is placed in direct relation to another discursive construction, namely, 'good' and 'innocent Americans'. Discourses may also be understood as a limited range of possible statements which promote a limited range of meaning; that is, discourses shape what it is possible and impossible to say in particular situations (Jorgensen and Phillips 2002: 157). In this sense, understanding specific discourses (like the 'war on terrorism') involves appreciating the rules guiding what can and cannot be said, and knowing what has been left out as well as what has been included. The silences of a text are often as important as its inclusions (Rosenberg 2003: 4). For example, within the discourse of the 'war on terrorism' there is no mention of negotiation as a method of dealing with terrorism (despite the fact that a great number of terrorist campaigns have been terminated in this manner), and to suggest that America negotiates with Osama bin Laden would seem somehow nonsensical.

Although language is crucial to the notion of discourse, society (and politics) is not reducible to language and linguistic analysis alone. Discourses are actually broader than just language, being constituted not just in texts or words, but also in definite institutional and organisational practices – what we call *discursive practices* (Hodgson 2000: 62). For example, an educational discourse includes not just the language and content of curriculum and school texts, but also the physical arrangement of the classrooms, the shape of the tables, school songs and mottos, disciplinary practices, school uniforms and dress codes, underlying teaching philosophies and the like. A political discourse similarly involves not just speeches by politicians, or their pamphlets and writings, but also the symbols they appropriate (flags, colours, dress codes, insignia), the myths and histories they refer to, the laws they pass, the organisational structures they create, the decision-making procedures they follow and the actions they undertake (marches, demonstrations, boycotts). Discourses can be considered to be an amalgam of material practices and forms of language and knowledge where each reinforces the other in a continuous cycle. In politics, for example, the presidential seal and the flag powerfully reinforce the words of any official speaking at the White House press office podium. When the words, symbols and traditional deference shown by attending journalists are all combined, a White House press conference becomes a powerful and authoritative act of truth creation in society – even if the 'facts' being discussed can later be shown to be false.

Political discourses are constructed and employed for specific purposes, most importantly, the creation, maintenance and extension of power. Discourses are an exercise of power; that is, they try to become dominant or *hegemonic* by discrediting alternative or rival discourses, by promoting themselves as the full and final truth and by drowning out the sound of any other discourse. A hegemonic political discourse then is one where the public debate uses mainly the language, terms, ideas and 'knowledge' of the dominant discourse, and where alternative words and meanings are rarely found and dissenting voices are almost never heard. The 'war on terrorism' is currently one of a great many kinds of political discourses, and it is attempting – with considerable success – to become hegemonic over alternative discourses, such as pacifist, human rights based, feminist, environmentalist or anti-globalisation discourses.

Importantly, discourses, particularly political discourses, are not monolithic, nor are they ever totally hegemonic; there are always contestations and sites of resistance. The anti-communist discourse of the cold war is a case in point: while at times it dominated both politics and society in America (such as during the height of the McCarthy era), at other times it was highly contested and alternative discourses were heard (such as when the McCarthy-era measures were rescinded by Congress). This is the reason there is still criticism of and opposition to the administration, and why the administration, in a sense, has to remake and reaffirm the discourse every day. Having said this, as during the cold war, discourses can become powerfully institutionalised and embedded into the culture and practice of politics; in a sense, they can take on a life of their own. As I argue later, this is exactly what has occurred during the present 'war on terrorism' and is part of what makes the current discourse unique. Unlike the cold war which took many years to develop, the current (warm) 'war on terrorism' has become the most powerful political discourse in America in little over two years. As I have already mentioned, this is part of the reason it did not really matter who won the presidential elections in November 2004; the 'war on terrorism' was already deeply embedded in American political life and the wider society.

Related to this, discourses are not simply transmitted from speaker to listener in an uninterrupted fashion; it is not like pouring water (words) into an empty receptacle. Rather, there is a continual process of producing, reproducing, interpreting and retransmitting the language from speaker to listener to other speakers; every individual interprets what they hear and read in their own unique way, as does every group and institution. In addition, discourses often have to be mediated and retransmitted by other social actors: the media for example, interprets the language of politicians, fashions it into a familiar media frame and then transmits it to the wider public. Churches, universities, pressure groups, artists and countless other social actors follow the same progression. In the process, the original discourse is inevitably changed and moulded in sometimes unpredictable ways. One of the most surprising and unique aspects of the 'war on terrorism' is the surprising level of consistency in the discourse. There is very little deviation from the central discursive formations or the primary narratives – even when it is interpreted and retransmitted by other actors like the media or religious groups.

Unfortunately, the role of language and discourse in the construction of political processes is relatively poorly studied and consequently poorly understood. As noted earlier, most analyses of the 'war on terrorism' for example, focus on its geo-political aspects or attempt to examine its diplomatic, political or legal dimensions. A key purpose of this study is to redress this imbalance by examining the way the 'war on terrorism' uses language and other discursive practices to create and maintain hegemony, to impose its interpretation of political reality on the rest of society and to rationalise, legitimise and normalise the practice of counter-terrorism.

Language and politics: why words matter

Thus far I have explained how the 'war on terrorism' consists of both practice and language, or discourse. Furthermore, I have suggested that discourses form the foundation for the practice by establishing the underlying assumptions, beliefs and knowledge. But how exactly does language achieve this? Why are words so important to politics? The answer can be simply stated: words are never neutral; they don't just describe the world, they actually help to make the world. As such, words can never be employed in a purely objective sense. There are several reasons for this.

In the first place, as linguists and anthropologists have discovered, all language has a basic binary structure such that almost every noun, adjective and verb has its direct opposite. It is a feature of the underlying architecture of language. Critically, this opposition between terms usually implies a 'devaluation of one term and a favoring of the other' (Llorente 2002: 39). The natural inequality between terms, where one is lacking something the opposite embodies, is rarely questioned or challenged. Some of the well-known examples of the way the binary system works include: good/evil, love/hate, new/old, healthy/sick, normal/deviant, moderate/radical, primitive/modern, black/white, masculine/feminine, strong/weak, urban/rural, native/foreigner, believer/atheist, forward/backward and west/east. In each case, one of the terms is privileged over the other and has inherently positive connotations the other lacks. The employment of language therefore, can never be a truly neutral act. Speaking about 'civilisation' for example, is impossible without bringing to mind the concept of 'barbarism' as its negative opposite. Thus, when politicians and newspapers describe the September 11, 2001 attacks as an 'assault on civilisation', the reader knows that (bad) barbarians are somehow involved. A similar process occurs when words like 'evil', 'freedom', 'hate', 'western' and 'justice' are utilised.

There is another reason why language is not a neutral act: because our way of speaking plays an active role in creating and changing our perceptions, our cognition and our emotions. First, as something particularly human, language moulds how we see the world; it is the main determinant of our perceptions, our access to concrete reality. From knowing the difference between an apple and a hand grenade, to knowing what to do with each in relevant situations, language shapes our understanding of the world around us (Collins and Glover 2002: 4). The language of politics is actually founded on this assumption and is deliberately structured to shape our perceptions of the world and the types of people in it. Politicians, or more accurately, their propagandists or media relations officers, try to shape public perceptions through the strategic employment of certain words and grammatical formations. As Martha Crenshaw has noted about the language of terrorism: '[W]hat one calls things matters. There are few neutral terms in politics, because political language affects the perceptions of protagonists and audiences, and such effect acquires a greater urgency in the drama of terrorism' (Crenshaw 1995: 7).

More than affecting perceptions language also structures cognition – it affects the way we think, and particularly how we make strategic choices. By using a restricted set of words and word formations, some choices can appear perfectly reasonable and commonsensical while others appear absurd. Expressed another way, the language we use at any given moment privileges one viewpoint over others, naturalising some understandings as rational and others as nonsensical (Foucault 1977). For example, a political party may state that it aims to promote an environmentally friendly energy policy. It goes on to use ecological language to promote its policy, speaking about 'clean' energy, 'renewable sources', 'environmental safety', 'sustainability' and the like. Employing this language, the choice of wind or solar power would appear to be a natural and logical solution; to suggest more fossil fuel burners, or nuclear power stations would seem somehow inappropriate. The language of the 'war on terrorism' has a similar effect, namely, it makes some strategic options seem rational and logical and others seem absurd, even taboo: attacking those states that harbour and support terrorists seems reasonable, while engaging in any kind of dialogue with so-called terrorists would seem somehow nonsensical or even treasonous.

Third, because language structures both our perceptions and our cognition, it also affects our emotions. It is in an important sense, the place where our psychic and social lives intersect. Certain words or combinations of words can make us feel anxious, fearful, angry or joyful. This generates immense power for those that deploy them. Politicians and propagandists have known this for a long time, and in fact, we see it almost every day in people's reactions to the use of certain words in the media, such as 'paedophile', 'AIDS', 'murder', 'weapons of mass destruction' and 'terrorist'. The use of particular terms by politicians is most often directly intended to create a definite kind of public emotion, such as outrage, sympathy or fear. In the lead-up to the Second Gulf War, the danger posed by Saddam's 'weapons of mass destruction', with his 'chemical and biological agents' which were 'capable of being launched in forty-five minutes' was spoken of almost daily to create a sufficient level of public anxiety, and hence, support for a war against Iraq.

One final reason why words cannot be considered neutral is because words have histories. This is because in themselves, words have no inherent meaning; rather, they have to acquire meaning in their own discursive setting (Collins and Glover 2002: 9–10). The process by which words obtain meaning is often lengthy and takes place through repetition and their careful and selective use in specific contexts. For example, the use of the terms 'civilised' and 'barbarous' cannot avoid invoking the history of these words as they were applied by Christian Europe in the Middle Ages, and by imperialists and colonists in the last century. There is a history to their meaning that affects their usage in a contemporary context. In other cases, words can take on new meanings. The history of the word 'terrorist' or 'terrorism' is a pertinent example of this process. Initially, the word was used to describe the actions of states against their own people: the Great Terror of the French Revolution; Stalin's purges; the Nazi terror state. To a lesser extent, it was also used to describe the actions of some anarchists of the late nineteenth century. Since the 1960s however, government officials, the media and many academics have used the term to characterise the use of violence by small groups of dissidents or revolutionaries to intimidate or influence the state. This strategic and repetitious usage has given the term a new popular meaning: the word 'terrorist' is hardly ever used now to describe state policies of repression or intimidation, but instead is almost exclusively used to describe the illegitimate acts of individuals or small groups of dissidents. Although there are some who contest this new popular meaning of 'terrorism' and who think it should be applied equally to certain kinds of governments and government policies (see Chomsky 2001, 2002), in most people's minds the term applies to individuals and small groups engaged in violently opposing the state.

Because words have histories, the act of naming things is always a highly charged process that can have serious political and social consequences. For example, a march by anti-globalisation protesters may be described as a 'mainly peaceful protest' by the media and politicians, in which case it will be thought of as orderly and legitimate. Other similar events may then be treated sensitively and proportionately by the police. The same event however, may also be described as an 'anarchist riot', which will then mark it as disorderly, unlawful and illegitimate. The police may then respond by using disproportionate force against subsequent marches. The different names for the same event may generate contrasting perceptions and responses. This effect of naming is especially powerful in terms of political violence because to 'call an act of political violence terrorist is not merely to describe it but to judge it' (Rubenstein 1987: 17). Consider the difference between calling the killing of an abortion doctor 'a murder' and calling it 'an act of terrorism'; the two names for the same act have very contrasting meanings and would likely elicit very different responses. The 'murder' of the doctor would most likely result in a police investigation, while the 'terrorist killing' of the doctor would result in the mobilisation of the FBI counter-terrorism unit.

Expressed another way, we can say that language has a reality-making effect; it is a way of constructing reality and not merely reflecting it. Because language affects perception, cognition and emotion, it inevitably also affects concrete political action; it has consequences for social processes and structures. In the study of other forms of political violence – wars, genocide, insurgency – for example, scholars have started to recognise that wars cannot be fought without the willing participation of large numbers of individuals from across the social spectrum. Enlisting such support requires altering the perception of individuals to comprehend the need for employing force, structuring their cognition so it appears as a reasonable and logical course of action and arousing them emotionally so they will participate or at least acquiesce to the violence. Bringing about such a profound change in so many individuals entails the construction of an entire vocabulary – a whole new language – which comes to replace normal modes of talking and thinking. For example, to make possible the civil war in the former Yugoslavia, people had to start talking about themselves as 'Croats', 'Serbs' and 'Muslims', instead of 'Yugoslavs'. They then had to talk about each other as 'historical enemies' rather than as friends and neighbours. Finally, they had to start thinking about each other as 'threats' and a 'danger' as opposed to fellow citizens (see Wilmer 2002). The leader of Yugoslavia, Slobodan Milosevic, achieved this transformation in people's speech through the public repetition over several years of a new kind of vocabulary based on these ideas that deliberately manipulated peoples' perceptions and emotions; he was aided by a media that endlessly repeated and amplified the words, and by supporters in the churches, schools, universities, cultural associations, unions and other places of social interaction.

In sum, speaking or writing is never a neutral act; language can never be used objectively. The deployment of language has concrete and tangible consequences; it creates or constructs reality. Above all, language is the medium of politics and politicians have always employed certain types and forms of language to generate public support and consent for their actions. As Martin Wight noted, power is a social phenomenon and constantly needs to be legitimated (Wight 1978; see also Hurrell 2002). For these reasons, it is crucial to our understanding of the 'war on terrorism' to examine and explain how the discourse of counter-terrorism constructs the practice of counter-terrorism.

The analysis of discourse

The method I have employed to examine the language of the 'war on terrorism' is known broadly as critical discourse analysis. This approach is at once both a technique for analysing specific texts or speech acts, and a way of understanding the relationship between discourse and social and political phenomena. By engaging in concrete, linguistic textual analysis – that is, by doing systematic analyses of spoken and written language – critical discourse analysis aims to shed light on the links between texts and societal practices and structures, or, the linguistic-discursive dimension of social action (Jorgensen and Phillips 2002: 60–71). The approach is based on a number of crucial assumptions. It assumes that discourse is a form of social practice which both makes or constitutes the social world, and is at the same time constituted by other social practices. Discourses both contribute to the shaping of social structures and are also shaped by them; there is a dialectical relationship between the two. Of even greater import, critical discourse analysis assumes that discursive practices are never neutral, but rather they contribute to the creation and reproduction of unequal power relations between social groups; discourses are an exercise in power. Thus, a central aim of critical discourse analysis lies in revealing the means by which language is deployed to maintain power; what makes critical discourse analysis 'critical' is its normative commitment to positive social change. In this case, my concern lies in facilitating the emergence of more effective and long-term solutions to the problem of political violence.

In terms of studying the role and use of language, there are two levels at which critical discourse analysis functions. First, it engages directly with specific texts in an effort to discover how discursive practices operate linguistically within those texts. Second, because individual text analysis is not sufficient on its own to shed light on the relationship between discourse and social processes, critical discourse analysis adds a wider interdisciplinary perspective which combines textual and social analysis (see Fairclough 1992). Thus, in the following chapters the reader will find examples of both specific text analysis focusing on formal features such as vocabulary, grammar, syntax and sentence coherence, as well as broader interdisciplinary analysis focusing more generally on culture, politics and society. In effect, critical discourse analysis involves carefully reading a specific text – such as a speech, interview, radio address or report – and employing a series of analytical questions. For instance, in examining the texts of the 'war on terrorism', I applied the following questions:

- What assumptions, beliefs and values underlie the language in the text?
- How does the grammar, syntax and sentence construction reinforce the meanings and effects of the discursive constructions contained in the text?
- What are the histories and embedded meanings of the important words in the text?
- What meanings are implied by the context of the text, and in turn, how does the context alter the meaning of the words?
- What patterns can be observed in the language, and how do different parts of the text relate to each other?
- How stable and internally consistent are the discursive constructions within the text?
- How is the language in the text reinforced or affected by discursive actions?
- What knowledge or practices are normalised by the language in the text?
- What are the political or power functions of the discursive constructions?
- How does the language create, reinforce or challenge power relations in society?

Note how these questions are directed at both the specific text itself, and the wider social and cultural context. Thus, finding answers to these questions goes some

25

way towards understanding how discourses work to construct social processes and structures in ways that reproduce power relations.

In my analysis of the language of the 'war on terrorism' I chose to focus mainly on the speeches, interviews and public addresses given by senior members of the Bush administration. Using critical discourse analysis I studied over 100 speeches, interviews, radio broadcasts and reports to Congress between September 11, 2001 and January 31, 2004; these texts were a representative sample of more than 6,000 such texts on the subject of America's 'war on terrorism' for that period. I began by examining all the important speeches that garnered major public attention or were of great symbolic importance, such as the September 11 and September 20, 2001 addresses to the American people, the State of the Union addresses and anniversary and commemorative speeches. Next, I tried to ensure a selection of different speakers, from the president to senior ambassadors, as well as texts from the entire period. I sought to examine whether the language remained consistent over both different speakers and different times, and only ended my analysis of new speeches when I felt I had obtained a thorough understanding of the discourse. The reason for focusing on these particular texts and not the documents of law-enforcement officials or the content of websites, for example, is partly logistical and partly that these speeches represent the source of the discourse. The 'war on terrorism' is an elite-led project and these elites have provided the primary justifications and overall vision. It thus seemed logical to focus primarily on their words.

Finally, it is important to note that while some discourses may occur fairly subconsciously or simply as evolutionary processes of discursive (re)production, the 'war on terrorism' is an instance of a deliberately and carefully constructed discourse. In the first instance, modern politics is extremely sensitive to the importance of media projection and it is well known how politicians take extreme care in formulating public language to ensure that precisely the right message is conveyed. We know for example, that President Bush is carefully and thoroughly primed by advisers and media handlers before every public appearance, and that from the first day following the terrorist attacks he 'wanted a daily meeting to shape the administration's message to Americans about the fight against terrorism' (Woodward 2002: 41). Bush then appointed Karen Hughes, Counsellor to the President, to be in charge of communicating the war, arguing that the way in which the White House explained its goals and thinking about the war effort would be critical to the overall success of the campaign: 'I knew full well that if we could rally the American people behind a long and difficult chore, that our job would be easier' Bush said (Woodward 2002: 95). Donald Rumsfeld agreed: in a war that was going to be lengthy and relatively secret, they would need 'message discipline', because sustaining such a war 'requires a broad base of domestic support' (Woodward 2002: 88–9). In addition, the 'war on terrorism' explicitly engages in 'public diplomacy' – the effort to influence public opinion through projecting positive images and communicating the right 'message' about America. Simply put, information management and message manipulation is a central plank of the counter-terrorism campaign. Thus, in no way can we assume that the words of these ranking officials are unconscious, accidental or unplanned. Besides, as I demonstrate throughout this book, there were a great many alternative narratives available to officials; the Bush administration could have employed any number of different approaches or paradigms and there is no reason for thinking they were unaware of these alternatives. The fact that the construction of the 'war on terrorism' has meshed so closely with the pre-existing policy agenda of the neoconservatives within the Bush administration also suggests it was deliberately formulated in pursuit of those goals.

This is not to say that the Bush administration was necessarily being disingenuous or deliberately misleading – that there was some kind of conspiracy. We know from insider accounts that President Bush and his cabinet genuinely believe what they say publicly about terrorism; they employ exactly the same language in private. For example, President Bush wrote in his personal diary on September 11, 2001: 'The **Pearl Harbor** of the 21st century took place today' and 'This was **a war** in which people were going to die' (Woodward 2002: 37). These words echo his later speeches to the American people. Nor is it to suggest there are no unconscious aspects to the discourse, or that it does not contain a number of continuities with previous counter-terrorism approaches. As I demonstrate in Chapter 6, there are clear links between the present 'war on terrorism' and the two earlier 'wars on terrorism' declared by President Clinton and President Reagan. It is not that there was some kind of plot to manipulate and deceive the public; rather, administration officials deliberately deployed language to try to persuade the American people of the logic, reason and rightness of their decisions. At the same time, the language they used drew upon pre-existing and deeply held beliefs, as well as earlier institutional discourses of counter-terrorism.

Conclusion

There are important and unambiguous connections between the language and the practice of counter-terrorism; critical discourse analysis permits us to analyse both the specific features of the language and the deeper relationship between discourse and the exercise of power. My aim in the following chapters is first to explain the discursive construction of the 'war on terrorism' by uncovering the kinds of rhetorical and grammatical strategies which are employed, the histories and genealogies of the key terms in the discourse and the myths, narratives and tropes used by the main speakers. The study is carried out in a thematic rather than a chronological fashion. The divisions between chapters are founded on the primary themes observed in the official texts. Second, I explore how the discourse affects the practice of the 'war on terrorism' – particularly, how the language of counter-terrorism has consequences for the moral community, for democratic participation and for the practice of counter-terrorism. Throughout the analysis, I stress that the language chosen by American officials was not natural or neutral; there were other available words and narratives they could have employed. Additionally, the 'war on terrorism' as a geo-political and strategic project is as much driven by the internal logic and effect of the discourse as it is by concrete political events. Language is extremely important for political understanding; words really do matter.

2

Writing September 11, 2001

THERE IS A TEMPTATION to think that large-scale human events can be readily understood and interpreted – that 'the facts speak for themselves', as it were. The reality is far more complex. While it may be possible to establish who the main actors were and the exact sequence of actions (although even this basic information may not always be clear – as the assassination of John F. Kennedy illustrates), it is far more difficult to determine the *meaning* of the events or how they are to be interpreted. Establishing the wider social or cultural significance of an event is a contested and complicated process which can never be completely settled or firmly fixed; over time and place meanings and interpretations can and often do change. This is where language comes in; the significance and implication of the experience, its wider social 'reading' as it were, has to be established afterwards through the use and deployment of words, and different words can result in different 'readings' for the same set of facts.

The events of September 11, 2001 are a perfect illustration of this process. While it was immediately obvious what had taken place – what the 'facts' were (hijacked planes had crashed into prominent buildings which had subsequently been destroyed) – it was far from obvious what these events meant or signified. At the time, reporters, television anchors and onlookers struggled to say anything more than what they could see in front of them; there appeared to be no accurate words, no appropriate vocabulary to express what the events signified or meant. In an important sense, the events created a 'void of meaning' (Campbell 2002; Der Derian 2002a); language itself appeared to collapse along with the Twin Towers, and the anguished cries of 'Oh, my God!' repeated over and over on the video footage seemed to be all that was left to say.

The 'void of meaning' left in the empty spaces where the towers had once stood was a direct consequence of the sheer visceral horror of the images – the massive explosions and walls of flame when the planes smashed into the structures, the bodies falling like rain as people leapt to their deaths, the unimaginable vision of two of the world's biggest buildings falling down in a massive cloud of dust and debris. Such sights are inherently horrifying and extremely rare, being hardly ever captured on film as they occur; as such, they inevitably produce a moment of verbal paralysis and linguistic dyslexia as onlookers struggle to express the powerful emotions and thoughts engendered by the spectacle. Usually, we only see the aftermath of this kind of violence: burning buildings, stunned survivors, emergency services attending the wounded.

However, this is only part of the explanation. A more important reason for the abrupt 'void of meaning' created by the attacks can be found in the perennial sense of 'hyper-reality' – the blurring of the lines between the virtual and real worlds through excessive media saturation – which characterises modern and, particularly, American society. For many onlookers, the sense that what they were seeing was only a movie (with the same spectacular special effects as any Hollywood blockbuster), but that it was even more 'real' than a movie, caused deep confusion and a genuine sense of epistemic anxiety. It was real but unreal at the same time; it was both surreal and hyper-real. After all, most Americans had actually seen the same images of the destruction of New York before in countless disaster movies like *Godzilla*, *Final Fantasy* and *AI*. In *Deep Impact*, for example, a massive wave unleashed by a meteor knocks over the Twin Towers in a chilling cinematic preview of the September 11, 2001 events. To those who observed the attacks as they occurred, it seemed more like a remake of *Towering Inferno* than actual events or news, as these excerpts from eyewitnesses attest (quoted in Nacos 2002: 35):

> I looked over my shoulder and saw the United Airlines plane coming. It came over the Statue of Liberty. It was just like a movie. It just directly was guided into the second tower. (Laksman Achuthan, managing director of the Economic Cycles Research Institute)

> I looked up and saw this hole in the World Trade Center building. And I – I couldn't believe it. I thought, you know, this can't be happening. This is a special effect; it's a movie. (Clifton Cloud, who filmed the attacks with his video camera)

> It's insane. It's just like a movie. It's, it's actually surreal to me to see it on TV and see major buildings collapse. (Unidentified man in Canada)

> This is very surreal. Well, it's out of a bad sci-fi film, but every morning we wake up and you're like it wasn't a dream, it wasn't a movie. It actually happened. (Unidentified woman in New York)

President Bush, speaking on the day of the attacks, expressed the same sense of unreality: 'The pictures of airplanes flying into buildings, fires burning, huge structures collapsing, have filled us with disbelief' (Bush, 11 September, 2001b). In essence, the spectacle of the attacks viewed through the medium of television fractured the common rhetorical resources of a society raised on a steady diet of virtual violence. There seemed to be no words to express fully what was taking place because its realness was in doubt – most of what appears on television is after all, unreal. How could anyone be absolutely certain that this wasn't unreal too?

My argument in this chapter is simple: into this 'void of meaning' – this failure of language due to the blurred line between virtual and real violence – administration officials inserted a politically driven narrative that has since come to dominate public interpretation of the events. National leaders constructed a narrative or story that would give meaning to the events and answer all the questions they engendered: why did they do it? What kind of people would do such a thing? Were there more such attacks to come? What was the appropriate response? The language used to explain these attacks was not a neutral or inevitable interpretation of what happened; rather, it worked to enforce a particular understanding or reading of the political, military and cultural meaning of the attacks. Other words and narratives could have been chosen which would have given the events quite a different 'reading'. Most importantly, the narrative worked to justify and normalise the military response at the heart of the 'war on terrorism'.

There are four notable features of the language I wish to examine here. First, and unsurprisingly, the attacks are discursively constructed as an exceptional tragedy and a grievous harm. In this aspect of the narrative, America is assigned a special status as the primary victim of the 'war on terrorism'. Second, the official language constructs the attacks as primarily an 'act of war' rather than a crime against humanity or an act of mass murder. This is arguably the most important rhetorical construction of the entire discourse. Third, the attacks are described in ways which allow them to fit into a number of pre-existing and highly popular meta-narratives: World War II (the Pearl Harbor analogy), the cold war, the struggle of civilisation against barbarism and the globalisation narrative. These fashionable political and cultural narratives assign particular meanings to the events and provide a very specific kind of contextual framework for their interpretation. Finally, I will briefly examine how the discourse explicitly attempts to deny or suppress any alternative reading of the events, particularly those which implicate American foreign policy. There was a sustained effort by administration officials to ensure the attacks could not be understood as anything but an unprovoked and treacherous attack on an innocent and peaceful nation.

An exceptional tragedy: grievance and victim-hood

One of the most noticeable aspects of the language surrounding the attacks of September 11, 2001 is its constant reference to tragedy, grievance and the exceptional suffering of the American people. This is not at all surprising, as it was the most devastating attack by non-state terrorists in history in which 2,998 people lost their lives. It was also the worst ever act of political violence on American soil. Among the many ways in which the events are talked about, three aspects are particularly important. In the first instance, the events are discursively constructed and fixed as a national 'tragedy' and as 'calamity', 'loss' and 'horror'; these words appear hundreds of times in speeches about the attacks. For example, at 9.30am on September 11, 2001, the day of the attacks, President Bush states: 'Today we've had **a national tragedy**. Two airplanes have crashed into the World Trade Center in an apparent terrorist attack on our country' (Bush, 11 September, 2001a). Importantly, the attacks are being constructed here as a 'national' (American) tragedy, rather than a local (New York) tragedy, or as they latterly were, a global tragedy. A few months on, Bush restates that the attack was '**a terrible national shock**, an act of evil that caused, and continues to cause **so much suffering**' (Bush, 24 November, 2001). The large number of people from other countries who died, and the fact that it was the 'World' Trade Center (WTC) which was attacked could have allowed a slightly different linguistic construction: it could have been an 'international tragedy', an attack on humanity, instead of solely an American tragedy. Accordingly, the language is being used in this instance to fix ownership of the tragedy; America (collectively) is the primary victim.

Ambassador Howard Baker discursively constructs the events in a similar mode: 'Few people will forget where they were when they first learned of **the calamities** in New York and Washington. It was like **a nightmare** from which we all wished to awake' (Baker, 23 September, 2001). A year after the events, Bush began his anniversary speech by stating: 'A long year has passed since enemies attacked our country. We've seen the images so many times they are seared on our souls, and remembering **the horror**, reliving **the anguish**, reimagining **the terror**, is hard – and painful' (Bush, 11 September, 2002). The effect of this language is to construct the attacks as a wound on the body politic of the nation itself, to identify the whole nation with the suffering. It is echoed in the statement: 'I will not forget **this wound to our country** or those who inflicted it' (Bush, 20 September, 2001). It is not just a wound to the country (and not just New York and Washington), but to '*our* country': Americans are all wounded by this, he is saying. This is a powerful discursive act which goes some way to constructing a collective sense of exceptional grievance.

More than simply a tragedy, an atrocity or a horrific calamity however, the discourse goes on to emphasise how September 11, 2001 was now a day that would never be forgotten. On the day of the attacks, Bush maintained that 'None of us will ever forget this day' (Bush, 11 September, 2001b). A few days later he reflects: 'Each of us will **remember what happened that day**, and to whom it happened. We'll **remember the moment** the news came – where we were and what we were doing' (Bush, 20 September, 2001). In expressing these words,

Bush and all the other officials who restated the same sentiment were in fact making sure that it did indeed become a day never to be forgotten. Significantly, this construction of an unforgettable day is similar to the construction by President Roosevelt of December 7, 1941, the day Japan attacked Pearl Harbor, as 'a date which will live in infamy' (quoted in Silberstein 2002: 29). This is the discursive construction of a national myth which gives meaning to a collective experience: just as the 'day of infamy' is now a part of American national identity, so too are officials attempting to fix September 11, 2001 as a defining moment in the national memory. In fact, as I demonstrate below, there is a deliberate and sustained effort to discursively link September 11, 2001 to the attack on Pearl Harbor itself.

Ambassador Baker follows this same strategy by contending: '**September 11 will now be known as a horrible defining date in history**. Few people will forget where they were when they first learned of the calamities in New York and Washington' (Baker, 23 September, 2001). Interestingly, this discursive rendering links the terrorist attacks on the WTC to the assassination of John F. Kennedy; that is, just as the act of remembering where one was on 22 November, 1963 has been mythologised in hundreds of movies, television programmes, books, plays and speeches, so too are officials attempting to construct a similar iconic status for September 11, 2001. In this way, the representation of the date can be etched into the national memory with a predetermined set of implicit meanings.

The power and success of this discursive construction of September 11, 2001 as a day of national American tragedy can be seen in the manner in which the actual date has become linguistically iconic and divorced from its temporal moorings. It is no longer necessary to add the year (2001) or even the month (September) to its designation; simply uttering the numbers '9-11' is now enough to communicate the significance of the date. In effect, the notation '9-11' is no longer fixed in time or geography; it is rhetorical shorthand for the day of America's tragedy and suffering – a date whose meaning is no longer contested. This could not have been achieved without the powerful and continuous construction of the attacks as a special day of tragedy with its own distinctive meaning. After all, few remember the actual date of the Omagh bombing in Northern Ireland, the Oklahoma City bombing, or even the start of the Rwandan genocide. This is because there was not the same powerful discursive construction of those dates as something to be remembered and mythologised.

Another theme in the discourse emphasises the great suffering and grief experienced by Americans as a result of the attacks. At the National Day of Prayer, Bush makes a great number of references to the nation's suffering and the sorrow of the people:

> We are here in the middle hour of **our grief**. So many have **suffered so great a loss**, and today we express **our nation's sorrow**.

33

We will read all these names. We will linger over them, and learn their stories, and many Americans will **weep**.

[T]he prayers of private **suffering**, whether in our homes or in this great cathedral, are known and heard, and understood. [...] we are not spared from **suffering**. (Bush, 14 September, 2001)

A month later, in the midst of the bombing campaign in Afghanistan, Bush once again reiterates America's great suffering: 'One month after **great suffering and sorrow**, America is strong and determined and generous. [...] I was standing up there at the Pentagon today, and I saw the **tears** of the families whose lives were lost in the Pentagon' (Bush, 11 October, 2001). In this instance, Bush is drawing attention to the fact that he personally is connected to this national and individual suffering – he sees their tears, he feels their suffering. In fact, in virtually every major political speech or press interview in the following months, the president and his senior officials make a point of remembering the attacks and mentioning their tragic effects. This constant repetition, while perfectly understandable and a form of national catharsis, also works to fix the meaning of the events as one of terrible grievance and tragedy. Constructing the events in this fashion, particularly in such evocative settings – the speech on the anniversary of the attacks on Ellis Island with the Statue of Liberty as a backdrop, for example – conveys a powerful set of emotions to the listeners and fixes their tragic quality.

Related to this is the potent construction of the victims of the attacks. In particular, there is a deliberate effort to establish the everyday humanity of the victims through personalised accounts. This is a way of creating empathy and eliciting sympathy – seeing the casualties as both ordinary people and innocent victims. In many cases, there is an emphasis on the affects of the attacks on children, who are the most innocent members of society. On the day of the attacks for example, Bush says 'Tonight, I ask for your prayers for all those who grieve, **for the children whose worlds have been shattered**, for all whose sense of safety and security has been threatened' (Bush, 11 September, 2001). It is in the September 20 national address however, that Bush most powerfully constructs the victims of the attacks:

We have seen it in the courage of passengers, who rushed terrorists to save others on the ground – passengers like **an exceptional man named Todd Beamer**. And would you please help me to welcome **his wife, Lisa Beamer**, here tonight.

Even grief recedes with time and grace. But our resolve must not pass. Each of us will remember what happened that day, and to whom it happened. We'll remember the moment the news came – where we were and what we were doing. Some will remember an image of a fire, or a story of rescue. Some will carry memories of **a face and a voice gone forever**. And I will carry this: It is the police shield of **a man**

named George Howard, who died at the World Trade Center trying to save others. It was given to me by **his mom**, Arlene, as a proud memorial to **her son**. This is my reminder of **lives that ended** [...] (Bush, 20 September, 2001)

This is a very powerful act of discourse creation. At both the start of the speech and at its conclusion, Bush mentions the names of one individual victim, as well as a surviving wife and a surviving mother. The fact that Todd Beamer's wife Lisa is there at the speech powerfully reinforces the language, as does the police shield Bush holds up as he speaks about George Howard and which he carries with him as a personal reminder of the tragedy.

Again, in his State of the Union address in January 2002, Bush provides another set of individual portraits:

For many Americans, these four months have brought sorrow, and pain that will never completely go away. Every day a retired firefighter returns to Ground Zero, to feel closer to **his two sons** who died there. At a memorial in New York, **a little boy** left his football with a note for **his lost father**: Dear Daddy, please take this to heaven. I don't want to play football until I can play with you again some day. [...] Beyond all differences of race or creed, we are one country, mourning together and facing danger together. (Bush, 29 January, 2002)

Notice again the reference to children, to a father and to the unity of grief and the mourning of the nation. Bush is saying that all Americans have been injured and are united in sorrow – as both a nation and as individuals, Americans are the victims and the injured party.

The main consequence of this sacralising language is to create *a myth of exceptional grievance* – and to establish America's status as the primary victim. It is not uncommon to think of myths as stories that are untrue or made-up. In actual fact, myths are stories or narratives which give meaning and purpose to experience; and national myths are the stories which convey commonly shared convictions on the purposes and meaning of the nation (Hughes 2003: 2). As such, myths are the discursive glue that keeps a nation of different groups and individuals together; leaders create and re-create myths, especially in times of crisis, as a means of reinforcing unity. In this case, the myth of exceptional suffering constructed around the events of '9-11' provides the American people with a story through which they can make sense of their collective experience. In part, the notion of 'exceptional' or special suffering is linked to well-established national myths that are often referred to as 'American exceptionalism' – the belief that America is a special or unique nation among the world's countries. Specifically, the myths that America is God's chosen nation and 'Nature's nation' – God and Nature established a new and different kind of political community unconnected to the European history and culture that the Pilgrim Fathers escaped from – expresses the collective belief that Americans are a special people (see Hughes 2003). Officials have tapped into this national myth by suggesting that the suffering caused by the attacks is unique and special; America is an exceptional kind of victim.

One of the purposes of constructing a myth of exceptional grievance is to divest the nation of the moral responsibility for counter-violence. Thus, as Donald Rumsfeld states in a press conference concerning the US attacks on Afghanistan, 'There are going to be loss of life – there already have been. It started on **September 11th** in this building. And there are going to be more' (Rumsfeld, 24 October, 2001). This message is powerfully reinforced by the physical and symbolic location of the speech – the Pentagon, a building attacked by the terrorists. The next day, in response to a question about whether the US ought to have done more to avoid civilian casualties in Afghanistan, Rumsfeld stated: 'We did not start this war. So understand, responsibility for every single casualty in this war, whether they're innocent Afghans or innocent Americans, rests at the feet of the al-Qaeda and the Taliban' (quoted in Wheeler 2002: 217). Significantly, there is an explicit effort here to use the tragedy of the September 11, 2001 attacks as a moral abdication for the civilian deaths in Afghanistan: the terrorists started it, and if they hadn't attacked first there would be no war in Afghanistan. This is the deliberate use of America's status of 'victim' to justify actions which harm other innocent civilians. America's exceptional status as the primary victim was then reinforced by the decision of television networks to avoid showing pictures of any bombed Afghan civilians, or even mentioning them without also recalling the American victims of September 11, 2001.

I am not suggesting that there was no real tragedy, or that it was not as bad as it seemed. It was a terrible event in which thousands of ordinary people were killed – the most deadly and horrific attack by non-state terrorists in history. What I am suggesting however, is that the discourse of grievance and victim-hood fulfils certain functions and has a genuine political value to officials. Other scholars have shown that one way to promote a discourse of violence which can motivate ordinary people to engage in or acquiesce to war, is to create or sustain a powerful sense of grievance and victim-hood (see Bowman 1994; Jabri 1996; Kaufman 2001; Wilmer 2002). This induces anger, hatred, fear and a desire for revenge – which then translates into support for the violent policies of leaders. In some cases, this sense of being a victim of another groups' injustice or violence has to be invented or created out of existing histories and myths. In the former Yugoslavia for example, both the Serbs and Croats went to great efforts to paint themselves as being the victims of the other's aggression, and relied on reinterpretations of historical events in World War II and previous conflicts (see MacDonald 2002).

In contrast, the September 11, 2001 attacks provided officials with a ready-made and exceptional grievance – in this case, a sense of victim-hood did not have to be in any way 'invented'. It did however, have to be nurtured and firmly embedded in peoples' minds. Consequently, the discourse surrounding the tragedy is an important foundation stone in the discursive creation of a 'war against terrorism'; being the victim constructs American military retaliation as justified self-defence and its treatment of terrorist suspects as proportionate – an act of justice rather than revenge. Additionally, it places the moral responsibility for consequent suffering on the original attackers rather than on American policy.

Maintaining a sense of victim-hood however, requires a constant reiteration of the grievance, which is why the horrors of September 11, 2001 are constantly referred to in official texts. It is also why military recruits are shown video footage of the WTC attacks as part of their induction; it is to remind them of the victim status of America. This is important because victims have a special status – they can be forgiven excesses, their anger can be understood and tolerated. One of the most disturbing consequences of this iconicisation of American suffering however, is a loss of moral perspective and the kinds of human rights violations seen in the Iraqi prisoner abuse scandal. The language of administration officials and the practice of showing recruits video footage of the terrorist attacks not only acted to stoke soldiers' outrage and desire for revenge, it also reinforced the belief that they were the main victims and that they were not the aggressors. In this way, the discursive construction of exceptional suffering made the daily humiliations handed out to prisoners in Abu Ghraib prison seem inconsequential compared with the atrocity of '9-11'.

Even if it was understandable, it was not inevitable that the attacks were constructed in such a way as to create exceptional (American) victim-hood and grievance. Other rhetorical resources were available. For example, the Omagh bombing in Northern Ireland in 1998 which killed 29 people and wounded another 220 could have been used by leaders in Britain and Northern Ireland to create another powerful grievance, as could other terrorist attacks by the Real IRA during this period. Such language however, would probably have upset the fragile peace process at the time and would have renewed the cycle of violence, which is why it was avoided by British officials. The attacks of September 11, 2001 and the suffering they caused in America were in reality far from exceptional: more than double the number of people killed by al Qaeda were killed every day for a hundred days in Rwanda in 1994, leaving upwards of 800,000 civilians dead; the UN estimates that more than three million people have died in the ongoing war in the Democratic Republic of Congo since 1998; terrorists have killed tens of thousands of civilians in the last few years in Algeria, Sri Lanka, Israel and Chechnya; and on September 11, 2001 itself, an estimated 30,000 children died of hunger and preventable diseases across the developing world – as they do every day. In this sense, the myth of exceptional suffering represents something of an obfuscation of global realities.

To summarise, it is possible that an alternative discourse regarding the September 11, 2001 attacks – perhaps, for example, one which emphasised solidarity with the victims of violence in other countries – might have created a less vengeful and more broad-based sense of victim-hood and grievance. Such a rendering might have even created the discursive basis for a global movement to end the terrible conflicts in Israel, Kashmir, Chechnya, the Democratic Republic of Congo and other countries blighted by violence. It might also have created the necessary political will to turn the International Criminal Court (ICC) into a fully effective mechanism of international justice for victims of crimes against humanity everywhere. Instead, the focus on American victim-hood and grievance set the basis for military retaliation and a global 'war on terrorism' that resulted in tens of thousands of civilian deaths and the systematic abuse of thousands of terrorist suspects.

From acts of terrorism to acts of war

It was not enough to construct the attacks as a tragedy and to fix America as the primary victim, however. It was also important to fix the exact nature and meaning of the events. In probably the most important discursive move of all, the attacks were remade from acts of terrorism, symbolic violence and political murder by non-state actors, to acts of 'war'. At 9.30am on September 11, 2001, Bush addressed the nation and referred to them as 'an apparent **terrorist attack**' (Bush, 11 September, 2001a). In his address to the nation on television the same day, Bush said: 'Today, our fellow citizens, our way of life, our very freedom came under attack in a series of deliberate and deadly **terrorist acts**' (Bush, 11 September, 2001b). In the same speech, he referred to them as '**acts of mass murder**', and 'despicable **acts of terror**', a phrase he repeated a few days later.

Almost simultaneously, the attacks began to be grammatically reconstructed as acts of 'war' rather than terrorism or criminal exploits. For example, only three days after the attacks, Bush dramatically changed his words: '**War has been waged against us** by stealth and deceit' (Bush, 14 September, 2001). The next day, he repeated this construction several times in one speech. He stated that 'the wreckage of New York City' was 'the signs of **the first battle of war**', and that 'There has been **an act of war** declared upon America [...] a group of barbarians have **declared war** on the American people' (Bush, 15 September, 2001). In a short space of time then, the terrorist attacks were remade linguistically from 'acts of terror' and 'murder' to a 'battle of war' and an 'act of war'. Directly related to this, the victims of the September 11, 2001 attacks were reclaimed in a powerful discursive act as 'combat casualties' rather than 'terrorist victims'. Donald Rumsfeld achieved this by announcing that the members of the armed forces killed in the attacks would be given war medals, as if they had been injured or killed in an official military operation:

> They were **acts of war**, **military strikes** against the United States of America. As such, those Department of Defense employees who were injured or killed were **not just victims of terror**. They were **combat casualties** [...] [T]he members of the armed forces that were killed or injured in the September 11th attack on the Pentagon and on the World Trade Center towers **will receive the Purple Heart**. As you know, the Purple Heart is given to those **killed or wounded in combat**. (Rumsfeld, 27 September, 2001)

This is a powerful symbolic act that remakes the attacks as fully 'war' and the victims as 'casualties of war'. There can be little doubt the attacks were acts of war if the Pentagon is awarding military medals to the victims. This linguistic evolution had immediate and concrete political effects, such as allowing the response to be framed in terms of accepted international legal norms.

The main problem with constructing the attacks as 'war' however, was that it imbued the attackers with a certain sense of legitimacy; it turned them into warriors (instead of terrorists and criminals), or at the very least, into legitimate international actors (because only legitimate and recognised states can wage war). Thus, officials had to modify their language and recreate the attacks from acts of war in the old, traditional sense, to acts of a 'new' and 'different' kind of war. This is what is called a *reflexive* discursive move – going back and linguistically remaking the original object into something new. The main strategy for reflexively reconstructing this 'act of war' was to suggest that while it was an act of war, it was a 'different' and 'new' kind of war quite unlike the old kind of war. As American officials such as Donald Rumsfeld constantly reiterated: 'I've therefore characterized this conflict, this campaign, this so-called war, as being **notably different** from others' (Rumsfeld, 7 October, 2001); '[...] **this new war** will be a conflict "without battlefields and beachheads," in short, an **unconventional war**' (Dam, 22 October, 2001). This construction of the September 11, 2001 attacks as a 'new' kind of warfare by a 'new' kind of enemy makes it an act of war, but not in the normal sense. Therefore, the attackers are not warriors, nor do they possess any legitimacy whatsoever.

This discursive construction provides policy-makers with a great deal of flexibility. It allows them to reconstruct the September 11, 2001 attacks as acts of war, but without conferring the commensurate legitimacy or status on the terrorists. At the same time, the 'war' context allows the American government to act in ways which would be difficult and probably unacceptable in peacetime or if engaged in a law-enforcement exercise. This is because 'behaviour that is unacceptable in peacetime becomes legitimate in time of war' (Jabri 1996: 6); the war framework allows a wider freedom of action. This is also partly how Bush justifies the creation of a new category of legal subjects in this 'war on terrorism'. A 'new' kind of war can obviously have new kinds of combatants without any major contradiction: 'Non-citizens, non-US citizens who plan and/or commit mass murder are **more than criminal suspects**. They are **unlawful combatants**' (Bush, 29 November, 2001). Bush is suggesting that these are not normal acts of war and the attackers are not normal soldiers. Rather, his words imply that it was a special kind of 'unlawful' or illegal warfare by 'unlawful' combatants.

The important point is that this construction of the attacks as 'war' (in both its initial and later 'new' sense) was probably the most significant and far-reaching aspect of the entire official discourse. It set the foundations for almost everything that followed – it made a counter-'war' against terrorism possible. But, as I have already indicated, it was in no sense inevitable and the use of different words would have given an entirely different understanding to September 11, 2001 – which in turn, would have altered the entire response to the attacks. For example, imagine that the attacks had been discursively constructed as 'the crime of the century'. Suppose that every senior official spoke of this 'crime', the 'criminals' who perpetrated it and the international 'law-enforcement campaign' that was being launched to find those responsible; that every newspaper and television network had headlines proclaiming 'the crime of the century'; and that the word 'war' was not mentioned in any references to either the attack or the American response. Such a discursive rendering could have altered the way the subsequent campaign against terrorism was structured and prosecuted. Preventive invasions of other countries, assassinations, secret military trials and a massive global military campaign would not have appeared to be so logical or reasonable within such a discursive framework. As well, a whole range of alternative counter-terrorist strategies would have become possible. Critically, other terrorist attacks – the Lockerbie bombing being one example – were discursively constructed as crimes and prosecuted through legal means. Although the Lockerbie process took decades, suspects were eventually handed over for trial, sentences were carried out and compensation paid. If it had been constructed as an 'act of war' in the way September 11, 2001 was, the outcome could have been destructively different.

Four meta-narratives

A significant aspect of the discourse surrounding September 11, 2001 is the way in which the events were (and still are) discursively linked to a number of popular meta-narratives. In fact, it is quite common for politicians to make use of historical analogies to try to explain current events. It is one way of rendering current events understandable, by providing them with a context and a historical comparison. As Emily Rosenberg expresses it, 'Amid the completely unexpected, it may seem reassuring to discern some familiar pattern, to domesticate the strangeness of the present by invoking the familiarity of a past shared and reconstituted in memory' (Rosenberg 2003: 175). Discursively however, the use of these analogies actually constructs particular meanings and profoundly affects the way they are subsequently understood. In addition, analogies are so powerful because they work to suppress relevant questions. In the First Gulf War, it was not unusual to hear President Bush Sr and his top officials refer to the analogy of World War II and in particular, Chamberlain's appeasement of Hitler following the invasion of Czechoslovakia. Iraq's invasion of Kuwait was explained by officials as being an identical case: President Bush Sr stated at the time that Saddam was 'Hitler re-visited' (quoted in Glassner 1999: 154). Attributing this meaning to the events implied that just as Hitler needed to be opposed, so too did Saddam: the only real option in dealing with these kinds of people involved the application of military force. The analogy with Hitler suppressed questions such as why Iraq attacked Kuwait in the first instance or whether diplomacy could have resolved the issue: if Saddam was just like Hitler, he was a ruthless, evil, expansionist dictator. There was no need for any other explanations.

Unsurprisingly, the September 11, 2001 attacks were also given meaning and context by comparing them with great historical narratives and linking them with other struggles. And in the same way, these analogies and myths attached particular interpretations and understandings to the events. For example, Donald Rumsfeld explained that the attacks on Washington in particular were 'the first attack on our capital by a foreign enemy since the **War of 1812**' (Rumsfeld, 27 September, 2001). This analogy discursively linked the events of September 11, 2001 with the story of the American struggle for independence. It suggested that the September 11, 2001 attacks were similar to the British attack on Washington, and therefore the struggle against the terrorists was similar to the historic struggle for liberty from colonial Britain.

Although there were a great number of popular narratives used to explain the attacks, I will focus here on the four most commonly occurring cases: the comparison drawn between the September 11, 2001 attacks and World War II and the attack on Pearl Harbor; the struggle against communism during the cold war; the eternal battle between civilisation and barbarism; and the threat posed by terrorism to the progressive benefits of globalisation. These powerful analogies are the most common and most well-articulated meta-narratives in the discourse.

World War II and the attack on Pearl Harbor

The first meta-narrative, and one of the most frequently invoked by political leaders, scholars and pundits, is the analogy of Pearl Harbor and World War II. The following examples are only a small sample of the many instances in which the terrorist attacks are compared with the attack on Pearl Harbor:

> Americans have known wars – but for the past 136 years, they have been wars on foreign soil, except for **one Sunday in 1941**. (Bush, 20 September, 2001)

> For my country, the events of **September the 11th** were as decisive as **the attack on Pearl Harbor** and the treachery of another September in 1939. (Bush, 31 May, 2003)

In the first instance, this can be seen as part of the discursive reconstruction of the events in a 'war' narrative; just as the Pearl Harbor attack was an act of war and the start of America's involvement in the Great War, so too are the September 11, 2001 attacks an 'act of war'. As Congressman Tom Lantos constructed it, '**September 11th was Pearl Harbor**' (Lantos, 10 October, 2001). Simply put, the Pearl Harbor analogy is one more (oblique) way of remaking the attacks as an act of war. More significantly, the World War II narrative recalls the heroic role of America in defeating fascism and saving the world from the axis powers. Bush alludes to this aspect of the analogy when he maintains:

> We have seen their kind before. They are the heirs of all the murderous ideologies of the 20th century. By sacrificing human life to serve their radical visions – by abandoning every value except the will to power – they follow in the path of **fascism**, and **Nazism**, and totalitarianism. And they will follow that path all the way [...] to history's unmarked grave of discarded lies. (Bush, 20 September, 2001)

Interestingly, Bush quotes Nietzsche's 'will to power' – an indirect allusion to the nazis. In this speech he is trying to impress upon his listeners that not only was this attack just like the attacks on the free world by previous 'murderous ideologies', but that America will once again save the world and consign terrorism to the grave of history. This part of the language is a reference to America's view of itself as the 'indispensable nation' (see Chapter 5). In addition, the notion of 'history's unmarked grave' is an appropriation of Marxism's formulation that capitalism would be consigned to the grave of history. Thus, it is a way of turning the meaning of language against itself and demonstrating discursively the earlier victory of capitalism over communism.

In yet another sense, there is also the notion that this was a criminal and 'treacherous' attack, even if it was an act of 'war'. As President Roosevelt originally said about the attack on Pearl Harbor on December 9, 1941:

> The sudden **criminal attacks** perpetrated by the Japanese in the Pacific provide the climax of a decade of international immorality. [...] The Japanese have **treacherously** violated the longstanding peace between us. [...] And no honest person, today or a thousand years hence, will be able to suppress a sense of indignation and horror at the **treachery** committed by the military dictators of Japan [...]. (Roosevelt, quoted in Silberstein, 2002: 30–1)

The effect of this characterisation is to establish something of the nature of the attackers; just like the treacherous and cruel Japanese in World War II, the terrorists also reveal themselves as deceitful criminals. Apart from the treachery association, another effect of this construction is to disconnect the September 11, 2001 attacks by al Qaeda from any of its past actions. It decontextualises them and makes it appear that this assault was part of some diabolical deception that came like a bolt from the blue. There is no sense here that this attack is just the latest in a long-running cycle of violence and counter-violence between the American government and al Qaeda. In fact, al Qaeda had been gradually escalating their attacks against American military and political targets since the early 1990s. The group has been implicated in a long list of attacks on American interests including: various airliner and car bombings; the Khobar Towers bombing in Saudi Arabia; the East African Embassies bombings; the ramming of the USS Cole in Yemen; and the September 11, 2001 attacks. The Clinton administration responded militarily in 1998 by bombing al Qaeda camps in Afghanistan and a chemical factory in Sudan.

The World War II meta-narrative can also be seen in the designation of the site of the Twin Towers collapse as 'ground zero', a highly condensed and charged appellation first used to describe the point of detonation of the atomic bomb over Hiroshima. There are several fascinating aspects to the use of this evocative spatial metaphor. In the first place, it is singularly ironic that America's greatest crime against humanity is discursively remade as a crime against America: where it once represented the incineration of more than 90,000 Japanese civilians, 'ground zero' is now transformed into the symbolic representation of a terrorist attack, an 'act of war' against America, a place of untold American suffering, an absence of the Twin Towers and heroic rescue work by New York EMS personnel (Kaplan 2003: 82). At the same time, the term 'ground zero' relies on an historical analogy which cannot be openly acknowledged because it would, among other things, destabilise the precariously established status of America as the primary victim. In a sense, the term 'both evokes and eclipses the prior historical reference, using it as a yardstick of terror – to claim that this was just like the horrific experience of a nuclear bomb – while at the same time consigning the prior reference to historical amnesia' (Kaplan 2003: 84). This is because 'ground zero' contains echoes of an earlier form of terror perpetuated by America itself. At the very least, it is a device for turning condemnation of previous US policies into sympathy for its suffering; at 'ground zero' the memory of Hiroshima is obliterated and replaced by the memory of '9-11'.

Another definition of 'ground zero' is of going back to square one, or starting again from scratch. In this sense, it is a chilling echo of the Khmer Rouge's proclamation of 'year zero' in Kampuchea – the attempt to restart history from scratch; almost unnoticed, the usage of the term also obliterates America's role in that conflict. Discursively, it is tied to the notion that the world changed on September 11, 2001 and that everything is thereafter 'new'. As such, it taps into a cultural and political myth which lies at the heart of American self-understanding, namely, the 'myth of nature's nation' (Hughes 2003: 45–65). In this narrative, it is self-evident that the American founders designed a new political system rooted in Nature and God that transcended the particularities of time and space, and which owed no debt to history or culture. America was given a new beginning and history was irrelevant to the American experience. This myth still holds a great deal of currency in American political and cultural discourse; 'History is bunk', as Henry Ford famously expressed it. In these senses then, the notion of 'ground zero' is a crucial discursive strategy in establishing the attacks as a special kind of war, and in historically and politically decontextualising them from concrete political events.

One of the most famous and most repeated World War II constructions comes from Bush's State of the Union address in January 2002 when he called North Korea, Iraq and Iran an **'axis of evil'** (Bush, 29 January 2002). This appellation is actually an ingenious new hybrid construction that discursively combines the meta-narratives of World War II, where the Allies fought the Axis powers (Germany, Japan and Italy), and the cold war struggle against the Soviet Union – which Reagan famously referred to as the 'evil empire'. Here, two great historical 'evils' are combined into one powerful new enemy. This implies not only the vast threat posed by terrorism (it is like fascism and communism combined), but also that the United States has a historic role to play in protecting the world from this menace.

In summary, the World War II meta-narrative imbues the September 11, 2001 attacks with a very particular set of meanings and constructs their interpretation in a unique and constrictive manner. In a sense, it makes the attacks instantly understandable to a public immersed in the 'good war' mythology surrounding World War II, popularised over decades of movies and television programmes such as *From Here to Eternity*, *Thirty Seconds Over Tokyo*, *Patton*, *The Longest Day*, *Schindler's List*, *Saving Private Ryan*, *The Thin Red Line*, *Band of Brothers*, *U-571* and the blockbuster of 2001, *Pearl Harbor* (see Pollard 2003; Rosenberg 2003). The most important effect of this discursive frame is to (re)contextualise the events in a military or 'war' narrative, which then makes a military-force-based response appear normal. In part, what makes this particular discursive construction so compelling is the failure of the policy of appeasement and the necessity for the use of force to defeat an evil system. Within this discourse, the attackers are demonised as treacherous, murderous and expansionist totalitarians; it can simply be assumed that they will not be deterred or dissuaded, but must be forcefully challenged by the one nation that has saved the world before; the words call for another Great Generation.

The cold war

Another important meta-narrative employed to discursively construct the September 11, 2001 attacks is the struggle against communism during the cold war. As Deputy Secretary of Defense, Paul Wolfowitz stated in prepared testimony to the Senate Armed Services Committee:

> The American people breathed a sigh of relief when **the Cold War** ended a decade ago. [...] And there was a temptation to believe that this favorable circumstance was a permanent condition. On September 11th, America learned that it was not. The **September 11th attacks** have awakened us to a fundamental reality: [...] This threat is as great as any we faced during **the Cold War**. (Wolfowitz, 4 October, 2001)

In this speech, Wolfowitz first links the September 11, 2001 attacks to the cold war in an opaque and indirect way. He draws a chronological line from the end of the cold war to the WTC attacks, thereby placing them in a single historical narrative. In addition, simply by mentioning the two events in such close proximity an association between them is formed. Next, Wolfowitz directly and explicitly compares the two conflicts, stating that they are different on one level, but the same on another – they are 'just as dangerous' as each other. Extraordinarily, he goes on to explicitly state that the attacks and the cold war pose a comparable level of threat: the threat posed by terrorism is equal to the threat of global nuclear annihilation at the height of the cold war. And, the terrorists, like the Soviets, are attempting to foment a global revolution against capitalism and democracy by toppling regimes one after the other. In both cases, one of the main effects of this construction is to fix the massive level of threat posed by terrorism (see Chapter 4).

Another important effect of linking the cold war meta-narrative with the September 11, 2001 attacks is to characterise the enemy in a particular way. Just as the World War II analogy suggests that terrorists are evil, treacherous, expansionist, murderous and unreasonable, so the cold war framework paints them as totalitarians and soulless ideologues seeking to impose their 'way of life' on subject populations. As Bush spelled it out: 'Because the war on terror will require resolve and patience, it will also require firm moral purpose. In this way **our struggle is similar to the Cold War**. Now, as then, our enemies are totalitarians, holding a creed of power with no place for human dignity' (Bush, 1 June, 2002). Here, Bush is saying that terrorists and communists are essentially the same kind of enemy and the 'war on terrorism' is just like the cold war. In one sense, Bush is redeploying the old cold war argument in which the enemy is seeking to overthrow the American 'way of life'. In addition to constructing the terrorists as a certain kind of enemy, he is also suggesting that the 'war on terrorism' must be fought in a particular manner and that it will require the same qualities of resolve, patience and 'firm moral purpose' that characterised the cold war struggle. This is an attempt to rewrite the history of the cold war, as well as pre-write the history of the 'war on terrorism'. In addition, as with the language of Wolfowitz, the discourse implies that the fight against tiny groups of terrorists (who do not possess a fraction of the power and resources that even a small state can muster) will be like the struggle against a superpower such as the Soviet Union, with its massive conventional army and gigantic nuclear arsenal. This would normally be seen as an absurd statement, except that, as Chapter 4 demonstrates, the threat of terrorism has been constructed in such a way that it appears to be a reasonable comparison.

A final aspect of the cold war analogy is the notion that America, through determined struggle, will ultimately triumph over terrorism in the same way it triumphed over communism. This is an important theme to which I will return in Chapter 5: wars must be constructed as winnable or they are unlikely to garner the requisite level of support. Donald Rumsfeld, often described as a 'cold war warrior' due to his role during the Reagan administration, gives an exposition of how the 'war on terrorism' compares with the struggle against communism: 'If you think about it, 50 years, 40 years, however long it was with **the Cold War** ... but here we are. No Soviet Union' (Rumsfeld, 24 October, 2001). Again, we have an association being constructed between the terrorist attacks and the cold war; at the same time, a powerful narrative of the coming struggle is constructed. It may take several decades, but victory is assured. Vice President Cheney (another cold war veteran) also enlists the analogy of the defeat of communism to demonstrate the certainty of victory: 'Your faith in freedom's ultimate triumph was vindicated when **the Berlin Wall** was toppled, when **an evil empire** vanished from the face of the earth. Today, freedom has a new set of **totalitarian enemies**' (Cheney, 1 May, 2003). Apart from the theme of winning the 'war against terrorism', Cheney once again uses the 'evil empire' construction. This is Reagan's anti-communist language, and is linked here to the notion of 'evil' terrorists (see Chapter 3), as well as the 'axis of evil' appellation mentioned earlier. The language employed is categorical – 'your faith in freedom's triumph *will* be vindicated' – and imbued with a sense of its own certainty of interpretation – 'the Berlin Wall *was* toppled', 'an evil empire vanished from the face of the earth'. This conveys a powerful sense of what is known about history, it leaves no room for alternative interpretations of either the ending of the cold war or the possible end of the 'war on terrorism'.

The cold war meta-narrative was for a long time a powerful theme in American politics and popular culture. In a sense, given the number of senior officials in the Bush administration who worked for Ronald Reagan at the height of the cold war, it is not surprising that it is once again a common frame of reference in political speech making. Apart from the direct references to the cold war, there is a constant theme in the official discourse that terrorism represents a 'threat to **our way of life**' (Bush, 20 September, 2001). This is itself a reference to the anti-communist struggle as it echoes the language of American leaders throughout the cold war: it was the primary reason why Americans had to be vigilant and get behind the struggle against the Soviet Union – communism endangered the 'American way of life'.

Put another way, the deployment of the cold war analogy in interpreting and ascribing meaning to the September 11, 2001 attacks would have brought to mind a number of images for many Americans: the threat of 'reds' spying everywhere and trying to take over the country; the danger of nuclear war and global annihilation; the anti-communist wars in Korea and Vietnam; and the eventual victory vividly captured by the fall of the Berlin Wall. Within this discourse then, they would have understood the terrible and fearful danger posed by terrorism, the likely presence of terrorist 'moles' in American society and the necessity of building up American military power to protect the American way of life. At the same time, they would also feel that just as the cold war ended in eventual victory, so too the 'war on terrorism' would be decided in America's favour. In a sense, '*terrorism* now occupies the place and function that *fascism* held in World War II and that *communism* held within the discourse of the cold war' (Singh 2003: 173; original emphasis). It is a way of mobilising and organising the nation behind a common cause.

As I have already maintained, the use of alternative historical analogies and meta-narratives would have evoked different kinds of interpretations and meanings. If, for example, the terrorist attacks had been compared repeatedly with the still ongoing 'war on drugs', Americans might have drawn a completely contrasting set of interpretations. They might have thought it would be a war involving primarily law enforcement and a war which was unlikely to have a clear end. Given the record of American anti-narcotic efforts in Latin America, there might also have been a suspicion that victory was not in fact, guaranteed. It is also interesting to consider the understandings that might have resulted if senior officials had said that the 'war on terrorism' would be akin to the war on poverty, or the historic struggle against racial inequality in America.

Civilisation versus barbarism

One of the most common appeals in the discourse, and one which has received a great deal of public attention, is the construction of the struggle between the terrorists and America as explicitly linked to the ongoing struggle between civilisation and barbarism. This meta-narrative has a long genealogy in international relations (see Salter 2002) which can be seen most recently in the so-called 'clash of civilisations' thesis (see El Fadl 2002), and in parts of the globalisation discourse (see below). In both popular culture and the counter-terrorism discourse, terrorists are seen as 'the new barbarians', the epitome of savagery for the western psyche (Zulaika and Douglass 1996: 156). Linguistically, this is achieved through the natural functioning of the binary structure of language: employing the concept 'civilisation' instinctively brings to mind its opposite concept, 'barbarism'. In its textual usage in political and social conversation, the civilisation-barbarism dichotomy has a number of different layers of meaning. For example, on one level it evokes images of menacing nomadic armies attempting to conquer Christian Europe. In the context of today's terrorists it implies that 'the behavior of these new "barbarians" is uncontrollably guided by the same cruel instincts that motivated some of the most infamous "barbarians" of past centuries, including Attila the Hun and the Mongol leader Genghis Khan' (Llorente 2002: 41, 45).

On another level, the civilisation narrative is, for Americans at least, embedded in its foundational myths: 'The myth represents American history as an Indian war, in which white Christian civilization is opposed by a "savage" racial enemy: an enemy whose hostility to civilization is part of its nature or fundamental character, an enemy who is not just opposed to our interests but to "civilization itself"' (Slotkin 2001, quoted in Sardar and Davies 2002: 190–1). In Freudian terms, we might say that the barbarians are representative of the id force: libidinous, irrational, violent and dangerous. At a cultural-political level, the civilised western world is contrasted with the violent and barbaric eastern world. It is a function of the way that our cultural identity has been constructed, according to Edward Said; the western person only exists as a contrast with the 'Oriental other' (Said 1978). In yet another sense, globalisation has come to be seen as the late-modern, sociological term for the 'civilising process'. In this respect, terrorism – as a form of barbarism – can be seen as a challenge to international order and the civilising process of globalisation (Rasmussen 2002: 337).

The initial step in fixing the 'war on terrorism' firmly within the civilisation-barbarism framework was the designation of the September 11, 2001 attacks as 'barbaric' and as attacks on 'civilisation' itself. Ambassador Baker asserted that the attacks were 'an attack not just on the United States but on **enlightened, civilized societies** everywhere. It was a strike against those values that separate us from **animals** – compassion, tolerance, mercy' (Baker, 23 September, 2001). Note that he is also suggesting that the terrorists (by implication, the 'barbarians') are little more than animals. This is a continuation of recent imperial and colonial attitudes, reinforced by Social Darwinism, which divided the world into a hierarchy of superior and inferior races. In this schema, some races were lower down the evolutionary ladder, close to the level of animals. In a related sense, the language of civilisation used here also connotes that there are bad nations of people and not just guilty individuals (El Fadl 2002: 29). It is a way of collectivising both identity and guilt; the uncivilised nations are terrorists.

In a speech that was symbolically delivered in Shanghai near the Great

Wall of China, built to keep out the barbarian Mongolian hordes from the great Confucian civilisation, Bush goes into some detail about the values that define civilisation and distinguish it from the barbarian 'other'. He begins by pointing out that the barbarians 'hate all **civilization** and culture and progress', and that:

> Throughout the world, people value their families – and nowhere do **civilized** people rejoice in the murder of children or the creation of orphans. By their **cruelty**, the terrorists have chosen to live on the hunted margin of mankind. By their **hatred**, they have divorced themselves from the values that define **civilization** itself. (Bush, 20 October, 2001)

Thus, while civilisation is associated with culture, progress, values and love of family, barbarism is defined by its cruelty, hatred, the murder of children and the creation of orphans. As a natural consequence, the barbarians are banished to the 'hunted margin of mankind' – the world of animals and sub-humans. This is a powerful act of identity creation – the civilised 'us' and the barbaric 'them' – as well as an essential dehumanisation and demonisation of the terrorists.

This linguistic boundary drawing is reiterated in a forceful passage from Attorney General John Ashcroft:

> Ladies and Gentlemen of the Judiciary Committee, the attacks of September 11 drew a bright line of demarcation between **the civil and the savage**, and our nation will never be the same. On one side of this line are **freedom's enemies**, **murderers of innocents** in the name of a **barbarous** cause. On the other side are friends of freedom; ... Today I call upon Congress to act to strengthen our ability to fight this evil wherever it exists, and to ensure that **the line between the civil and the savage**, so brightly drawn on September 11, is never crossed again. (Ashcroft, 24 September, 2001)

Ashcroft is suggesting that a clear line exists between civility and savagery and that the terrorists are 'savages' and 'barbarians'. Such a rendering clearly echoes the imperial mind-set in the age of colonialism and taps into the narrative of the 'civilising mission' towards the colonial savages. There is a clear sense here that it is America's mission to prevent the terrorist savages from crossing that metaphysical line. Disturbingly, an important real-world effect of this language is to create the conditions for abuse and torture against terrorist suspects: if they are animals, barbarians and savages then they have no 'human' qualities and no 'human' rights and can be treated as animals without regret or pity. The image of the naked prisoner being dragged on a leash is the elemental realisation of this discursively constructed relationship – the civilised American soldier subduing the savage barbarian. It is a disturbing mirror image of colonial-era photographs of African-American slaves tied together by ropes to the neck.

More than simply locating the September 11, 2001 attacks within the civilisation-barbarism narrative, there is also a powerful attempt to construct the purpose of the 'war against terrorism' as a fight for civilisation itself. In his major address to Congress following the September 11, 2001 attacks, Bush assured: 'This is not, however, just America's fight. And what is at stake is not just America's freedom. This is the world's fight. **This is civilization's fight**. This is the fight of all who believe in progress and pluralism, tolerance and freedom' (Bush, 20 September, 2001). A month later in Shanghai, Bush reiterated that the counter-terrorism campaign was '**a fight to save the civilized world**, and values common to the West, to Asia, to Islam' (Bush, 20 October, 2001). Following the military campaign in Afghanistan, the outcome was again located within the civilisation-barbarism narrative: 'In the battle of Afghanistan, we destroyed one of the most **barbaric** regimes in the history of mankind. A regime so **barbaric**, they would not allow young girls to go to school. A regime so **barbaric**, they were willing to house al Qaeda' (Bush, 2 May, 2003). In one sense, the use of the terms 'civilisation' and 'barbarism' in this context is a reiteration of the European cultural mythology of modernity. It is an appeal to a deeply pervasive and long-running historical narrative that also provides a crucial dividing line between the 'civilised' European world and the 'uncivilised' and 'barbarous' non-western, non-European 'other'. The narrative of European civilisation and modernity is frequently invoked to explain the brutal behaviour found in (non-western) contemporary warfare; apart from the cruel and backward Taliban regime, Rwanda's genocide was widely interpreted as ancient tribal (pre-modern and irrational) hatred, and Yugoslavia's bestiality was seen as the result of eastern and central European backwardness, primitiveness and blood-feuding.

Constructing the September 11, 2001 attacks as an expression of the 'barbarous', 'uncivilised' world and as part of the long-running struggle between savagery and civility fulfils a number of functions. First, it locates the act in a long-running historical narrative about the noble struggle to civilise the non-western, non-European world; it makes it a part of the struggle to bring modernity to the colonies, to save the Somalis and Rwandans from their primitive blood-letting, and to rescue the Kosovas, the Afghans and most recently the Iraqis from their savage rulers. Second, it provides clear-cut identity markers for 'us' and 'them': we are the 'civilised' who only use violence in the pursuit of good and just goals, while they are clearly 'uncivilised', 'savage', 'barbarians' who have no belief in the value of human life. It suggests that there is a clear line that distinctly sets them apart. At the same time, this construction obliterates any reference to western civilisation's savagery and brutality in two World Wars, the Holocaust, the atomic attacks against Japan, numerous colonial wars and many recent wars where cluster bombs and other 'barbaric' weapons were used – or the barbarous and savage treatment of prisoners in Iraq, Afghanistan and Guantanamo Bay.

This powerful meta-narrative has deep roots in western politics and culture and fixes the September 11, 2001 events within a very particular set of meanings. As with the other meta-narratives, it was not inevitable that the attacks were constructed in this way. The use of alternative narrative frameworks would have helped to create a different set of meanings and interpretations. For example, the attacks could have been interpreted as part of the long historical conflict between states and revolutionary actors. There is a long line of revolutionaries – anarchists, communists, abolitionists, guerrillas, resistance fighters, revolutionaries and terrorists – who have fought the power of the state employing asymmetric modes of warfare. Or, the attacks could have been located within the narrative of the north–south conflict. These other analogies would have imbued the attacks with a wholly different set of meanings.

Globalisation

A final meta-narrative common to the discourse is the construction of the September 11, 2001 attacks as an attack on globalisation and world economic progress. In part, this interpretation is inferred because the terrorists attacked the World Trade Center, a potent symbol of the global economic system. In another sense, the globalisation narrative is part of the civilisation-barbarism theme: globalisation *is* civilisation because western society rests on the achievements and prosperity of global interconnectedness. Therefore, according to the discourse, an attack on civilisation is an attack on globalisation. Soon after the attacks, Bush gave voice to this construction when he stated that, 'In every generation, the world has produced enemies of **human freedom**. They have attacked America, because we are **freedom's** home and defender' (Bush, 14 September, 2001). In American political culture, the notion of 'freedom' is inextricably linked to economic freedom – the so-called 'free market'. When Bush speaks about America in these terms, he knows that his listeners will understand that he is speaking about more than simply political freedom; he is also referring to economic prosperity, opportunity and globalisation.

The notion that the September 11, 2001 attacks were an attack on globalisation is initially inferred by Paul Wolfowitz: 'The American people breathed a sigh of relief when the Cold War ended a decade ago. [...] They saw **a powerful economic expansion creating unprecedented prosperity**. And there was a temptation to believe that this favorable circumstance was a permanent condition. On September 11th, America learned that it was not' (Wolfowitz, 4 October, 2001). This speech is actually constructed as a sort of story of the post-cold war period. It has a simple chronology, a central character (the lone superpower) and a climax (the attacks). The narrative implies that globalisation, the 'powerful economic expansion creating unprecedented prosperity', was steadily spreading its positive benefits around the world until it was interrupted by the terrorist attacks. In this way, we are provided with a simple narrative structure into which the attacks can be neatly inserted. Moreover, this construction actually works to suppress any notion that the attacks were in any way caused by globalisation itself – a reaction to the negative effects of globalisation in peripheral regions. Democracy and unprecedented prosperity are the effects of globalisation; the language does not allow any additions, such as a widening gap between the rich and poor, increasing debt burdens or even increasing technological vulnerabilities.

Beyond these implicit and rather opaque references to globalisation, there are also more explicit and direct references. For example, in his Shanghai speech to the CEO Summit, President Bush deliberately and forcefully constructs the terrorist attacks as being directed specifically against the progress of globalisation:

> The stakes of this fight for all nations are high – our lives, our way of life, and **our economic future**. By **attacking two great economic symbols**, the terrorists tried to shatter confidence in the **world economic system**.
>
> The terrorists hoped **world markets** would collapse.
>
> And this week in these halls, we return to the steady work of building the **market-based economic system** that has brought more prosperity more quickly to more people than at any time in human history.
>
> When nations accept the rules of the **modern** world, they discover the benefits of the **modern** world.
>
> ... our governments must keep the path of **economic progress**. That progress begins with freer trade. Trade is the engine of **economic advancement**.
>
> **Terrorists want to turn the openness of the global economy against itself**. We must not let them. We need customs, financial, immigration, and transportation systems that makes it easier for us to do our business, and much harder for terrorists to do theirs. (Bush, 20 October, 2001)

There are several interesting features in this speech. First, the attacks are constructed as assaults on the 'world' economic system – as symbolised by the Twin Towers of the WTC – rather than as attacks on the 'American' economy. This discursive construction also omits and obscures any notion of American hegemony or dominance of the world economic system, or the possibility that the terrorists, by attacking a symbol located on US soil, might have actually been signalling opposition to specifically *American* hegemony. Second, the attacks are constructed as being aimed at 'world markets'; also, that they threaten 'our' (the world's) economic future. Again, there is no room to suggest that they might have been directed solely at America. This is also a powerful construction of threat and danger: terrorism, even by such tiny groups, threatens the entire global economy and the prosperity of everyone. Lastly, there are two references to the 'modern world' in the speech, inferring that the terrorists are primitive or anti-modern. This is another opaque reference to the civilisation-barbarism narrative; it suggests that al Qaeda (and their Taliban allies) belong to the ancient past and are mere reactionaries to the modern world – they are primitives and 'luddites'.

Bush reiterates this construction of the benefits of globalisation and the opposition of terrorists to the modern world in a more recent speech: 'America's national ambition is the spread of **free markets**, **free trade**, and **free societies**. These goals are not achieved at the expense of other nations, they are achieved for **the benefit of all nations**' (Bush, 21 May, 2003). In this case, Bush brings American aims to the forefront, and takes pains to make the point that America's role in the global economy is to benefit 'all nations'. In this sense, he is suggesting that by opposing the American vision, the 'terrorists and tyrants' are really against prosperity and freedom. In other words, '9-11' was an act of anti-globalisation, as well as an act of war; it was 'the battle of Seattle' but in New York and Washington. Again, what is left out of the discourse is as important as what is left in: there is no acknowledgement that globalisation has a dark side, and that the terrorists came from a region that has yet to experience any of the 'palpable gains' of globalisation – at least for the majority of its citizens.

As before, this construction of the September 11, 2001 attacks and their location within a simple narrative of expanding global economic prosperity creates a precise understanding and meaning of the events. It constructs them as reactionary, anti-modern, and in a way, highly irrational. After all, why attack something which is bringing prosperity and freedom to millions? It also constructs them as being a threat to the entire global economic system which underpins 'our way of life'. As before, this interpretation was not inevitable or natural, but rather it serves the (political) function of suppressing awkward questions, demonising the attackers and amplifying the threat of terrorism. It would have been equally credible to locate the attacks within an entirely different rendering of globalisation. For example, the attacks could have been described and explained as a manifestation of globalisation's dark side: the attackers, representing a constituency blighted by the global economic system, attacking the symbols of that system by turning the vulnerabilities of a globalised society against itself. Such a rendering would have fixed a different interpretation of the September 11, 2001 events, perhaps one which forced a reconsideration of the current realities and long-term consequences of present economic conditions and policies. It may even have opened up a debate about the need to regulate and reform the unhindered operation of global capitalism which is proving so damaging to developing regions.

Why was America attacked?

As the preceding analysis suggests, one of the key functions of the discourse surrounding the September 11, 2001 attacks was to deny or suppress any alternative reading of the events, particularly those that might implicate American foreign policy. It was important for senior officials to ensure that the attacks could not be understood as anything but an unprovoked and undeserved assault on an innocent and peaceful nation. As a consequence, a sustained effort was made to establish firmly the reasons why America was attacked. The meta-narratives described above imply that America was attacked simply because the attackers were totalitarian and expansionist, they were barbarians and they were primitive reactionaries against progress; they attacked because it was in their nature to attack. The reasons for the assaults therefore are firmly rooted in the identity and nature of the attackers and not in any concrete political grievances. Beyond this implicit reading of the reasons for the attacks, there are also more explicit attempts to fix the motives of the terrorists.

In the first instance, there is an effort by senior officials to establish that America was attacked for its virtues rather than its failings and that any claims by the terrorists (or their sympathisers) that US foreign policy was to blame are false. As Bush asserted on the day of the attacks, 'America was targeted for attack because we're the brightest beacon for freedom and opportunity in the world' (Bush, 11 September, 2001b). From the very first hours, Bush is trying to suppress any alternative readings and firmly establish America as an innocent victim, attacked because it is a symbol of freedom and democracy. He elucidates this construction a few days later when he suggests that the terrorists attacked the WTC because they hate 'American' freedoms: '**They hate what we see right here in this chamber** – a democratically elected government. Their leaders are self-appointed. **They hate our freedoms** – our freedom of religion, our freedom of speech, our freedom to vote and assemble and disagree with each other' (Bush, 20 September, 2001). Bush is stating that the reasons for the attacks lie within the terrorist's nature and their hatred and envy of America. This not only negates alternative readings, such as that they attacked because of American support of Israeli attacks on Palestinians for example, but it also fixes the notion that America was attacked for its virtuous qualities rather than its policy choices.

In a more personalised construction, Bush expresses his amazement that anyone would hate the United States:

> [H]ow do I respond when I see that in some Islamic countries there is vitriolic hatred for America? I'll tell you how I respond: I'm amazed that there is such misunderstanding of what our country is about, that people would hate us. I am, I am – like most Americans, I just can't believe it. Because I know how good we are ... (Bush, 11 October, 2001)

This is an ingenious discursive strategy, because it implies there could be no real reason for such hatred, that America has done nothing to deserve it, and that even the president (who presumably has access to all the relevant information) cannot think why anyone would dislike America. Bush is offering no possible political reasons for such hatred; therefore, it must be because the attackers are envious or naturally full of hate. Bush repeats this same construction in a more folksy style when he remarks: '**They can't stand what America stands for**. It must bother them greatly to know we're such a free and wonderful place – a place where all religions can flourish; a place where women are free; a place where children can be educated. It must grate on them greatly' (Bush, 29 November, 2001). The grammatical construction of this narrative implies that by their very nature, terrorists hate freedom and the mere existence of a wonderful place like America 'must grate on them'. There is no concrete reason for this; it is merely a part of their character. Also, it echoes the civilisation-barbarism discourse; these are clearly primitive, barbarous people who despise progress, education and advancement.

Ironically, this formulation of the terrorist's motives is at odds with the American government's own definition of terrorism. The State Department defines terrorism as 'politically motivated violence perpetrated against non-combatant targets' – implying that the September 11, 2001 attackers were not really terrorists at all because they were, according to Bush, motivated by hate and envy. Without realising it, the administration's attempt to deny a political rationale for al Qaeda's campaign contradicts its initial efforts to demonise them as terrorists; depoliticising the aims of terrorists destabilises the very term itself.

Another discursive strategy involves deliberately denying alternative readings of the attacks. The following quote from Marc Grossman for example, is an explicit attempt to deny one alternative interpretation. In response to the question of whether the attacks could have been linked to American military support for Israel, Grossman asserts that the attacks 'don't have anything to do with the Middle East peace process', and that they were 'Totally irrelevant to the question of pluses or minuses in the Middle East peace process' (Grossman, 19 October, 2001). This is a direct denial of statements made by al Qaeda and an effort to dismiss and suppress any possibility that the attacks could be read as being connected to American foreign policy. The attackers are thus denied a voice and their reasons are deconstructed and replaced by other (more acceptable) reasons (see Lincoln 2002: 27). The language implies that as the attacks were 'totally irrelevant' to the Middle East conflict, they must have been caused by hatred of democracy and freedom, anti-globalisation and anti-modernism. After all, as Bush and other senior officials reiterated again and again, America 'is a peaceful nation. This is a nation that wants nothing more than the world to be more free and more peaceful. We believe in the peace, in keeping the peace' (Bush, 2 May, 2003).

In fact, we know that al Qaeda's reasons for attacking American interests are deeply political and intimately connected to American foreign policy; they have very little to do with hatred, envy or anti-modernism. As Peter Bergen, one of the few people to have actually interviewed Osama bin Laden, concludes:

> In all the tens of thousands of words that bin Laden has uttered on the public record ... [H]e does not rail against the pernicious effects of Hollywood movies, or against Madonna's midriff, or against the pornography protected by the US Constitution ... [B]in Laden cares little about such cultural issues. What he condemns the United States for is simple: its policies in the Middle East ... [T]he continued US military presence in Arabia; US support for Israel; its continued bombing of Iraq; and its support for regimes such as Egypt and Saudi Arabia ... The hijackers who came to America did not attack the headquarters of a major brewery or AOL-Time Warner or Coca-Cola, nor did they attack Las Vegas or Manhattan's West Village or even the Supreme Court. They attacked the Pentagon and the World Trade Center, preeminent symbols of the United States' military and economic might. (Bergen 2001: 242)

In other words, bin Laden attacked America for clearly defined political reasons, in the belief that just as the 1983 suicide bombings drove American forces out of Lebanon, and just as a sustained terrorist campaign drove the Soviets out of Afghanistan, so too would terror attacks force America to change its policies in the Middle East. Within this alternative narrative, the reasons America was attacked take on a whole new meaning and the attackers actually emerge as rational and complex political actors rather than one-dimensional hate-filled anti-modernists.

A final discursive strategy by officials involves answering the question: what were the exact aims of the terrorist attack? As any terrorism scholar will attest, the aim of terrorism is first and foremost to gain publicity and force governments to pay attention to a political cause. In this sense, the WTC attacks were by any assessment a spectacular success (see Nacos 2002). They elevated Osama bin Laden and his followers from a minor irritant to the most famous and most talked about fugitives in the world. The American government was, for obvious reasons, unwilling to allow this situation to continue and attempts were made to try to suppress this reading of events. Instead, the attacks were reconstructed as being aimed at turning America into a traumatised coward. As Bush describes it:

> Their intention was not only to kill and maim and destroy. **Their intention was to frighten** to the point where our nation would not act. **Their intention was to so frighten** our government that we wouldn't seek justice; that somehow we would cower in the face of their threats and not respond abroad or at home. [...] I know their intended act was to destroy us and **make us cowards** and **make us not want to respond**. (Bush, 11 October, 2001)

Fundamentally, by remaking the intentions of the terrorists America can then proclaim that the attacks had not succeeded; that they were in fact a failure instead of a resounding success. This is more than simple self-deception; it is actually an ingenious strategy for enlisting support for a 'war against terrorism' because it implies that if America does not respond then the terrorists will have retrospectively won. The logic of the language thus predetermines the policy response; there is no other option but to fight back. At the same time, it makes anyone who opposes the policy appear like a coward who would give in to terrorism.

The combined effect of these discursive strategies is to fix the reading of the reasons for the attacks as lying within first, the nature of the terrorists; second, in the virtues (rather than the failings) of America; and third, in the hope that the US would cower and refrain from responding. The terrorists must have attacked America because it is in their barbaric nature and because it is such a powerful symbol of freedom and democracy. By implication, to fail to respond with a forceful counter-attack would be to allow the terrorists to win.

Conclusion

It is a common refrain that the events of September 11, 2001 were the day that everything changed, the end of one phase of human history; or simply, 'the beginning of World War III' (Friedman 2002: ix). While the devastation at 'ground zero' might appear to 'speak for itself' – as an inherently evil act or the start of a global war, for example – the reality is not quite so straightforward. After all, the Hiroshima explosion in 1945 was infinitely more horrific than the attack on New York; at face value, that assault by the US air force looks like the ultimate act of human evil. Yet, American popular understanding rejects this reading of it and sees it as an unfortunate but ultimately necessary action that ended World War II and saved American lives. That event has not been allowed to 'speak for itself' but has had a particular interpretation imposed on it. The same process has occurred in relation to the events of September 11, 2001: officials have constructed a particular reading or interpretation which serves a purposeful political agenda while simultaneously closing off other possible readings.

Simply put, the discursive associations drawn between the four meta-narratives – World War II, the cold war, civilisation versus barbarism and globalisation – and the September 11, 2001 attacks, affected to fix their meaning and establish the context of public knowledge of these events in very specific ways. For example, they establish American understanding of the events as part of a long and heroic struggle against totalitarian and murderous ideologies such as fascism and communism. This interpretation implies that just as America did not appease these evil regimes of the past, so too should America avoid appeasing the terrorists. In a historical perspective, the civilisation narrative, as well as the more recent globalisation story, enforces the understanding that the attacks on New York and Washington were part of the eternal struggle between the forces of enlightened progress and the dark forces of backwardness, primitivism and savagery.

One of the most important consequences of these constructions, and part of their intended function, is to de-historicise the events from the recent past, while simultaneously imposing a more distant historical reading with a radically different set of interpretations. That is, fixing the attacks within the World War II, cold war, and civilisation-barbarism meta-narratives actually works to remove all traces of more recent American actions or policies in the Middle East: there is no room here for any discussion about the murky policies of supporting and arming the Mujahaddin in Afghanistan out of which al Qaeda and Osama bin Laden emerged, or of the escalating cycle of attack and counter-attack between the US military and the terrorists since the First Gulf War. Similarly, it functions to deny a voice to the terrorists and the constituencies they represent and suppresses any discussion of what their real motives or aims might have been. For example, it is clear that the attackers were attempting to make a statement about American economic and military hegemony, and to provoke a reassessment of US policies in the Middle East. The overwhelming use of historical analogies suppresses any such questions.

Another key function of these discursive constructions is to fix the identities of the terrorists and their victims. This is examined in more detail in the following chapter. The attackers are firmly constructed as evil destroyers, totalitarians, barbarians and haters of freedom, democracy and progress. America by contrast, is discursively made as a beacon of freedom and democracy, and more importantly, as the innocent victim of hateful aggression. By denying certain readings of the attacks – for example, as revenge for American military support for Israeli attacks on Palestinian civilians – the US is able to maintain its identity as the injured and innocent victim. This is the reinforcement of a sense of exceptional victim-hood, which is a key component of constructing support for war violence.

Finally, and most importantly, these interpretations of the September 11, 2001 attacks were not necessarily inevitable or natural in any way; other narratives, other analogies, other myths – different kinds of words and language – could have been employed by officials. Employing a dissimilar vocabulary would have fixed a different set of meanings and a different set of options for responding to those attacks. Within alternative narratives, policies apart from war might have seemed more logical and commonsensical. Giving meaning to the September 11, 2001 attacks is not a case of simply 'letting the facts speak for themselves', but rather of deploying language in such a way that only certain interpretations are possible. These understandings were a necessary part of the discursive construction of the global 'war on terrorism'.

3

Writing identity:
evil terrorists, good Americans

O NE OF THE MOST NOTICEABLE and ubiquitous features of the language of counter-terrorism is its invariable appeal to identity: terrorists are endlessly demonised and vilified as being evil, barbaric and inhuman, while America and its coalition partners are described as heroic, decent and peaceful – the defenders of freedom. The clear implication of this language is that identity rather than deliberation is the basis of human action: terrorists behave as they do not because they are rationally calculating political actors but simply because it is in their nature to be evil. Similarly, the United States acts to bring the terrorists to justice and to secure freedom because that is what America is like – Americans are a freedom-loving and dependable nation. In large part, the Iraqi prisoner abuse scandal which began in May 2004 was disturbing because it upset the fundamental identities established through the official discourse; in those photos the American soldiers looked like the evil barbarians and the Iraqi suspects looked like the innocent victims – a reversal of the natural order constructed through the public rhetoric.

In this chapter I explore the unique and particular ways in which identity has been discursively constructed through the official language of counter-terrorism. I argue that the process of 'othering' so apparent in the discourse of the 'war on terrorism' – the discursive creation of an external 'other' who reinforces the identity of the 'self' – was not inevitable or a natural consequence of the horrific terrorist assault on September 11, 2001. Rather, it was carefully and deliberately created to satisfy a number of political objectives. At the simplest level, establishing the identities of the primary characters – the heroes and villains or the 'good guys' and the 'bad guys' – was a key element in constructing the overall narrative of the 'war on terrorism'. In a media-saturated society, establishing the identities of the 'good guys' and the 'bad guys' was essential to making the national story of America's war understandable to the wider public.

However, even more importantly, the social construction of war itself requires a unique kind of 'othering' process. This is because intensive political violence is actually very difficult to sustain otherwise; there are powerful in-built social and individual inhibitors to killing other human beings, like empathy. Constructing a large-scale project of political violence such as a global counter-terrorist war requires an extremely powerful process of demonisation and dehumanisation to overcome the natural reticence over the destruction of human life for political reasons. As James Der Derian expresses it: 'People go to war because of how they *see, perceive, picture, imagine,* and *speak* of others; that is, how they construct the difference of others as well as the sameness of themselves through representation' (Der Derian 2002b; original emphasis). For both soldiers and wider society the common everyday language of human recognition and respect has to be replaced by the language of hate and fear; perceptions and emotions have to be profoundly altered so ordinary people can more easily countenance the deliberate infliction of suffering. There is no better way to achieve this than by replacing the language they ordinarily use with a new language of hate and fear based on powerful categories of identity: them and us, citizen and foreigner, civilised and savage, terrorist and soldier. At its most basic level, the discursive construction of the depersonalised and dehumanised 'enemy other' can be seen in the commonly used derogatory terms that soldiers of every generation have employed. 'Hun', 'Japs', 'gooks', 'rag-heads' and 'skinnies' are the means by which fellow human beings – who are also husbands, sons, brothers, friends – are discursively transformed into a hateful and loathsome 'other' who can be killed and abused without remorse or regret. The term 'terrorist' is simply the latest manifestation of this discursive process – today's 'terrorists' are the new 'gooks'.

While warfare always necessitates the construction of an identifiable enemy, there were a number of unique problems facing American officials in this particular instance. In the first place, rewriting the terrorist attacks as 'acts of war' raised the possibility that the enemy would be seen as soldiers or warriors; this was unthinkable because in the contemporary setting non-state actors cannot be allowed to express legitimate violence (only states are allowed to have a monopoly on the legitimate instruments of violence). Similarly, the enemy needed to be stripped of any genuine and justifiable political grievances; they needed to be portrayed as simply evil or mad rather than as rationally calculating revolutionaries or political dissidents. Also, the highly unconventional nature of the war convinced officials that they needed greater flexibility in pursuing, capturing, interrogating and punishing terrorists. Thus the enemy should be exempt from both the laws of peacetime (due process) and the accepted laws of war (the Geneva Conventions); their normal human rights needed to be suspended. In the end, a very specific and unique kind of enemy 'other' had to be constructed for the kind of 'war on terrorism' that administration officials envisaged.

There is a deeper political purpose to the official language of identity, namely, the discursive construction of the 'enemy other' which is important for creating and maintaining national identity – it is a way of 'writing identity'. The construction of foreign enemies, external threats and war or crisis is enormously significant for preserving the internal/external, foreign/domestic, self/other boundaries that define the limits of the group (see Campbell 1998). The simple reason for this is that one's own identity is impossible without an external 'other'; the very notion of the 'self' depends on an 'enabling other'. To be more specific, American national identity and citizenship is dependent on the existence of other external nations and people who are *not* American citizens – what is called its negative justification.

Alternatively, a shared identity is a prerequisite for nationhood. As anthropologist Benedict Anderson describes it, the nation is 'an imagined political community' (Anderson 1983: 6); in order for a nation-state to remain intact and retain some kind of unity and coherence all of its members must believe or 'imagine' they belong to a common community, even though they cannot possibly meet or get to know all their fellow citizens personally. This sense of belonging to a special and exclusive political community must be continually maintained in every citizen's mind in order for the nation-state to exist and function properly. This is why governments invest so much time and effort in maintaining and reproducing the symbols of statehood – national flags, national anthems, pledges, citizenship ceremonies, emblems, mottos, seals, official currency, national sporting events, passports, national postage stamps, commemorative holidays, independence day ceremonies and the like. The continual use of these symbols (re)creates the nation's identity; it actualises and constitutes the 'imagined community' in everyday practice. Additionally, like all political groups, nations are exclusive and can only function whilst maintaining strict boundaries between citizens and non-citizens, the domestic and the foreign, the inside and the outside. Critical to maintaining the nation-state and the collective identity of its citizens therefore, is the notion of *difference*; there has to be a series of identity markers to differentiate those who belong to the community and those who do not.

In this chapter, I examine the way in which identity has been framed in the language of the 'war on terrorism'. In the first section, I focus on the strategies used to differentiate, demonise and dehumanise the terrorist 'other'. In this discourse, the enemy terrorists are constructed, among other designations, as evildoers, aliens and foreigners, and fundamentally inhuman. Their essential nature is defined by their savagery, madness, hatred and treachery. Such a rendering functions to create an enemy so heinous and so inhuman that large-scale violence against them seems perfectly normal and reasonable. In the second part of the chapter, I focus on the ways in which language is employed to establish clear boundary markers of identity, to make it clear that 'we' are different to 'them'. In direct contrast to the terrorists, Americans (and by implication, all 'civilised' people fighting on the side of the coalition) are discursively constructed first and foremost as 'innocent' victims; even the Pentagon casualties and the soldiers fighting in Afghanistan are remade as 'innocent Americans'. In addition, Americans are discursively reconstructed as 'heroic' and 'united'.

Constructing the terrorist enemy

The language of identity so infuses the official discourse of the 'war on terrorism' that it is not possible to describe each and every linguistic construction in one short chapter; a few examples must suffice. The language is not natural or normal, but is deliberately designed to essentialise, demonise and dehumanise the terrorist 'other' for specific political reasons. In the first place, the meta-narrative of defending civilisation examined in the previous chapter is a powerful way of constructing the essential nature of the terrorists as barbarians and savages. Simply by referring to an 'attack on **civilisation**' for example, the language brings to mind or naturalises its binary opposite – barbarism and savagery. Therefore, by implication, terrorists are characterised as inherently cruel, hateful, murderous and lacking in human values; they are savages living on the 'hunted margin of mankind'. As John Ashcroft affirms it, 'the attacks of September 11 drew a bright line of demarcation between **the civil and the savage**, and our nation will never be the same. On one side of this line are **freedom's enemies**, murderers of innocents in the name of a **barbarous** cause' (Ashcroft, 24 September, 2001). Notice how the language is used to mark a boundary 'between the civil and the savage' – between the 'self' and 'other', the 'good guys' and the 'bad guys'. Moreover, it is a 'bright line', a clear marker, easily identifiable. Ashcroft is saying that it is obvious to anyone what the difference is between civilised people and savage terrorists. The main problem with the pictures that emerged from Abu Ghraib prison was that they blurred this line and made the boundaries difficult to sustain. Critically, Ashcroft's description of terrorists as 'freedom's enemies' is a deliberate attempt to deny the possibility that they could be called 'freedom fighters'; it is a pre-emptive discursive assault on the commonly held notion that 'one person's terrorist is another person's freedom fighter'. In effect, this is an attempt to prevent the emergence of a certain kind of identity.

A related characterisation common to the official discourse is that terrorists are mad, treacherous and devious. For example, Bush alleged that 'the depth of their **hatred** is equalled by the **madness** of the destruction they design' (Bush, 29 January, 2002). This is a very popular cultural construction of terrorists, reflecting the widely held belief that they must be mentally unbalanced or psychologically ill to engage in such behaviour. Virtually every popular cultural depiction of terrorists makes them out to be pathological in one way or another – think of the mad and diabolical terrorist bad guys in movies like *Die Hard*, *True Lies*, *Air Force One*, *The Siege*, *Patriot Games* and *The Peacemaker*, or the pathological terrorist in Nelson DeMille's popular novel *The Lion's Game*. In actuality, most psychological studies on the terrorist personality reveal that terrorists are not psychologically abnormal in any identifiable way – that 'the most outstanding common characteristic of terrorists is their normality' (Crenshaw 1981: 379; see also Corrado 1981; Crenshaw 1992; Horgan 2003; Silke 1998). Making terrorists out to be mad is actually a powerful way of deflecting questions about their political beliefs or grievances, because their behaviour can be explained as being motivated by pathology rather than ideology. Their political statements, their grievances, and their programmes can then be dismissed as the product of a diseased mind, not to be taken seriously.

Another characteristic regularly assigned to terrorists is their treacherous nature. In an echo of Roosevelt's characterisation of the Japanese attack on Pearl Harbor in 1941 (see Chapter 2), Bush maintains that 'Our country has been attacked by **treachery** in our own cities – and that **treachery** continues in places like Riyadh and Casablanca' (Bush, 21 May, 2003). As the term treachery implies, the terrorists are here being constructed as perfidious and as betrayers of trust. This is considered to be a heinous crime in any society, because the very foundation of society is based on trust and mutual respect. If people begin treacherously to betray each others' trust, the entire basis of social cooperation is liable to break down. The Judas story is in part, a religious allegory for the social crime of treachery and betrayal, and a terrorist is therefore, a kind of Judas-like character. Related to this, there is in this language an inference of violating faith or allegiance: the terrorists are violating the faith they adhere to, as well as the societies they attack. Treachery, of course, is also associated with the trait of deviousness. Bush asserts, 'They are **devious** and ruthless' (Bush, 24 November, 2001). This is part of the invidious and diabolical personality of terrorists. They are 'the enemy within' who hides and plots evil, as seen in every popular novel or movie about terrorists.

In addition to these depictions, a major construction of the terrorist character is that they are motivated by intense hatred. This is a ubiquitous feature of the official language, which is partly designed to highlight the difference between 'them' and 'us': while we are loving and kind, the terrorist enemy is full of hate. As Bush expressed it, 'We understand they **hate** us because of what we **love**' (Bush, 25 November, 2002); it is a clear binary opposition, and one that firmly fixes the difference between the two sides. And what exactly is it that the terrorists hate? According to the official discourse, 'they **hate** our value system' (Powell, 23 September, 2001). This is related to the discursive construction of the September 11, 2001 attacks (see Chapter 2): the United States was attacked because the terrorists hate what they see in American society. This depiction of the terrorists' motivations completely depoliticises their aims: it is not about politics, ideology or foreign policy, but about irrational hatred. Bush spells it out most clearly in his first speech to Congress after the attacks: 'They **hate** what we see right here in this chamber – a democratically elected government. Their leaders are self-appointed. They **hate** our freedoms – our freedom of religion, our freedom of speech, our freedom to vote and assemble and disagree with each other' (Bush, 20 September, 2001). The terrorists are thus denied not only a political voice, but an alternative viewpoint. It is possible that the terrorists do hate what they see in that chamber, but what they see is different from President Bush. It is possible they see a chamber where decisions that affect the lives of millions around the world are carried out with callous indifference for the consequences, and where support for Israel is affirmed year after year no matter what illegal actions the Israeli government undertakes. Of course, the discursive rendering of their infantile hatred denies the attackers any such reading.

Another fascinating construction of the terrorists is the notion that they are 'traitors' to their own religion, that they have 'perverted' its teachings. This is a necessary part of the discourse in the eyes of US officials, because there was (and still is) a very real danger that terrorists would be viewed as being representative of Muslims in general. The American government had no wish to start a global religious war, thus it had carefully to fix the nature of the enemy terrorists in such a way that any possibility they might be considered essentially 'Muslim' terrorists was forestalled. The discursive strategy used to maintain this fine distinction was aimed at dismissing and suppressing the religious element of the terrorists' political agenda, as well as attempting to alienate them from wider Muslim support. Early on Bush assures us that: 'The terrorists practice a **fringe** form of Islamic extremism that has been rejected by Muslim scholars and the vast majority of Muslim clerics – a **fringe** movement that **perverts** the peaceful teachings of Islam ... The terrorists are **traitors** to their own faith' (Bush, 20 September, 2001). The language used here echoes earlier constructions of the terrorists. The notion that they practice a 'fringe' form of Islam is an oblique reference to the notion that they exist on the periphery of the religious community – and the 'hunted margins of mankind'. At the same time, it is related to the Orientalist stereotype of the 'mad Mullah' – 'a wild-eyed, turbaned, and bearded fanatic whose innate irrationality precludes taking him seriously but makes him a serious danger' (Lincoln 2002: 20). It is another way of saying that terrorists are outside the moral community. Moreover, that the terrorists are 'traitors' is related to their treachery; culturally, there is nothing worse than a traitor. Again, we might understand this construction, particularly its religious focus, as an oblique reference to the Judas narrative. Rumsfeld reiterates a similar line of thought:

> I think people in the Moslem world who think about it carefully ... understand that their religion's being **hijacked** and ... they're going to have to take back their religion and not allow people to **pervert** it the way the al Qaida leadership is **perverting** it.

They've got to worry also that the people in their countries start believing **this twisted approach** to the world. (Rumsfeld, 24 October, 2001)

In addition to the notion of terrorists who 'hijack' a great religion, the terrorists are also explicitly constructed as 'perverse' and 'twisted'. This reference to perversion is actually an echo of the cultural construction of the quintessential terrorist figure; most depictions of terrorists in literature and cinema paint them as morally and, very often, sexually deviant. In Nelson DeMille's *The Lion's Game*, the terrorist attempting to exact revenge on America is portrayed as being sexually abnormal due to a childhood experience; the implication is that this deviance lies at the root of his pathological behaviour. In this sense, terrorists are placed into that broader category of social deviants and degenerates which includes paedophiles and child pornographers, serial killers, rapists and other morally aberrant individuals. Obviously, this is yet another way of depoliticising and criminalising terrorists. After all, no one would pay attention to the political views of a convicted child molester; their status in society and their past actions prevents their voice from being heard.

Paradoxically, the language of the terrorists as 'traitors to their religion' contradicts to some extent another aspect of the discourse, namely, the idea that the terrorists are also 'godless' and 'unbelieving'. Colin Powell begins by suggesting that Osama bin Laden is 'unfaithful' to his religion: 'The reality is that Osama bin Laden has demonized himself. He is **unfaithful** to the religion that he says he is an adherent to' (Powell, 23 September, 2001). This is a continuation of the notion that the terrorists have rejected the teachings of their own faith. Powell then goes much further, alleging the terrorists actually have no faith at all: 'They are evil people. **They believe in no faith. They have adherence to no religion** ... The message I have for Osama bin Laden is that he can not hide behind **a faith in which he does not believe** because, if he believed in it, he would not be doing what he does' (Powell, 21 October, 2001). It is not simply that the terrorists have perverted their religion or hijacked it for evil purposes, but that they don't really believe in it at all. This is an attempt to say that Osama bin Laden is a fake and a charlatan who is trying to deceive Muslim people. As before, it is yet another way of constructing the terrorists as treacherous and as betrayers. In a repetition, Powell contends that 'it is terrorism that is directed against people; it represents **no faith, no religion**' (Powell, 26 October, 2001). In this turn of phrase, we can also hear echoes of the cold war language of the godless and atheistic communists.

Beyond these characterisations however, there are three other discursive constructions of the terrorist enemy that are crucially important. They are the most important depictions because they are the most common. They draw on pre-existing cultural constructions and they fit closely with broader narrative structures in the official discourse.

Evil terrorists

Perhaps the most frequent rhetorical construction of the terrorist enemy is that they are 'evil'. A subplot of the civilisation-barbarism meta-narrative, there are literally hundreds of references to 'evil' in the official discourse and President Bush in particular uses the term in almost every speech about terrorism. The good versus evil narrative is securely embedded in American rhetorical traditions and political life, and provides a deep reservoir of cultural forms and meanings for politicians to draw on (see Hariman 2003). At one level, America is a deeply religious society and the theologically burdened language of evil resonates with the very large conservative Christian audience of 70 million that George W. Bush – arguably the country's first fundamentalist president – mainly speaks to. At another level, the language of evil taps into popular culture and its steady diet of virtual evil: from slasher movies to serial killer films and all other variants of the horror genre in between, the popular theatre of darkness provides a cast of prototypical characters and cultural 'lessons' about the dangers of evil in modern society. Thus, 'when the president says that something or someone is evil, he places it within a well-known drama, one that not only provides convenient characterisations for all concerned, but that channels powerful emotions that have already been experienced virtually' (Hariman 2003: 513). Employing this language in public discourse therefore, allows the speaker to acquire rhetorical resources that are not available in normal democratic political language.

In grammatical usage by senior administration officials, this language conforms to an explicitly individual theory of evil, where evil exists as a force or principle residing within specific human beings, rather than in a complex set of structural conditions or as the moral outcome of a chain of events (Rediehs 2002: 66–7). The rhetorical strategy employed most often is one of personification – creating a human version of supernatural evil, or 'evil incarnate' (McDaniel 2003). For example, in his depiction of Osama bin Laden, Bush states: 'on our TV screens the other day, we saw **the evil one** threatening – calling for more destruction and death in America' (Bush, 11 October, 2001). This language is a way of suggesting that the terrorist mastermind is something like Damien in *The Omen* movies – a kind of Antichrist figure. The fact that he appeared virtually on television only reaffirms this discursive construction. In another famous quotation, Bush says: 'I like to remind people that **the evil ones** have roused a mighty nation, and they will pay a serious price' (Bush, 29 November, 2001). The phrase 'the evil one' is a term used in the Bible and is popular evangelical Christian usage for Satan, or the Devil. The use of this linguistic form is actually a way of saying that the terrorists are the Devil, or perhaps, are devils; in either case, they are a form of 'evil incarnate'. It is therefore a directly religiously oriented demonological move in which the terrorists are individually and collectively marked or essentialised as satanic and morally corrupt.

The construction of the terrorists and their acts as 'evil' began on the very first day of the attacks. On September 11, 2001, in his first major address to the nation, Bush declared they were '**evil**, despicable acts of terror', and 'Today, our nation saw **evil**, **the very worst of human nature** [...] The search is under way for those behind these **evil** acts' (Bush, 11 September, 2001b). In this discursive form, both the acts and those who committed them are evil and this evil is rooted in human nature. Such a construction implies that the evil is eschatological and cannot be dealt with except through destruction or a type of sacred cleansing. After all, human nature is immutable and cannot be changed simply through persuasion or punishment. As Donald Rumsfeld noted, 'Are we ever going to be able to stop people from wanting to terrorize each other? No, I suspect not ... [N]o one around the Pentagon's going to **change the nature of human beings**' (Rumsfeld, 24 October, 2001). In a similar kind of construction, National Security Advisor Condoleeza Rice propounds that the war on terrorism is 'a war against **evil people**' and 'a war against **the evil of terrorism**' (Rice, 15 October, 2001). In effect, the evil of terrorism is rooted inside certain people, in their very nature. This implies that rooting out terrorism actually requires the elimination of certain individuals and groups of people. It is a simple and theological construction – rid the world of evil people, and the world will be free of the evil of terrorism.

One of the consequences of employing the language of good and evil is that it leads inexorably towards a crusader or inquisitional mentality. As Bush candidly observes, 'We've come to know truths that we will never question: **evil is real**, and **it must be opposed**' (Bush, 29 January, 2002); and 'We are in **a conflict between good and evil**, and America will call **evil** by its name' (Bush, 1 June, 2002). The concrete existence of evil implies that we must make a conscious effort to be rid of it; indifference to evil is actually evil itself. There is an inbuilt logic: '[O]ur responsibility to history is already clear: to answer these attacks and **rid the world of evil**' (Bush, 14 September, 2001). In this sense, the repeated (and often retracted) reference to the 'war on terrorism' as a 'crusade', and which was for a short time called 'Infinite Justice', was no accident (Morris 2002: 152). If America really is battling evil (in its theological sense), then it is a divine calling to bring God's justice to bear; it is a necessary part of the 'conflict between good and evil'. The notion of 'our responsibility to history' is also an oblique reference to the role of America in ridding the world of the 'evil' Soviet threat. There is thus a dual meaning inherent in the language.

In another example of the discursive construction of evil, Bush explicitly draws out the binary contrast between the evil terrorists and good Americans: 'Anybody who tries to affect the lives of our **good** citizens is **evil**', and 'out of **evil** can come **good**' (Bush, 24 October, 2001). In these statements, Americans are first constructed as 'good citizens'. Then, in a surprising move, evil is defined as anybody (a personalised evil) who 'tries to affect the lives' of good American citizens. It is a very broad description which seems to suggest that any interference at all with the lives of American citizens must be evil. There is also the binding together of 'terror and evil', so that by association, any use of the term 'terror' or 'terrorist' is associated firmly with evil. Following this, Bush makes another allusion to Christianity and a theological formulation of evil by suggesting that 'out of evil can come good'. This is an opaque biblical reference, which normally would imply that redeeming an evil situation (or person) actually involves returning evil with good, turning the other cheek, loving your enemies, and showing mercy. In this context however, Bush is drawing out a more medieval Christian meaning: ridding the world of evil through a crusade will be for the good of all.

Strikingly, in the discourse, the evil of the terrorists is frequently linked to having no faith or religion, to being godless as well as evil. Apart from the historic religious narrative, this is another way of suggesting that the evil terrorists do not belong to the moral community; that they are on the margins of mankind. For example, Powell says that terrorism 'represents **no faith, no religion**. It is **evil**, it is murderous' (Powell, 26 October, 2001). In a theological construction of evil, being atheistic and godless is a common assumption. In terms of American political discourse, this formulation is also an echo of the Reaganesque cold war language condemning atheistic communism and the 'evil empire'. In other words, like the godless and atheistic communists we fought in the cold war, we are now fighting godless terrorists. This is a similar formulation to Bush's most famous reference to 'evil' in his State of the Union address when he called North Korea, Iraq and Iran an 'axis of evil' (Bush, 29 January, 2002). As I have noted, it is an incredibly powerful piece of rhetoric that recalls both the World War II coalition of fascist axis powers, Reagan's cold war appellation of the Soviet Union as the 'evil empire' and the theologically driven language of the 'evildoers'.

In perhaps his most comprehensive exposition of the 'evil' of terrorism, and using the term numerous times, Bush declared:

> [T]he truth of the matter is, in order to fully defend America, we must defeat the **evildoers** where they hide.
>
> We learned a **good** lesson on September the 11th, that there is **evil** in this world ... it's essential that all moms and dads and citizens tell their children we love them and there is love in the world, but also remind them there are **evil** people.
>
> I think that's one of the positives that have come from the **evildoers**. **The evil ones** have sparked an interesting change in America [...]
>
> We're fighting **evil**. And these murderers have hijacked a great religion in order to justify their **evil** deeds. (Bush, 11 October, 2001)

This speech combines a range of narratives and formulations, and is a good example of the intertextuality of the discourse. There are the biblical references to 'evildoers' and the 'evil ones' – the demonic terrorists. Of greater consequence, there is also the notion that Americans learned 'a **good** lesson' on September 11, 2001, namely, that evil really does exist in a concrete, religious sense. Parents should, according to Bush, try to instil in their children the belief in the absolute reality of evil. This evil is to found in hate, murder and prejudice, and in the form of 'the evil ones' – the terrorists. Paradoxically, this language inadvertently supernaturalises the terrorists, giving them powers beyond the realm of normal human beings. As such, it taps into the movie images of supernatural demonic characters like *Dracula*, *Warlock*, Freddy from the *Nightmare on Elm Street* movies or Damien from *The Omen* series. In this sense, it is also a way of constructing the kind of threat that terrorists pose to ordinary and decent people (see Chapter 4). Finally, Bush imbues the war on terrorism with a holy justification and a sense of divine sanction: 'we're fighting evil'. This means we are on the side of good and God and it is a noble and pure quest – like Arnold Schwarzenegger in *End of Days*.

The language of evil fulfils a number of important political functions. In the first place, it moralises the conflict, transforming it into a cosmic struggle between the forces of goodness and light against the forces of darkness and evil. No longer is this a political conflict, a cultural conflict or a conflict over specific policies, it is simply a struggle between good and evil. This is a powerful way of forcing people to choose the side of the United States; after all, no one deliberately chooses to be on the side of evil. In any moral conflict, one always wants to be on the side of good. At the same time, the radical evil argument is a familiar strategy for silencing liberal dissent: from Leo Strauss and Reinhold Neibuhr to Ronald Reagan, liberals have been charged with lacking both a realistic sense of human evil and the moral courage to confront it (Aune 2003).

Second, the language of good and evil suppresses questions: we don't need to ask what the motivations or aims of the terrorists were if they are 'evil', as 'evil' is its own motivation and its own self-contained explanation. Evil people do not have any politics and there is no need to examine their causes or grievances. Evil people do what they do simply *because* they are evil. Clearly, the use of this language is a way of encouraging quiescence and displacing more complex understandings of political and social events (Cloud 2003: 510). As such, it qualifies as demagoguery by appealing to ignorance and arrogance through a distorted representation of the nature of evil.

Third, the language of good and evil is also clearly a part of the representational project in which not only must the boundaries between 'them' and 'us' be clearly delineated, but the nature and qualities of ourselves and the enemy other must be affirmed (see Passavant and Dean 2002). This representational project moreover, is deliberately designed to dehumanise the enemy, because 'as agents of evil, they are by definition of less human worth'

(Sardar and Davies 2002: 174). The language of evil removes the need for self-reflection and the assessment of context and contributory circumstances. As Gunnell suggests:

> It is merely an invitation to identify our enemies. By talking of them as 'evil', we do not need to ask why they act as they do, feel outraged or oppressed, opt for suicidal terror rather than protest or political engagement. The questions to which we all need answers since 11 September fall off the agenda in the face of the description 'evil'. Evil simply demands opposition rather than analysis or understanding. (Gunnell 2002, quoted in Sardar and Davies 2002: 56)

This is actually one of the primary purposes of this language – to so demonise and dehumanise the terrorists that the only acceptable course of action is to kill and destroy them; to depoliticise and depersonalise them to such a degree that no one is tempted to find out their actual grievances and demands. As Condoleeza Rice explicitly stated: 'The one thing that we expect no one to do is to somehow negotiate with terrorists. It only emboldens them' (Rice, 14 May, 2003).

Lastly, designating terrorists as evil is a 'demonological move', which in this case is made easier by the fact that the terrorists were foreigners who did not belong to the political community. This notion of the terrorist enemy as 'alien' is explored in the following section. Demonising certain individuals and groups is an important part of both enlisting widespread support (if people hate enemy terrorists enough, they will support the use of massive and sustained violence against them), and ensuring flexibility (if the terrorists lose all sympathy as human beings, the authorities will have the freedom to treat them as they like – without the need for human rights conventions or lawyers).

'Alien' terrorists

The notion of the enemy as 'foreign' or 'alien' has always been a central element in the discursive construction of war; the enemy is characterised as belonging to an outside realm – they are not part of the 'homeland' and thus are positioned outside of the moral community in a space where civil rights have no relevance. The 'war' against terrorism is no different. There is a sustained attempt by senior American officials, both in language and institutional practice, to construct the terrorist enemy as something alien to America. This is clearly part of the representational project – the attempt to maintain a sense of 'Americanness' by maintaining boundaries between the inside and the outside – as well as an implicit means of dehumanising the terrorists. If they are different to ourselves as citizens (if they are 'aliens'), they are not entitled to the same rights and treatment by law-enforcement officials.

Within this context, the use of the term 'foreign' can also be read as a medical metaphor, as in 'foreign bodies' that infect the body (politic). This is part of the well-known construction of the 'enemy within' that every nation mythologises and fears. Similarly, the 'alien' characterisation has a double meaning in America's media-saturated society, reflecting both legal non-citizenship and the virtually ubiquitous non-human extraterrestrials. American officials cannot use the term 'alien' without their listeners recalling – at least at a subconscious level – hundreds of movies, television programmes, comics, novels and radio broadcasts (such as *War of the Worlds*) where space aliens attacked, invaded or subverted society from within. In a society immersed in the movie mythology of *Invasion of the Body Snatchers*, *Alien*, *Predator*, *Independence Day* and *The X-Files*, the meaning of the term 'alien terrorist' oscillates between 'extra-terrestrial parasite' and 'foreign enemy' without any sense of the absurd. Alien invasion movies are well-known metaphors for the fear of foreign invasion.

In the language of the 'war on terrorism, the discursive construction of the terrorists' alienness started with the notion of '**foreign** enemies' and '**foreign** terrorists'. This was a way of saying that they were external enemies who attacked the nation from without. However, this construction very quickly evolved into the notion of '**alien** terrorists' (Ashcroft, 24 September, 2001). This term is directly related to and deliberately echoes the notion of 'enemy alien', which has an extensive genealogy in American politics. For example, during the founding of the republic, fears about the 'enemy within' led to the passing of the *Enemy Alien Act of 1798*, which incidentally remains on the books today. During World War I, similar fears saw J. Edgar Hoover land his first job in 1917 working for the Justice Department's Alien Enemy Bureau where he administered the identification, regulation and internment of 'enemy aliens'. And in 1986 a secret Immigration and Naturalisation Service (INS) 'Contingency Plan' proposed that in a terrorist emergency 'alien terrorists' and 'alien activists' be interned at a federal detention centre in Oakdale, Louisiana (Cole 2003: 102, 116). The notion of the 'enemy alien', as both a legal category and a culturally meaningful metaphor, has been used by American officials on numerous occasions to detain or expel the so-called 'enemy within' – always with widespread public support. For example, it was used against British people during the war of 1812, against Germans, Austro-Hungarians and war resisters during World War I, against anarchists and radicals during the Palmer Raids, against Japanese people in World War II and against communists during the cold war. Thus, by appealing to these kinds of notions in relation to terrorists, American officials tap into a wellspring of latent xenophobia and reproduce hundreds of years of security practice.

In perhaps the most detailed construction of 'alien terrorists', Ashcroft expounds:

[A]s September the 11th vividly illustrates, **aliens** also come to our country with the intent to do great evil [...]

The Department of Justice will prevent **aliens** who engage in or support terrorist activity from entering our country. We will detain, prosecute, deport **terrorist aliens** who are already inside the nation's borders [...]

The **Foreign Terrorist** Tracking Task Force that Mr. McCraw will lead will ensure that federal agencies coordinate their efforts to bar from the United States all **aliens** who meet any of the following criteria: **aliens** who are representatives, members or supporters of **terrorist organizations**; **aliens** who are suspected of engaging in **terrorist activity**; or **aliens** who provide material support to **terrorist activity**. (Ashcroft, 31 October, 2001)

In this construction, Ashcroft is clearly attempting to heighten the sense of outrage in the community about these 'aliens' – these foreign and non-human creatures – who 'come to our country' to commit great evil. While Americans quietly go about their business and hurt no one, these aliens come to 'our' country and attack us; it is obviously a gross violation and an abuse of American tolerance. This is clearly designed to create fear and hatred of the enemy other sufficient to enlist support for a war against them or at the very least, their preventive detainment. There is also a powerful sense that a great number of these aliens, perhaps most of them, are in some way involved in terrorism. They are either engaged directly in terrorism, representatives or members of terrorist organisations or are providing material support for other terrorists. There is so much terrorist activity among aliens that a special federal agency has to be established to deal with them.

In a sense, this language of the 'alien terrorist' is also directly related to the notion of the American 'homeland' – as in 'Homeland Defence' and the 'Department of Homeland Security'. That is, it is the reinforcement of the idea that there are two groups of people in the world: American citizens and foreigners/aliens. There is an implicit meaning inherent in the binary structure of language that one group is basically good while the other is inherently bad: 'citizen' implies 'good' while 'alien' implies 'bad'. The discursive construction of the 'alien terrorist' is powerfully reinforced and reified in the institutional practice of US law enforcement. First, as the speech by John Ashcroft stated, a special federal organisation designed to deal with the foreign/alien terrorist was created – the Foreign Terrorist Tracking Task Force. In addition, in the months following the September 11, 2001 attacks, and with widespread public support, US law enforcement agencies immediately began to question and detain thousands of resident 'aliens' from Middle Eastern countries. Since then, it has been estimated that more than 5,000 Muslim and Arab 'aliens' have been preventively detained by the American government (Cole 2003: 25). Third, the essential difference between citizens and aliens was reinforced through the institutional practice of treating American citizens suspected of terrorism differently to non-US citizens. While US suspects were accorded their normal legal rights to representation and open trial in a US court, 'alien' suspects were denied any of these rights and were incarcerated under inhumane conditions while being interrogated in Guantanamo Bay, Baghram Airbase in Afghanistan, Iraq and other detention centres. This is a powerful discursive act that constructs some individuals as legal persons entitled to protection of their human rights and others as 'aliens' who are not entitled to even the minimal status of prisoners of war.

Inhuman terrorists

Another ubiquitous feature of the discourse is the use of descriptive terms that thoroughly dehumanise terrorists and those who support them. This is an extension of the language of 'evil', 'alien' and 'foreign' terrorists. It is a way of reinforcing the fact that terrorists are not like normal 'good' people; they are essentially different and not human in the way we are familiar with. As I noted in Chapter 2, the civilisation-barbarism meta-narrative constructs terrorists as 'savages' who choose to live on the 'hunted margin of mankind' (Bush, 20 October, 2001), rejecting 'those values that separate us from **animals** – compassion, tolerance, mercy' (Baker, 23 September, 2001). The implication is that terrorists are only marginally human, and are more like savage and wild animals. On this initial foundational narrative, the discourse then goes much further and deconstructs all traces of their humanity. For example, in an extension of the discourse of evil, President Bush speaks about 'the whole **curse of terrorism** that is upon the face of the earth' (Bush, 15 September, 2001). Apart from transforming terrorism from a particular type of political violence perpetuated by certain disenfranchised individuals into an abstract form of malevolence, this is another thoroughly religious construction which seeks to equate terrorism discursively with God's curse on the earth in the Garden of Eden following Adam and Eve's sin. The sin of humanity is thereby given form in the sin of terrorism. Additionally, this construction transports terrorism from its specific historical and geographical locations (terrorism is always rooted in the politics and history of a particular people and region) to an abstract moral plain that covers the entire 'face of the earth'.

In a similar kind of discursive construction, terrorism is translated through the language of disease into a plague upon the earth. Colin Powell for example, refers to 'the **scourge** of terrorism' (Powell, 26 October, 2001), which invokes notions of infection, dirt, squalor and sickness. More specifically, on October 7, 2001, the day that bombing operations commenced in Afghanistan, Rumsfeld declared that 'terrorism is **a cancer** on the human condition and we intend to oppose it' (Rumsfeld, 7 October, 2001). In its initial reading then, terrorism is like a sickness which can infect single countries – in this case, Afghanistan – but which is also a disease affecting the human condition as a whole. This is related to the language of evil, where terrorism is rooted in human nature. Ominously, in the context of the bombing of Afghanistan, the 'surgical strikes' against the Taliban are transformed from destructive military assaults into a medical procedure that will cut out the cancer from Afghanistan's infected society. Military 'operations', in this construction, are actually an act of healing and cleansing – a way of purifying and cleansing the human condition.

Implicit in this language is the notion that terrorists are like cancerous cells; they are not people with feelings or individuals capable of making political choices. Like the mysterious but horrifying disease of cancer (it attacks its host and turns the body against itself), we too should fear the terrorists who infect and destroy us from within our own body politic. This is an echo of the language of alien/foreign terrorists who come to 'our country' to plot great evil. Admiral Dennis Blair, Commander-in-Chief of the US Pacific Command, expands this construction: 'Over the years, the international community watched Al Qa'eda ... spread its **cancer** to over 60 countries, encouraging young men to come to Afghanistan for training in terrorist techniques [...] It sent its **spawn** to Chechnya, Central Asia, Xinyang, and the Kashmir' (Blair, 23 October, 2001). In this metaphor, the terrorists are not only a cancer, but a kind of infectious cancer that spreads to other bodies. Following this, terrorists are reconstructed into some kind of fungus or reptilian creature that 'spawns'. Another cultural reading might infer the 'spawn of Satan', or the demon-like superhero of the comic books. In either case, the terrorists are no longer human beings, but more of a disease or a non-human creature.

In another medical metaphor, Bush speaks of terrorists as '**parasites** that hide' in certain countries (Bush, 11 October, 2001). Later he reiterates that there is the danger posed by 'the terrorist **parasites** who threaten their countries and our own' (Bush, 29 January, 2002). Not only is this the construction of the terrorist enemy as a dangerous organism that makes its host ill, but of the foreign/alien enemy that hides within and spreads poison. Terrorists in this formulation draw the life-blood from their unsuspecting host, sucking it dry.

In sum, terrorists are 'an evil and **inhuman** group of men' (Baker, 23 September, 2001), and 'the **faceless** enemies of human dignity' (Bush, 21 May, 2003). Significantly, military policies in Iraq and Afghanistan of hooding prisoners and suspects is a way of physically and figuratively making them 'faceless' – it is an obliteration of their human features. In an important sense, the official practice of prisoner management is a discursive act that reinforces the language; combined, the language and practice creates the reality of the 'faceless' terrorist. Given this thorough dehumanisation and depersonalisation, it is not surprising that the 'terrorist other' were then rendered without legal status as 'unlawful combatants', not even subject to the Geneva Conventions. Nor is it surprising that a very public discussion in 2002 about whether the torture of terrorist suspects should be allowed was then followed by widespread instances of the abuse of prisoners. Notably, the Bush administration refused publicly to confirm that it would not use torture and admitted that terrorist suspects may be taken to countries where torture was legal so that interrogators would have a freer hand. During the initial invasion of Afghanistan, Donald Rumsfeld refused to allow the surrender or safe passage of Arab (al Qaeda) fighters, stating quite openly that it would be better if they were killed outright.

The truth is, once a group has been reduced to being an evil 'spawn', 'animals', 'parasites', 'a cancer' on the human condition, 'a scourge' on the world and 'a curse' on the face of the earth – once they have become 'faceless' both figuratively and literally – it is relatively easy to treat them in an unconscionable manner and without any regard for their human rights. After all, conscience is not required when dealing with parasites or cancerous disease. The use of animalistic imagery and dehumanising language to describe the enemy is a well-worn trope in America political discourse: after ordering the use of atomic bombs on Japan, President Truman opined, 'When you have to deal with a beast you have to treat him as a beast' (quoted in Rosenberg 2003: 55). Similarly, Ivan Frederick, one of the first guards from Abu Ghraib to be charged with abusing Iraqi prisoners, admitted that his favourite way of referring to the prisoners was as 'animals'. This was a direct repetition of the language of his superiors and it allowed him to dehumanise the prisoners and mistreat them without any feelings of remorse. This is the purpose of the discourse: to obliterate their humanity so that not only is it easier to commit violence against them, but there is a greater freedom of action in not having to take care to respect their human rights. This kind of behaviour would have been difficult to countenance if the enemy terrorists had not been characterised as 'terrorists' in the first place, and then as 'inhuman terrorists' in the second.

Again, this language was not a neutral reflection of who the terrorists actually were; rather, it was designed for precise political purposes. Studies by scholars for example, paint an entirely different picture of why and how ordinary people come to be involved in terrorist activities. In most cases, it is a complex mix of intense political grievances combined with frustration and a lack of opportunity for expression. Additionally, they are often subject to powerful feelings of helplessness, many have been traumatised by personal experiences of repressive violence, some have a desire to experience 'military action' (like many soldiers), and most come from communities that have normalised expressions of political violence for historical and sociological reasons.

In short, destroying the face of the terrorist, removing all traces of their personality or humanity and depoliticising their aims and goals was essential to constructing the massive counter-violence of the 'war on terrorism'. After all, it would be far more difficult to bomb, torture or hold in prison camps 'enemy combatants' who were seen as simply misguided or ordinary people with legitimate political grievances. Also, writing the identity of the terrorist enemy was relatively easy because the notion of the evil/cancerous/alien terrorist 'monster' is actually a cultural projection of the tabooed 'wild man' figure of the Western imagination – the veritable 'bogey man' (see Zulaika and Douglass 1996). Rooted in the fundamental need to control dangerous behaviour, taboos function to locate, identify and segregate transgressions and dangers. Terrorism has been a powerful taboo within western societies since the industrial revolution and provides a ready-made rhetorical resource for officials to draw upon. Additionally, the sheer visceral horror of the September 11, 2001 attacks formed the discursive foundation for constructing the enemy terrorist: the appalling images lent powerful emotional credence to the idea that only a truly inhuman and demonic creature could have contemplated, much less enacted such horror.

Constructing good Americans

The discursive construction of the 'other' is one half of the construction of the 'self'; the terrorist enemy is the 'enabling other' of the American 'self'. A great deal of the official discourse is devoted to essentialising Americans as the direct (binary) opposite of the terrorists. In part, this was an effort to reassure Americans following the terrorist attacks, which had severely challenged American self-belief. There was a feeling that America must have done some terrible things to be the object of such intense hatred. The US government wanted to disavow this notion and reassuring Americans that they really were good, kind and innocent of wrongdoing was one way of achieving this. Another reason it was important to construct Americans as essentially decent and peaceful was because the US was going to attack other nations and cause inevitable human suffering. These actions therefore, had to be carefully framed within a positive conception of American foreign policy; even if military action caused much suffering, it proceeded from noble and virtuous intentions; America was a force for good in the world despite television footage which might show otherwise.

The first major discursive construction of the American character comes in the Prayer and Remembrance Day service, when Bush contends:

> In this trial, we have been reminded, and the world has seen, that our fellow Americans are **generous** and **kind**, **resourceful** and **brave**. We see our **national character** in rescuers working past exhaustion; in long lines of blood donors; in thousands of citizens who have asked to work and serve in any way possible. And we have seen our national character in eloquent acts of **sacrifice**. Inside the World Trade Center, one man who could have saved himself stayed until the end at the side of his quadriplegic friend. A beloved priest died giving the last rites to a firefighter. Two office workers, finding a disabled stranger, carried her down sixty-eight floors to safety. [...] In these acts, and in many others, Americans showed a deep **commitment to one another**, and an abiding **love** for our country. (Bush, 14 September, 2001)

There are several important features of this language. First, there is the rendering of the nation – the 'imagined community' – in such a way that affirms unity and a sense of collective identity: 'we' have seen 'our' national character, and 'we' feel the warmth of 'national unity'. Second, there is the fixing of all the good qualities of 'the American people': generosity, kindness, resourcefulness, bravery, sacrifice, love and unity. These characteristics are identity markers; they are what make Americans stand out from the terrorist 'other'. In addition, there is the powerful deployment of examples of heroic and kind actions that then stand as exemplars of the nation as a whole.

Not long after America began bombing Afghanistan, Bush makes another speech in which he constructs America's good qualities. At one level, this is a way of reassuring and reminding Americans that they were still good people, in spite of the military assault against an impoverished nation in the midst of a humanitarian crisis:

> We've shown **great love** for our country, and great **tolerance** and **respect** for all our countrymen. I was struck by this: that in many cities, when Christian and Jewish women learnt that Muslim women – women of cover – were afraid of going out of their homes alone, that they went shopping with them, that they showed true friendship and support – an act that shows the world **the true nature of America**.

> One month after great suffering and sorrow, America is **strong** and **determined** and **generous**.

> [T]his **great nation**, a **freedom-loving nation**, a **compassionate nation**, a **nation that understands the values of life** [...]

> [H]ow do I respond when I see that in some Islamic countries there is vitriolic hatred for America? I'll tell you how I respond: **I'm amazed that there is such misunderstanding of what our country is about**, that people would hate us. I am, I am – like most Americans, I just can't believe it. Because **I know how good we are** [...]

> [O]ne of the truest weapons that we have against terrorism is to show the world **the true strength of character and kindness of the American people**. (Bush, 11 October, 2001)

The construction begins by listing America's good qualities – great love, great tolerance, great respect – followed by an example that proves it. Then there is the statement that these acts show 'the true nature of America'. What Bush is really saying here (given the timing and context of the speech) is that it is these actions rather than the military actions in Afghanistan that reveal America's *true* nature. This true character of America is then elucidated: it's a great nation, a freedom-loving nation, a compassionate nation, a strong nation, a united nation, a caring nation, a good nation and a tolerant nation. The amazement that Bush expresses over hatred for America in the Middle East is in part, an expression of the self-doubt engendered by the September 11, 2001 attacks. It is also a reflection of the deeply held view that Americans have of themselves as being essentially good and well-intentioned. Within this cultural understanding, it is inconceivable that anyone could hate America because America is so good, kind, peaceful and well-intentioned – and the number of immigrants trying to get in to America every year seems to prove it.

A key element in this discourse is the notion that America is a good society because of the values it holds. As Bush describes it, 'This is a great country. It's a great country because we share the same **values of respect** and **dignity** and **human worth**' (Bush, 17 September, 2001); and later, 'Ours is a great land, and we'll always **value freedom**. We're an **open** society' (Bush, 29 November, 2001). Again, this is a contrast to the terrorists who lack any civilised values. The values that define American society are also, according to the official discourse, the imperatives that drive US foreign policy. As Bush sets forth:

> As a people dedicated to **civil rights**, we are driven to defend the **human rights** of others. We are the nation that liberated continents and concentration camps. We are the nation of the Marshall Plan, the Berlin Airlift and the Peace Corps. We are the nation that ended the oppression of Afghan women, and we are the nation that closed the torture chambers of Iraq. (Bush, 21 May, 2003)

In this text, Bush constructs a powerful historical narrative that puts America's good qualities into a single story line that runs through World War II, the cold war, the Afghan war and the war against Iraq. It is the same imperative every time: America is so deeply permeated by the values of civil rights that it is 'driven' to defend the human rights of others. Within this construction, who could doubt the motives of US foreign policy? As such, this language is designed to suppress any suggestion that US foreign policy might have more nefarious motives, or that the terrorists attacked America in response to its cynical actions in the Middle East. At another level, it is also a rather overt attempt to write the current conflict into the 'good war' narrative of World War II – to suggest that the 'war on terrorism' has the same moral status as the liberation of the Nazi concentration camps.

An important and related aspect of the 'good Americans' narrative is the notion that the United States is an essentially peaceful nation inhabited by a peaceful people. This is linked to the construction of the September 11, 2001 attacks as unforeseen and undeserved; it is also an essential ingredient of America's self-image. Most Americans would be shocked and surprised to learn that the US had been involved in 134 military interventions between 1890 and

2001, and that following the end of the cold war, these foreign interventions have occurred on average two times per year (Grossman, quoted in Sardar and Davies 2002: 68). Nevertheless, at the announcement of the bombing campaign in Afghanistan, Bush asserts 'We're a **peaceful** nation' (Bush, 7 October, 2001). This is a discursive attempt to counter the image of the world's most powerful military attacking one of the world's weakest militaries. It is a way of saying that in spite of what you might see on television, America really is a peaceful nation.

Later, in a construction that tries to justify why the US had to attack two very poor countries, Bush says that America is '**a peaceful nation**. This is a nation that wants nothing more than the world to be more free and more **peaceful**. **We believe in the peace, in keeping the peace**' (Bush, 2 May, 2003). There is here a direct link between the names of the military campaigns – 'Operation Enduring Freedom' and 'Operation Iraqi Freedom' – and the reasons for going to war; namely, the promotion and the defending of freedom. In other words, reconciling the truly 'peaceful' nature of America with the aggression against two states in less than a year and a half requires that the attacks be rewritten as the pursuit of 'peace' through the bringing of 'freedom'. They are not really military assaults; they are 'the promotion of freedom'.

Beyond these broad characterisations of the American character however, there are three other crucial constructions that need to be examined. They are important because not only do they occur frequently in the official discourse, they are also linked to a number of deeply embedded cultural and political narratives.

American heroes

An important feature of the official language of identity was the ubiquitous 'hero' narrative that emerged after the attacks. In this story, everyone – victims, rescue workers, New York Mayor Rudy Giuliani and US military personnel – were all recast as quintessential American heroes. The hero narrative is modelled on popular entertainment scripts; every tale in American popular culture has a cast of heroes and villains and as a carefully scripted narrative the 'war on terrorism' is no different. In this script, every EMS worker is Bruce Willis in *Die Hard*, every member of the armed forces is Tom Hanks in *Saving Private Ryan* and every ordinary citizen is Mel Gibson in *The Patriot*. At another level, the hero narrative is also highly gendered: it evokes the popular entertainment images of the lone 'man's man' who has to use his masculine qualities to save innocent women and children from harm. Women are always cast in the role of potential victims and almost never in the role of hero; even Private Jessica Lynch was rewritten from wounded soldier to woman-in-need-of-rescuing. The notion of protecting the 'homeland' is also highly gendered, as the home is seen as a woman's domain – a feminine domestic sphere. In this reading, men are defenders while women are nurturers. What is also notable is how often American hero figures are linked to the military or police professions. This reflects America's powerful military-industrial complex and its highly militarised society; the maintenance of a national mythology of military heroism (from citizen militia in the war of independence, to the Normandy landings, to the Special Forces in Afghanistan) is essential for justifying extraordinarily high levels of military spending.

In the first instance, the casualties of the September 11, 2001 attacks were discursively reconstructed from being victims – as they were in the discourse of victim-hood and grievance (see Chapter 2) – into genuine heroes. As we saw earlier, the stories of the victims – the man who died after staying with his quadriplegic friend – were recast into a distinctly heroic frame. In an even more powerful discursive move, Donald Rumsfeld announced that the members of the armed forces killed in the terrorist attacks would be given war medals, as an official recognition of heroism in war: '[W]e're announcing today that the members of the armed forces that were killed or injured in the September 11th attack on the Pentagon and on the World Trade Center towers will receive **the Purple Heart**' (Rumsfeld, 27 September, 2001). This is a powerfully symbolic act that discursively remakes the casualties from victims to war heroes who have won medals for their bravery. In another careful and thorough construction, Rumsfeld personalises the hero-victims:

> We are gathered here to remember ... those lost to us on September 11th. We remember them as **heroes**.
>
> 'He was a **hero** long before the eleventh of September,' said a friend of one of those we have lost – 'a **hero** every single day, a **hero** to his family, to his friends and to his professional peers.'
>
> About him and those who served with him, his wife said: 'It's not just when a plane hits their building. They are **heroes** every day.' '**Heroes** every day.' We are here to affirm that. (Rumsfeld, 11 October, 2001)

In one sense, this is a way of giving meaning to the lives lost; in another, it is part of the discursive construction of the heroic 'good Americans' who are the opposite of the cowardly 'evil terrorists'.

The other main characters in the September 11, 2001 narrative, the emergency rescue personnel, are also cast as heroic figures that exhibited courage in the line of duty. This is a narrative that fits easily into America's popular culture where police officers, firefighters and rescue workers are the constant focus of hero worship through movies and television programmes – from *Hill Street Blues* to *Law and Order*, *NYPD Blue*, *ER* and *Third Watch*. Soon after the initial attacks on New York and Washington, John Ashcroft speaks about the bravery of the rescue workers who responded to the attacks: 'Among the high honors of my life has been ... to be in the company of **these heroes**, these friends of freedom; to meet with and work side-by-side with men and women who have exerted themselves beyond fatigue, who have set aside their own personal agendas and their personal safety to answer our nation's call' (Ashcroft, 24 September, 2001). In this passage, Ashcroft associates heroism with the love of freedom. This is an attempt to discursively link the actions of the rescue workers with the subsequent military operations 'Enduring Freedom' and 'Iraqi Freedom'. Simultaneously, it is the antithesis of the terrorists who are said to 'hate freedom'. In a similar construction, Bush praises the efforts of 'our heroic police and firefighters' and states that: 'The American people have responded magnificently, with **courage** and **compassion**, **strength** and **resolve**. As I have met **the heroes**, hugged the families, and looked into the tired faces of rescuers, I have stood in awe of the American people' (Bush, 29 January, 2002). In this construction, he assigns all the main heroic (and masculine) qualities to the police and firefighters: courage, strength and resolve – mixed with compassion. At the same time, the grammar suggests that all Americans – the 'American people' – are heroes.

In a powerful discursive act, a benefit concert was given to honour the firefighters, police officers and rescue workers who died in the attacks and to raise money for their families; more than 5,000 emergency personnel were invited. New York Governor George Pataki, speaking at the Concert for New York, also constructs a broad array of (American) heroes:

> And we're inspired by the **courage** of others, people like the passengers on Flight 93, who risked their lives ... the **courage** of our children, the **brave** schoolchildren in lower Manhattan who saw horror before their eyes and nine days later went back into their classrooms with incredible **courage** and **resolve** to continue their education. And we look to **the quiet heroes** of this crisis. The fathers and mothers, the husbands and wives, the sons and daughters of those who have lost their loved ones, the innocent victims. We are inspired with their **strength**, with their **faith** and the **courage** they have shown ... (Pataki, 20 September, 2001, quoted in Silberstein 2002: 95)

This narrative is similar to President Bush's construction in which almost everyone is affirmed as a courageous hero: passengers, schoolchildren, fathers, mothers, husbands, wives, sons and daughters. At the same time, the qualities of heroism are affirmed: courage, resolve, strength and faith. While from one perspective this language functions to comfort and inspire a country that has experienced terrible suffering, it is also a powerful means of creating unity and establishing national identity.

Lastly, the hero story rewrites the invading US soldiers in Afghanistan and Iraq as heroic defenders of the homeland and the bringers of freedom and human rights. This is a more opaque construction which emphasises the noble and heroic qualities of America's soldiers. Interestingly, it can also be read as an attempt to obliterate the image of the military's impotence on September 11, 2001 when despite its awesome fire power it failed to protect the American people. The heroism of the military in Afghanistan and Iraq rewrites their failure as success and restores their iconic status as true defenders of the 'homeland'. For example, speaking about the military action in Afghanistan, Bush affirms that the Armed Forces 'are **dedicated**, they are **honorable**' and they 'represent the best of our country' (Bush, 7 October, 2001). Later, he says that in the invasion of Iraq 'our men and women in uniform showed their **decency** and kept their **honor**' (Bush, 21 May, 2003). In other words, the military forces are also heroes who are dedicated and who keep their honour and decency; simultaneously, the binary structure of language implies that the enemy must be indecent and dishonourable.

The hero discourse is more than simply a way of discursively constructing the identity of 'good Americans'; it is also a way of redeeming the tragic story of September 11, 2001 through a careful rewriting of public memory. Instead of a massive failure of intelligence that resulted in the most spectacular terrorist success of all time and the worst loss of life in a single attack in US history, the story is rewritten like the script of a Hollywood disaster movie: although there is some tragic loss of life along the way, the heroic rescue workers save some civilians and demonstrate their true (American) character, while the bad guys are blown away. A photo taken on September 11, 2001 shows a firefighter rushing up the stairs in Tower One as frightened civilians descend. In the story accompanying the photo, *Time* magazine aptly noted that: 'The photograph fast became part of the redemptive fairy tale spun by Americans to make some rough sense of Sept. 11. The good guys ... saved the day, the evil ones were blotted out' (quoted in Silberstein 2002: 95–6). In a similar and simultaneous discursive move, the story of Afghanistan and Iraq is also rewritten from one where the most powerful military on earth mercilessly pulverises two of the weakest, most ill-equipped and poorly trained conscript armies in the world, to one where true American heroes risk their lives against a ruthless and vicious enemy to protect the homeland from attack.

From one perspective, the language of heroism is a common psychological reaction to death and tragedy. No one wants to face the idea that loved ones died needlessly or meaninglessly; narratives of survival and redemption are therefore an instrument for exorcising the mantle of victimisation and vulnerability. In this sense, they are a normal part of the collective ritual of mourning. At the same time however, they are a powerful means of writing cultural identity and demonising the enemy. This is because to probe the notion of courage and heroism is to find its opposite: cowardice (Silberstein 2002: 94). The narratives about American heroes therefore, are a means of stripping the terrorists of any vestige of courage; instead, the attacks are characterised as 'cowardly acts' (Bush, 11 September, 2001). The words used to write the character of Americans during the tragedy are more than simply a set of neutral or natural characterisations; they are a political act of identity creation – both in terms of Americans and the terrorists.

Innocent Americans

The official discourse makes a concerted effort to write the American victims of terrorism, as well as the combat casualties in the wars against Afghanistan and Iraq, as 'innocent'. In a sense, it is the attempt to construct a particular kind of victim-hood (see Chapter 2): not only is America the primary victim, it is an 'innocent' victim. The language is designed to evoke a sense of outrage. The term is at once both a powerful cultural descriptor (everyone understands implicitly that 'innocent' civilians refers to children, women, the elderly, the infirm and the defenceless), as well as a highly relative and rather unstable property (Townshend 2002: 7). After all, just as German citizens worked in munitions factories during World War II, it is possible to argue that the civilian workers in the Pentagon could not strictly be considered 'innocent'. Post-modernists and anti-globalisation critics have demonstrated that everyone is implicated to some degree in global structures of power and domination, which undermines any notion of true innocence. The workers in the Twin Towers, in some readings, could be considered guilty of promoting a global economic system that oppresses millions around the globe. For these reasons, there was a powerful imperative from US officials first to establish, and then maintain, the 'innocence' of Americans against other possible readings or interpretations.

This is another component of the discursive construction of the September 11, 2001 attacks as unprovoked and undeserved and in large part it is a strategy for maintaining grievance and victim-hood. At the same time, the discourse of innocence is a way of constructing the terrorists' guilt: if America is innocent, then the terrorists and anyone who supports them must be guilty. And as everyone knows, the guilty must be brought to justice. In the speeches I examined, there are countless references to 'innocent' Americans, 'innocent' civilians and 'innocent' victims. In virtually every case, this appellation was used to describe the American victims of terrorist attacks or the potential victims of terrorism, and *not* the 'collateral damage' of US military action in Afghanistan and Iraq. In effect, there is here a veiled attempt to deny the quality of 'innocence' to the victims of US military actions because this would obscure the clear distinctions that the US government wishes to maintain between the 'guilty' under attack and the 'innocent' Americans attacking them. The Iraqi prisoner abuse scandal was so destabilising because it upset this carefully constructed notion of American innocence: the images in the photos actually reversed the natural order to make Americans appear unequivocally guilty.

The construction of American casualties of terrorism or war as 'innocent' is a long-running feature of American political discourse: for example, the soldiers killed in the 1983 marine barracks bombing in Lebanon are recorded in official State Department records as 'innocent civilians' (see Livingston 1994), as are the military personnel killed in the 1996 Khobar Towers bombing in Saudi Arabia. This is reflective of what Richard Hughes calls a 'cult of innocence' in American political life (Hughes 2003: 154). In its foundational myths America emerges as innocent child among nations, untainted by the finite dimensions of human history – it is the embodiment of a new golden age of liberty and justice. As Ronald Reagan expressed it in his State of the Union address in 1987, 'The calendar can't measure America because we were meant to be an endless experiment in freedom, with no limit to our reaches, no boundaries to what we can do, no end point to our hopes' (quoted in Hughes 2003: 155–6). Rooted in a rejection of history then – 'History is bunk' – American political discourse has always sought to portray its motives as being free from self-interest or the normal machinations of foreign policy. In this sense, America genuinely believes itself to be 'innocent' of anything but pure motives and noble aspirations.

One of the indispensable aspects of this discourse therefore is the construction of the victims as not just 'innocent', but innocent 'Americans'. There is a clear sense that Americans are by implication, if not by definition, 'innocent'. For example, Rumsfeld says, 'Think of the thousands of **innocent Americans** that were killed by the terrorists.' Without any clarifications, the grammatical construction of this implies that the Pentagon workers killed in Washington are also 'innocent Americans', even though many of them were soldiers or ex-military personnel. Rumsfeld repeats the construction later in the same speech: 'We're not going to allow a thousand or thousands of **innocent Americans** to be killed and not do anything about it' (Rumsfeld, 16 October, 2001). The failure to disaggregate the soldiers from the civilians among the 'innocent civilians' here is not just a failure to be more semantically precise; in the context of the Purple Heart medals awarded to the Pentagon casualties (given to soldiers in combat), it is a deliberate attempt to affix the condition of 'innocence' to them as well. Thus, even America's soldiers are considered innocent victims of war.

Actually, the establishment of innocence takes on more unequivocal forms in the language of senior officials. For example, in response to a question about whether the US ought to have done more to avoid 'civilian' casualties (not 'innocent' civilian casualties) in Afghanistan, Rumsfeld stated: 'We did not start this war. So understand, responsibility for every single casualty in this war, whether they're **innocent Afghans or innocent Americans**, rests at the feet of the al-Qaeda and the Taliban' (quoted in Wheeler 2002: 217). On one level, Rumsfeld's statement can be read as meaning that the US forces killed in 'this war' (Afghanistan) are 'innocent Americans' (alongside the 'innocent Afghans'), despite the fact that any US personnel killed in Afghanistan would have most likely been armed combatants. More explicitly, Rumsfeld is deflecting moral guilt onto the terrorists by placing the blame for any 'innocent' deaths on their decision

84

to attack America in the first place. In a similar vein, but with a much more elaborate construction, Condoleeza Rice attempts to establish the automatic innocence of victims of terrorism:

> Islam is a religion that respects **innocent human life**. So we cannot believe that Islam would countenance the kind of **destruction of innocence** that we saw on September 11th.

> It is a war against people who take the lives of **innocents** willingly in terrorist attacks against office buildings or against the Pentagon. This is a war against the evil of terrorism. The President of the United States understands Islam to be a faith of peace, a faith that protects **innocents**, and the policy of the United States is to do the same. (Rice, 15 October, 2001)

There is here an effort to establish that all victims of terrorism are by definition 'innocent' – even if they work in the headquarters of the most powerful military in the world. The phrase 'destruction of innocence' is a powerfully emotive discursive construction which holds echoes of rape and violence towards children (the symbolic embodiment of innocence in our society). It can be seen therefore as an attempt to construct the September 11, 2001 attacks as a kind of rape of America's innocence. Likewise, the grammatical form of 'people who take the lives of *innocents* willingly in terrorist attacks against office buildings or *against the Pentagon*' is an explicit way of remaking the soldiers who received Purple Hearts for being wounded in combat into 'innocents'.

A consequence of this language is that once even the military is established as an innocent victim, it becomes relatively easy to excuse even the worst American actions. After all, it is reasonable and perhaps even human nature that the completely innocent victims of such a heinous assault would respond so forcefully. The status of innocent victim is actually a very powerful position to hold. In western culture, the revenge meted out by such victims is not only very often tolerated, but in some cases, it is applauded.

The 'United' States of America

As I have noted, in order for nations to maintain stability and avoid violently fracturing (as a number of states have tragically done in the post-cold-war period), unity has to be remade and sustained on a daily basis. Virtually every country in the world is made up of different communities, cultures, religions, language groups, classes and belief systems; maintaining overall unity in the political union called 'the State' takes a great deal of effort. Sometimes the need for unity appears overwhelming, particularly in large and diverse countries like America where there are deep and pervasive social divisions based on race, gender, class, region and political opinion – among others. This partly explains the comparatively high levels of patriotism in the United States, and the many state and federal initiatives that promote patriotism in schools, sporting events, official ceremonies, popular culture, social activities, religion and the like. Without the glue of patriotism to hold it together, the United States would be in danger of fragmenting, perhaps violently.

In times of conflict, unity becomes even more of a moral imperative. This is because policy makers in particular believe that modern wars cannot be won without a combined national effort, and that any expressions of disunity will undermine the struggle, thereby endangering the community's existence. In America, this is related to the mythology surrounding the Vietnam War – the so-called 'Vietnam syndrome'; a great many officials believe that the war in Indochina was lost because social and political divisions undermined America's unity of purpose. There is therefore, in the discursive construction of war, a major attempt to create and enforce the discipline of unity.

There are several strategies that are commonly employed to sustain unity. In the following chapter, I examine how unity is enforced by constructing a powerful sense of threat and danger. Most often however, the call to unity begins with a choice: either you are with us, or you are with the enemy. This is an attempt to polarise the world and draw up clear and unambiguous boundaries between friends and enemies, good guys and bad guys. It is called bifurcation – simplifying a complex situation into only two options. We have already seen how on one level the language of good and evil surreptitiously forces people to choose sides: if one side is definitely 'good' and the other is inherently 'evil', then unconsciously people want to be on the side of good.

The language of the 'war on terrorism' goes much further than this however, in distilling differences of all kinds into what has been called 'the moral logic of unity' (Stoddard and Cornwell 2002: 175). That is, the diversity and demarcations of political and social life are reduced into a simple binary logic: 'Every nation, in every region, now has a decision to make. **Either you are with us, or you are with the terrorists**' (Bush, 20 September, 2001). This stark choice was repeated over and over in the following months: '**Every nation has a choice to make**. In this conflict, **there is no neutral ground**. If any government sponsors the outlaws and killers of innocents, they have become outlaws and murderers, themselves' (Bush, 7 October, 2001). The grammatical construction of this choice is extremely powerful. On the one hand, it obliterates all neutral ground and denies any possibility of withholding judgment or weighing up the evidence. As Bush stated on another occasion, 'I don't see any shades of grey in the war against terror' (quoted in Hariman 2003: 517). On the other hand, it is loaded in such a way that any choice other than fully supporting the United States results in condemnation: if you do not choose America (for any reason at all), then 'you are with the terrorists'. Of course, being consigned to the 'terrorists' is to share in their evil, their savagery and their inhumanity. This language therefore, functions both to simplify the world – removing its ambiguities and its morally grey areas – and to enforce a set of clear identities – those with the good Americans and those with the evil terrorists. Interestingly, Bush's moral catch-22 echoes earlier words from Prime Minister Margaret Thatcher; she too warned against ethical ambivalence in the struggle against the IRA: 'Either one is on the side of justice ... or one is on the side of terrorism' (quoted in Carruthers 2000: 195).

In addition to the external world beyond America's borders however, there is a parallel and simultaneous effort to enforce unity at home. The same choice is presented to every American citizen: 'People who have information about terrorist activity **must make a choice**: either they will come forward to save American lives, or they will remain silent against evil' (Ashcroft, 29 November, 2001). Again, there is in the grammatical construction a highly loaded choice: if a person chooses for any reason not to support the US government, then they are on the side of evil. It is a stark moral choice: every person is either on the side of good or they have chosen evil – there is no option to remain neutral. The logic of this moral imperative for unity is to be found in the peril facing the community (see Chapter 4), and the fact that everyone's help is needed to fight the evil of terrorism: '**Every American must help us defend our nation** against this enemy. Every state, every county, every municipality **must join together** to form **a common defense** against terrorism' (Ashcroft, 25 October, 2001). In this construction, there is an implicit assumption that if a person considers themselves to be a true 'American', then they have a moral duty to join the fight against the enemy. It also implies that it would be disloyal, even treacherous, not to join the common defence of the community. On another level, the appeal for help is a way of making individuals feel important and thereby enlisting their support; it echoes earlier appeals during times of national need – 'Uncle Sam needs you!'

Another discursive strategy for enforcing the discipline of national unity is to construct a communal narrative that ascribes it as a national characteristic; that is, to write it into the community's history and mythology. In large part, the identity of the 'imagined community' – the things that bind a group together – are the stories the group tells about itself. As the previous chapter demonstrated, the events of September 11, 2001 have now become an important part of America's story. As such, they are identity defining events: they are the things Americans have in common at this time in history, and 'unity' means sharing in this moment (Stoddard and Cornwell 2002: 175). At the National Day of Prayer – itself a powerful discursive act of 'national' uniting – Bush stated:

> In these acts, and in many others, Americans showed **a deep commitment to one another**, and an abiding **love for our country**. Today, we feel what Franklin Roosevelt called the warm courage of **national unity**. This is a **unity** of every faith, and every background. (Bush, 14 September, 2001)

In this construction, Bush is writing the qualities of unity into the story of the actions of Americans following the attacks of September 11, 2001: these acts prove that Americans have 'a deep commitment to one another'. In addition, they prove that Americans really do love their country. The grammar enforces a certain interpretation of the meaning of peoples' actions following the attacks and is a clear effort to generate unity for the purpose of fighting the war. There is also an attempt to speak for the whole community and linguistically force everyone into the same emotion: 'Today, *we* feel'. Again, by stating it as a fact, despite the impossibility of knowing how everyone in America feels, Bush is trying to create it as a reality. The reference to Franklin Roosevelt moreover, is an attempt to appeal to the mythical past when America was (supposedly) truly united; it is a way of connecting the present story with other historical stories, thereby writing a single continuous national narrative.

At a popular level, this call to unity in the discourse of the 'war on terrorism' is repeated in the rhetoric of the advertising campaign, 'We are all Americans'. Interestingly, we can see the reconstruction of the September 11, 2001 story for the purposes of enforcing national unity in the way that 'We are all **New Yorkers** now' quickly transformed into 'We are all **Americans** now'. As we saw in the previous chapter, the attacks had to be remade from a local (New York) tragedy to a national (American) tragedy. Popular displays of the American flag on houses, cars, clothing, advertising, and news broadcasting are another powerful discursive act of unity creation, and following the attacks on New York and Washington, most stores across the country quickly sold out of American flags.

In summary, writing American identity in the 'war on terrorism' was in no way natural or neutral. Rather, the language was carefully designed to fulfil a number of specific political functions. In the first instance, it was intended to justify the use of counter-violence and reassure Americans of the moral purpose of the war. This was particularly important when the victims of the war – bombed civilians and abused Iraqi prisoners – began to look identical to the victims of the terrorist attack. At this point, there was a danger that the identities of the protagonists would become blurred. In this sense, the language was being used to create and enforce a difference between the images of bombed Afghan homes and the images of 'ground zero', despite the fact they looked virtually identical. The language of identity also worked to simplify the war and bifurcate the moral universe in which it operated. Related to this, the writing of identity was a means of enforcing national unity and social discipline. The writing of identity in the official discourse was relatively easy for officials because identity is deeply rooted in psychology and human emotion. Politicians have always appealed to patriotism and identity as a way of mobilising support. In addition, during times of group crisis there is a normal human need for psychological reassurance and support; as a consequence, groups tend to draw together or corral in times of danger or common threat.

Conclusion

Employing the language of identity was a necessity for American officials; the construction of a 'war' against terrorism would not have been possible without it. However, there were two important unforeseen consequences or 'reality effects' of this language, which have subsequently proved damaging to the war's prosecution. The first was the Iraqi prisoner abuse scandal which broke out in April 2004. Actually, concerns over the mistreatment of suspects in the 'war on terrorism' went back to the early stages of the Afghan campaign; human rights groups are still waiting for the UN to investigate American involvement in war crimes during that conflict, including the massacre of thousands of foreign fighters in the infamous 'convoy of death' incident. As early as March 2002, US officials openly admitted to using cruel, inhuman and degrading treatment on terrorist suspects held in Cuba – what they called 'rigorous' interrogation techniques. According to Amnesty International the statements by US officials were an admission of complicity in torture, a view shared by several noted international jurists. In any case, it was well known that when US interrogators wanted to use more forceful torture methods, they simply transported prisoners to the custody of countries where torture was more openly employed.

Apart from the sexual abuse, humiliation and ritual domination of terrorised captives seen in the initial photos from Abu Ghraib, the full horror of coalition prison practices has now been documented in numerous reports by the US military, the Red Cross and human rights groups: casual and serious beatings (including with a broomstick and pistol-whipping); prolonged hooding; sleep deprivation and exposure to bright lights and loud music; prolonged restraint in painful positions; keeping prisoners naked and bound for days at a time; the denial of medical treatment to wounded prisoners, including one who had been shot; the pouring of phosphoric acid over prisoners' genitals; unleashing attack dogs on naked prisoners; pouring cold water on naked detainees; the sodomy of prisoners with chemical lights and broomsticks; rape and its threat; mutilation of corpses; and even murder (dozens of suspicious deaths in custody are currently being investigated by military authorities). The abuse seems to fall into two main categories: the 'normal' and officially sanctioned practice of softening prisoners up for questioning and their subsequent interrogation employing a 'stress matrix' of techniques – known colloquially as torture 'lite'; and the casually inflicted abuse of over-eager, angry and sadistic soldiers taking their cue from their peers, but more importantly, from the environment created by their superiors.

It is clear that the discourse of counter-terrorism created an institutional environment where abuse became normalised and where the actions and language of senior officials undermined and destabilised previously held norms of ethical behaviour among ordinary soldiers; it created a culture of impunity. At the most fundamental level, the abuse is the direct result of the official discourse that paints all terrorists (and by extension all 'terrorist suspects' held in custody) as inherently 'evil', 'alien' and 'inhuman'. When George Bush and his senior officials come on television day after day stating that terrorists are 'barbarians' and 'savages', that they are 'a scourge' and 'a cancer on the human condition', and that they are 'the faceless enemies of freedom' who live on 'the hunted margins of mankind', then it is little wonder their jailors think of them as less than human and treat them accordingly. The official discourse simultaneously paints American and coalition forces as essentially 'good', 'decent', 'courageous' and 'honourable'. One result of such moral essentialising is an acceptance of behaviour that would normally be considered repugnant; this is because the logical outcome of the belief in one's inherent moral infallibility is a failure to engage in ethical reflection.

Apart from an official discourse that powerfully essentialised, demonised and dehumanised the 'enemy other' there are also institutional factors that created an environment in which abuse became normalised. For example, officials sanctioned the use of 'harsh' interrogation techniques, deliberately creating an environment where prisoners would be routinely abused in the belief that it would aid the gathering of intelligence. In a perversely ironic twist, it is fairly well known by intelligence experts that torture is a poor tool for gathering information, and very little useful or useable intelligence is ever gained by such practices. The atmosphere of impunity was further reinforced by the administration's public assertion that the Geneva Conventions did not apply to prisoners in the 'war on terrorism'. During the war in Afghanistan, Donald Rumsfeld stated publicly that he would prefer that members of al Qaeda and foreign fighters be killed rather than allowed to surrender. In other words, soldiers in Iraq took their cue from these powerful discursive actions: if suspects had no internationally recognised rights, and if it was acceptable to kill suspected terrorists rather than let them surrender, then what was the harm in a little prisoner abuse here and there? Added to this, the practice of American domestic law enforcement, with its unconstitutional denial of civil liberties to thousands of detainees, sent another powerful message to the troops serving in Iraq. Finally, it is clear that specific modes of military practice in Iraq also played a role in creating a situation ripe for abuse. In combination with the dehumanising discourse, the official policies of handling prisoners – hooding them so they become 'faceless' and inhuman, keeping them tied up for hours while they are processed, denying suspects any appeal against detention, instructing prison guards to soften prisoners up for interrogation – merely compounded the potential for abuse.

When the ingredients are all added together – a public discourse that vilifies the 'enemy other', the failure of moral reflection, officially sanctioned torture 'lite' interrogation techniques and orders to kill suspects, the abrogation of the Geneva Conventions, the policies of prisoner management in Iraq and the example set by domestic law enforcement – the abuse is easily explained. Such an environment normalises actions that would otherwise be considered morally repugnant and transforms human rights violations into routine. In fact, what is most surprising about the whole situation is that there isn't even greater evidence of abuse. It seems obvious that without a complete transformation of the entire language and practice of the 'war on terrorism' such abuses will continue to occur; no amount of prosecution of individual guards will reform such a powerfully constructed system.

Disturbingly, the abuse of prisoners in the 'war on terrorism' has become mimetic; terrorists and insurgents have started to mimic the behaviour of the American forces by deliberately capturing and then publicly abusing Coalition soldiers and civilian workers. In a horrifying pantomime of discursive mirroring, the terrorists dress their captives in the orange jumpsuits of the Guantanamo Bay detainees, hood them to make them 'faceless' and in some cases, murder them. Then, like the photos from Abu Ghraib showing Arab humiliation, they also post the images of the American dead and mistreated on the internet for the entire world to see. In a sense, this imitative war of images is a predictable outcome of the language of identity. In the end, the process of 'othering' makes everyone faceless and inhuman.

A second unforeseen consequence of the discourse of identity was the entrenchment and institutionalisation of an approach to counter-terrorism that has historically proved to be largely ineffective. The language makes it completely inflexible because it precludes the consideration of other potentially more effective options; it is an intellectual cul-de-sac. Once the enemy has been so thoroughly demonised and dehumanised, there is little possibility of anything but annihilation; logically, there is only one way to deal with evil, inhuman terrorists and it is to eradicate them. In addition, the moral absolutism of the discourse induces a kind of political amnesia about the failures and lessons from other counter-terrorist campaigns such as Britain's struggle against the IRA: until Tony Blair stopped referring to the IRA as evil terrorists, it was not possible to even explore other counter-terrorist strategies. Until then, just like in America's 'war on terrorism' today, the language of identity locked the British government into relying solely on (ineffective) retaliatory violence.

4

Writing threat and danger

T HERE IS LITTLE DOUBT that terrorism is now considered the greatest danger to western security since the threat of superpower confrontation at the height of the cold war. In May 2003 the G8 Summit affirmed that terrorism remains a 'pervasive and global threat' (Pfaff 2003); more recently, Eliza Manningham-Buller, the Director-General of MI5 stated that a terrorist attack in Britain using crude weapons of mass destruction was 'inevitable'; politicians and terrorism experts echo this warning almost weekly. Many ordinary people in both America and Europe rate the danger of terrorist attack as their number one security concern, and there is a great deal of generalised anxiety about the risks of air travel, public transport and large public gatherings. In the glow of the graphic images of bodies falling from the Twin Towers, the scenes of apocalyptic destruction at 'Ground Zero' and the twisted metal of the Madrid train bombings, this fear would appear to be justified.

And yet, there is an inherent puzzle at work here. The actual risk from terrorism is minute: in statistical terms the risk of being killed in a terrorist attack ranks somewhere near the risk of being killed by DIY accidents, lightning strikes or bee stings (Barker 2002: 37). Certainly, it does not even begin to compare America's annual death toll from gun violence: since 1965 close to a million Americans have died from gunshot wounds and in 2000 a total of 28,117 people died in weapons-related incidents – more than 10,000 of whom were murdered (North 2002: 162). Even in 2001, America's worst year on record, the casualties from terrorism were still vastly outnumbered by deaths from automobile accidents and pedestrian deaths, alcohol and tobacco-related illnesses, suicides and a great many diseases like influenza, cancer, rabies and liver disease. At a global level, the estimated 1,000–7,000 yearly deaths from terrorism pales into insignificance next to the 40,000 people who die every *day* from hunger, the 500,000 people who are killed every year by light weapons and the millions who die annually from diseases like influenza (3.9 million annual deaths), HIV-AIDS (2.9 million annual deaths), diarrhoeal (2.1 million annual deaths) and tuberculosis (1.7 million annual deaths) (Hough 2004: 155). The United Nations recently estimated that 150,000 people die every year from increased diseases caused by global warming; Dr David King, Britain's chief scientist has suggested that global warming is really a much greater threat to humanity than terrorism (Lynas 2004).

A study of the location and nature of terrorist attacks themselves confirms the view that terrorism actually poses a negligible risk to the personal safety of Americans or Europeans. In geographical terms, the vast majority of terrorist attacks occur in a very small number of countries – Israel, Russia, Colombia, Kashmir, Algeria, Afghanistan and since May 2003, Iraq. Terrorism, in other words, is almost always linked to a relatively small number of ongoing political conflicts; the vast majority of the world's 200 or so states face extremely low levels of risk. The nature of terrorist attacks reveals a similar kind of picture: proportionally, most terrorist violence is directed at property rather than persons and the majority of attacks involve few or no fatalities at all. For example, of the fifty terrorist incidents reported for the entire Latin American region in 2003, forty-one of them were bombings of an American-owned oil pipeline in Colombia (Pfaff 2003). Significantly, of the more than 10,000 terrorist incidents between 1968 and 1998, fewer than a dozen involved more than 100 fatalities (Jenkins 1998: 244–5). Overall, the number of terrorist attacks worldwide has been stable or falling for some time. The random mass casualty terrorism that we are constantly told to expect is actually extremely rare. This is because, as one terrorism expert put it, 'terrorists want a lot of people watching, not a lot of people dead' (Jenkins 1998: 230). Mass casualties are often counter-productive to terrorist aims – they alienate their supporters and can provoke harsh reprisals from the authorities – as well as being unnecessary – a phoned-in bomb threat is usually sufficient to cause widespread panic. In reality, most terrorist violence is directed at symbolic targets; its aim is to create a media spectacle in order to communicate some kind of political message. It is instrumental violence, or 'propaganda of the deed'.

None of this is meant to imply that terrorism is not a threat; the dangers can plainly be seen in the haunting images we are now so familiar with. Experts have noted that while the number of terrorist attacks is falling overall, they are becoming increasingly lethal, as the recent bombings in Iraq and Madrid attest. The real question we need to ask is why terrorism should be considered the pre-eminent public threat when there are so many more immediate and proximate dangers. Why do a few dozen 'terrorist' murders arouse the sense of social panic that tens of thousands of 'ordinary' murders do not? How exactly did the fear of terrorism become so widespread and so pervasive when the actual risk for most people is negligible? Part of the answer to this puzzle rests in the character of terrorist violence itself, in particular the sheer visceral horror of the September 11, 2001 attacks. Such seemingly random violence, packaged as media spectacle, creates an initial shock that is difficult to transcend. As Zulaika and Douglass explain:

> The reporting of innocent travellers killed in the bombing of an airplane is so brutally factual that no possible explanation makes sense; indeed it is so 'real' that it requires no frame, so 'true' that no interpretation is necessary, so 'concrete' that no meaning need be inferred. Its reality appears to belong more to nature than to society. This is discourse so over-whelmed by the 'reality effect' of the facts that the very suggestion that it authenticate itself appears ridiculous. (Zulaika and Douglass 1996: 5)

The 'reality effect' of terrorist violence induces an anxiety that no amount of rationalising can counteract; the visual pictures of violence are far more powerful than any counter-factual statistics could ever be. The violence seems to 'speak for itself' and the threat appears self-evident in the act. Additionally, terrorism touches our deepest cultural fears of random death at the hands of strangers, chaos and disorder, and wild, uncontrollable, faceless people; it is one of western society's strongest taboos.

This is only part of the rejoinder, however. A greater part of the explanation lies in the role of political discourse in creating public dangers and threats. Although there are 'real' dangers in the world – disease, accidents and violence (among others) all have life and death consequences – not all dangers are equal and not all risks are interpreted as dangers (Campbell 1998: 2). The world contains a multitude of dangers (so many that we cannot even begin to know all that threatens us), but it is only those that are *interpreted* as threats that society learns to fear. The necessarily interpretive nature of threat and danger can be seen in the fact that different societies fear different things: in some societies, danger can be associated with breaking religious taboos (which can result in curses or illness sent by deities). In western society, illicit drugs are considered to be a major public danger (there is even a 'war on drugs' being waged by America costing billions of dollars), despite the fact that the number of deaths resulting from the consumption of licit drugs exceeds by several magnitudes the deaths caused by illicit drugs. In this case, as in many other modern 'dangers' (serial killers, paedophiles, meteors, flesh-eating diseases, killer kids, road rage – among others), there is little correspondence between the socially accepted level of threat and the actual risk to individuals. This gap between society's perception and the physical reality is created by a 'discourse of danger' (Campbell 1998) that constructs and normalises the fear.

To put it another way, the main reason terrorism is so greatly feared in our society is because a 'discourse of danger' continues to surround virtually all public rhetoric about the subject, which in turn normalises public anxiety (despite the actual low risks). The authorities have deliberately and carefully constructed a deep and widespread fear of terrorism and the language used to describe the threat posed by terrorism makes it seem perfectly rational and reasonable to be afraid. According to politicians and security experts (like the head of MI5), one would need to be a fool *not* to be frightened. This is why a great many people feel more afraid stepping onto a plane than they do stepping onto a zebra crossing – despite the fact that the risk of being killed crossing the road is several hundred times greater than being killed in a terrorist hijack. Actually, the current fear of terrorism did not begin with September 11, 2001; it began in the early 1980s when officials started to apply the term 'terrorism' to acts of violence that they had previously called hijackings, bombings, assassinations, kidnappings and sabotage. As a result of this reclassification, it appeared there was a new plague of terrorist violence. The media quickly adopted the same language, and news stories about terrorism soon became a staple of television and print media news. In addition, the fear of spectacular terrorist atrocities made their way into hundreds of movies, television programmes and works of popular fiction. From books like Larry Collins and Dominique Lapierre's *The Fifth Horseman* and Nelson DeMille's *Cathedral*, to movies like *Black Sunday*, the public was primed to expect sudden horrific death at the hands of crazed terrorists. Not surprisingly, by 1987 surveys in America revealed that 68–80 per cent of the public regarded terrorism as a 'serious' or 'extreme' threat – despite only seventeen deaths attributable to terrorist activities (Zulaika and Douglass 1996: 6; see also Livingston 1994: 1–2). Today's anxiety is built on decades of public fear that was deliberately encouraged by the authorities, and which is continually experienced in the virtual dangers seen in *24*, *XXX*, *The Sum of All Fears*, *The Peacemaker*, *True Lies* and countless other movies, television programmes and books.

In this chapter, I examine the way the threat of terrorism facing America since September 11, 2001 has been constructed discursively and the reasons it is so crucial to the prosecution of the 'war on terrorism'. In the language currently employed by officials, terrorism is scripted as being a danger of colossal proportions; it threatens civilisation itself, democracy, freedom and America's very way of life. Despite this obvious hyperbole, creating such a monstrous threat is actually essential to the practice of the 'war on terrorism' because without the overwhelming 'reality' of the threat, the massive effort and expenditure of a global war would be impossible to sustain. The threat of terrorism, in other words, co-constitutes the war against terrorism; it makes it appear reasonable, it makes it seem normal; it makes it real. Critically, the creation of social fear also has a great many political functions and can provide the authorities with resources unavailable to them under normal circumstances.

Writing the threat of terrorism

The language of threat and danger saturates the discourse of the 'war on terrorism'. In fact, this kind of language is far more prevalent than most of the other aspects we have examined. One indication of the vast extent of this rhetorical onslaught lies in the frequencies with which certain words appear. In the speeches I examined, there were 328 uses of the word 'threat' and 110 uses of the word 'danger' in reference to terrorism and the nations who support them. In addition, the word 'risk' is used 90 times in conjunction with the words 'terrorist' or 'terrorism', as in 'the risk posed by terrorism'. In a related move, the highly emotive and alarming phrases 'weapons of mass destruction' and 'weapons of mass murder' appear 100 times, while the terms 'nuclear weapons', 'chemical weapons' and 'biological weapons' appear 92 times. These are very high frequencies and they add up to a kind of discursive offensive against the listeners' sense of safety; such continuous repetition creates a whole new world full of 'threat', 'danger' and the 'risk' of 'nuclear weapons', 'chemical weapons', 'biological weapons' and 'weapons of mass destruction'. In such a world, it appears reasonable and logical to be afraid.

In the following sections, I examine the discursive construction or 'writing' of threat and danger under five headings: (1) the construction of the 'new' threat of terrorism; (2) the making of the supreme emergency; (3) the construction of 'super-terrorists' and their links to 'rogue states' and weapons of mass destruction; (4) the creation of an extremely dangerous terrorist enemy; and (5) the reintroduction of the notion of 'the enemy within'. Following this, I will examine the reasons it is necessary for officials to construct threat and fear.

The 'new' terrorist threat

The initial construction of the threat of terrorism involved fixing the attacks of September 11, 2001 as the start of a whole 'new age of terror' – the dawning of 'a new era' of terrorist violence which contained 'unprecedented dangers'. This was the manufacture of a world of danger from the images of destruction seen on September 11, 2001. This is one of the most crucial steps in creating a discourse of danger and is a frequent rhetorical strategy for officials. It is very common for authorities to claim that a crisis is totally unprecedented and unforeseen, because such language provides resources not normally available to politicians. In the first instance, it can be a way of wiping the slate clean and absolving officials of any blame for the catastrophe; after all, by definition no-one can be blamed for failing to anticipate an unanticipated event. Second, officials can claim wider powers than would normally be available to them by stressing that 'new' and 'unprecedented' threats require 'new' and 'unprecedented' powers and resources to respond. In addition, the regular systems of institutional constraints and checks and balances can be resisted – a 'new' situation has no precedents, uncharted territory needs no compass. In short, writing events like the WTC tragedy as the signifier of 'new' threats and dangers allows the authorities to construct a new world and in a sense, to control the future. It is an extremely powerful discursive strategy.

Within the discourse of the 'war on terrorism', this construction of the 'new age of terror' started almost immediately. President Bush stated in his first major address to the nation: 'All of this was brought upon us in a single day – and night fell on **a different world**' (Bush, 20 September, 2001). Bush is here reconstructing the world Americans have always known. He does this by attaching significance and meaning to the attacks that goes far beyond their physical and psychological impacts: these were not just acts of dissident violence or the exposure of American vulnerability; they were a dawning, a revelation, a rupture in time. The use of this language transforms them into a powerful historical signifier – an event of metaphysical proportions, the marker of a new age of human existence. Even more crucially, this moment of transformation is linked specifically to danger and threat rather than to anything positive: 'The safety and security of America also faces **a new threat**, and that is the threat of terror' (Bush, 29 November, 2001); Ashcroft calls it a new 'reign of terror' (Ashcroft, 25 October, 2001). Vice President Cheney constructs an even clearer image of the new age: 'Today, we are not just looking at **a new era** in national security policy, we are actually living through it. The exact nature of **the new dangers** revealed themselves on September 11, 2001, with the murder of 3,000 innocent, unsuspecting men, women and children right here at home' (Cheney, 9 April, 2003). The language of senior officials constructs a new world in the foundations of the WTC where there is 'a new enemy' and 'new terrorist threats to Americans'; unlike the past, this is 'a new kind of threat' involving 'new dangers' and 'unprecedented dangers'. The 'new terrorist technologies' moreover, mean that 'we are in a new era'. It is 'a new world' and 'a new chapter in American history' with 'new reasons to fear'.

This rhetorical association between the dawn of the new age and the threats posed by terrorists is deliberate and specifically designed to script a discourse of danger. As I have already suggested, this construct of a 'new' era of terrorism was only possible by severing all links between this act of terrorism and the countless others preceding it, and in particular, by decontextualising it from the history of al Qaeda's previous attacks: '9/11' was constructed without a pre-history; it stands alone as a defining act of cruelty and evil. Given the spectacular nature of the WTC and Pentagon attacks, it was a relatively small and easy discursive step to weld them to a new world of danger. After all, it is a common psychological reflex to assume a spectacular event heralds the beginning of a new trend (rather than just being an exception). Once the authorities started encouraging this interpretation it soon seemed self-evident. The 'reality effect' of the attacks therefore, overwhelmed all other discursive possibilities.

The crucial point is that this construction was not natural or inevitable; it could have been written differently. For example, instead of the start of a new age of terror it could have been constructed as the start of a new age of global cooperation and multilateralism in tackling poverty, crimes against humanity, human rights abuse, injustice and the like; and instead of completely unprecedented attacks they might have been seen as part of a message of rage that the developing world has been trying to communicate to the developed world for many decades. In actuality, the events were extraordinary not because they signified a whole new era, but because there was a profound breakdown of intelligence and security procedures. Many similar plots have been hatched in the past, but they had all failed due to the work of the intelligence agencies and terrorist incompetence. The truth is that tiny groups of terrorists do not have a fraction of the resources or expertise available to states (especially superpowers such as America) and most terrorist groups are kept under fairly tight surveillance. In the case of September 11, 2001, the attackers would have certainly failed if there had not been a series of intelligence breakdowns and bureaucratic blunders; from this perspective, the hijackers were incredibly lucky not to have been arrested and deported well before the day of the attacks.

From another perspective, the attacks could have been written as simply part of the ongoing conflict between al Qaeda and America in progress since 1991. In this sense, the attacks were not the start of a new phase of terrorist violence but the continuation of a well-established one; they need not have signified a new age at all. In addition, the methods that the terrorists employed, far from being 'new terrorist technologies', were actually modelled on familiar terrorist strategies of the past. The Palestinian Liberation Organisation (PLO), for example, hijacked four airplanes simultaneously in September 1970; there have also been several publicised plots to fly planes into buildings. Ilich Ramirez Sanchez, 'Carlos the Jackal', admitted that the idea of using hijacked planes to target buildings had been discussed in terrorist circles since 1991 (Gupta 2002: 20).

The authorities could have written the nature of the terrorist threat in a completely different way; they need not have constructed a whole new world of catastrophic violence and unimaginable terror. However, wiping the slate clean and insisting that we were living in a 'new world' provided political resources that would normally have been unavailable to the Bush administration. It laid the foundation for constructing a whole new kind of discourse of danger and a new 'war on terrorism' that went far beyond the previous Clinton administration's 'war on terrorism'.

Constructing the supreme emergency

Another feature of the discourse of threat and danger involves the construction of numerous and seemingly catastrophic threats and dangers. The purpose of this language is to suggest that not only is the threat 'new' and 'unprecedented', but it is of such massive proportions that it endangers our physical, psychological, cultural and political lives. Moreover, it is a present, ongoing and imminent threat.

Neither is it just about physical safety or a passing danger. Rather, it is a fundamental threat – a threat to our collective and individual existence, to our very essence. Constructing a danger this great is extremely useful for authorities because it creates a situation of extreme crisis – the 'supreme emergency' – where normal politics is suspended and where the usual checks and balances on the exercise of power can be dispensed with. In international law, the notion of 'supreme emergency' denotes a situation where the very existence of the state is under threat; that is, where the national security, foreign policy and economy of the state is at risk. Under such circumstances, states are permitted to take any measures deemed necessary for their survival – including pre-emptive war, the suspension of constitutional rights, preventive detention or any other extraordinary measure. Thus, it gives a government immense power and freedom of action if they can construct their crisis as being so severe that it constitutes a 'supreme emergency'.

There is no question that the architects of the 'war on terrorism' have discursively constructed the crisis brought on by the terrorist attacks as being a 'supreme emergency'. The following phrases are taken directly from speeches and appear frequently; collectively, they construct a threat of titanic proportions. Terrorism, officials insist is: a 'threat to the national security, foreign policy, and economy of the United States'; a 'threat to the Middle East peace process'; a 'threat to international peace and stability'; a 'threat to the stability of legitimate governments'; a 'threat to America and our friends and allies'; a 'threat to the world'; a 'threat to all of us who believe in peace and freedom'; a 'threat to those who seek a modern society'; a 'threat to the welfare of millions of people'; a 'threat to national security'; and a 'threat to peace and liberty'. Colin Powell, for example, states that terrorism is actually a 'threat to **civilization**' and a 'threat to **the very essence of what you do**' (Powell, 26 October, 2001). Bush often describes terrorism as a 'threat to our **way of life**' (Bush, 20 September, 2001), and a threat to 'the peace of the world' (Bush, 29 January, 2002). The notion of a 'threat to our way of life' is actually a well-worn cold war expression that serves two functions. First, it vastly inflates the danger and constructs the magnitude of the threat: instead of a tiny group of dissidents with resources that do not even begin to rival that of the world's smallest countries, it implies they are as powerful as the Soviet empire was once thought to be with its tens of thousands of nuclear missiles and its massive conventional army. Astonishingly, it implies the terrorists could do what the Soviet Union failed to achieve over forty years of trying. Second, as we saw in Chapter 2, it discursively links the terrorist threat to a popular narrative in American politics, namely, the long struggle against international communism. During the cold war, one of the most common rhetorical refrains was that agents of communism – both within and without the American homeland – threatened 'the American way of life'. The construction here is that terrorists have both the means and the desire to do the same: they want to turn America into a pure Islamic state similar to Afghanistan under the Taliban; they want to destroy the American way of life.

In reality, terrorists have never truly threatened a state, or democracy, or freedom or the way of life of an entire people; nor have they ever threatened the peace of the world or the existence of any civilisation. On the other hand, there are numerous examples where the reaction of the authorities to terrorist attacks has endangered democracy and freedom by withdrawing civil and political rights, and where the state's eagerness to suppress dissidents has led to miscarriages of justice and human rights abuses by the security forces. In reality, it is not terrorism that threatens the essence of our societies – terrorists are tiny groups of desperate people able to do little more than commit symbolic acts of violence – but rather counter-terrorism and the dangers of over-reaction.

In addition to the vast number of ideals and institutions that terrorism purportedly threatens, the discourse also establishes the temporal dimensions of the threat. That is, terrorism is not a passing or ephemeral threat, but one that inhabits all of our time: present and future, the immediate and the imminent. For example, it is not uncommon to hear officials state that America (and the world) face 'daily threats', 'immediate threats', 'imminent threats', 'potential threats', 'emerging threats', 'ongoing threats', 'clear and present threats', 'even greater threats to come', 'likely threats' and 'predictable threats' – to name just a few. In other words, the threat of terrorism is in a way timeless; there is no escape from it. John Ashcroft constructs a more classical formulation: 'Terrorism is **a clear and present danger** to Americans today' (Ashcroft, 24 September, 2001). The phrase 'clear and present danger' implies that it is obvious to everyone that a danger exists – it is 'clear' to all who can see – and that it is 'present', which could mean it is temporarily present (now), or spatially present (here). It is also an echo of the language used against communists during one of America's early 'red scares'. Emotionally, the phrase resonates powerfully because it echoes earlier moments of peril in the nation's history: the attack on Pearl Harbor, the Cuban Missile Crisis and the Vietnam War. It is also fixed in popular culture as the title of a Tom Clancy book and movie of the same name. As the language reverberates through our collective consciousness, we recognise that we are living through a moment of genuine peril. Cofer Black, Spokesman Coordinator for Counter-terrorism, expands the danger even further: 'The threat of international terrorism **knows no boundaries**' (Black, 30 April, 2003). This is the logical conclusion of the language: it is in fact, an infinite threat. This rhetorical construction implies that we should not even try to measure its dimensions or calculate its probabilities. Rather, we should just accept it is everywhere at all times – it is a 'super-supreme emergency'.

An example of the way in which the threat is typically constructed in official speeches can be seen in President Bush's Press Conference on 11 October, 2001, exactly a month after the WTC attacks. In the process of one short speech and a

Q & A with the press, Bush uses the word 'threat' fourteen times – in addition to references to 'danger', 'weapons of mass destruction', 'chemical weapons' and 'biological weapons'. More than simply trying to overwhelm the listener with the imminence of danger, the text is also notable for the use of specific rhetorical strategies. For example, in his opening statement Bush assures: 'Americans tonight can know that while **the threat is ongoing, we are taking every possible step** to protect our country from danger. **Your government is doing everything we can** to recover from these attacks, and to try to prevent others.' This is a familiar discursive device in politics where the speaker simultaneously provokes and allays anxiety. He reminds the listeners that the threat is 'ongoing' and real; there is genuine reason to fear, in other words. At the same time, he tells them that 'we' (he associates the person and office of President with the effort), 'your government' (the people you trust to look after you) are doing everything possible to ensure your safety. This is a clever manipulation of emotions creating an artificial dependency on the government: the listener feels grateful to the state for relieving an anxiety which was encouraged by officials in the first place. This reinforcement of the threat followed by a comforting reassurance occurs several times:

> The Justice Department did issue a blanket alert. It was in recognition of **a general threat** we received. [...] I have urged our fellow Americans to go about their lives, to fly on airplanes, to travel, to go to work. But **I also want to encourage them by telling them that our government is on full alert**.

> Now, if we receive specific intelligence, where we – **a credible threat** that targets a specific building or city or facility, **I can assure you our government will do everything possible** to protect the citizens around and in, or near that facility.

> I think it is **important for the American people to know their government is on full alert**. And that's what that warning showed. **We take every threat seriously**. And the American people shouldn't be surprised that we're issuing alerts. After all, on our TV screens the other day, we saw the evil one threatening – calling for more destruction and death in America. And so **we should take these threats seriously**. Had it been specific, we would have dealt with the specifics of **the threat**. I think **the American people should take comfort** in the fact that their government is doing everything we possibly can do to run down every possible lead, and take threats – and **we take threats seriously**.

In the following segment, Bush reinforces the threat/reassurance rhetorical format by giving a concrete example of how the government received a threat and then acted strongly and appropriately to counter it:

And let me give you one example of **a specific threat** we received ... We received knowledge that perhaps an al Qaeda operative was prepared to use a crop duster to **spray a biological weapon or a chemical weapon on American people**. And so we responded. We contacted every crop-dust location, airports from which crop dusters leave, we notified crop duster manufactures to a potential threat. We knew full well that in order for a crop duster to become **a weapon of mass destruction** would require a retrofitting, and so we talked to machine shops around where crop dusters are located. We took **strong and appropriate action**. And we will do so any time we receive **a credible threat**.

Critically, in explaining how responsible and appropriate the government is being in protecting the American people from these 'ongoing threats', Bush simultaneously ratchets up the level of fear by invoking an image of crop dusters (a symbol of rural life, quiet agriculture and the production of life-giving nourishment) raining down biological and chemical weapons on the American people. It is a terrifying spectre: an instrument of progress, a life-affirming application of technology (and the opposite of a military plane, for example) transformed into a weapon of mass destruction.

These contradictions – creating terror and reassurance at the same time – are given even greater power by the symbolic act of hiding the Vice President in a secure bunker every time a threat is issued. A reporter questions Bush about it:

Question: Mr. President, you've tried very hard to assure Americans that the country is safe, and yet your own Vice President has spent most of this week in a secure location. Can you explain why that is, and also how long that will last?

The President: [...] We take very seriously the notion of the continuity of government. It's a responsibility we share, to make sure that under situations such as this, when there are **possible threats facing our government**, that we separate ourselves, for the sake of continuity of our government.

In effect, the answer to the question is the production of even more fear: the government that you trust to keep you safe is actually at risk – even the Vice President does not feel safe, so how are ordinary people going to feel safe?

Finally, there is a less than subtle attempt to remake and reconstruct normal life by introducing an element of terror into everyday activities:

The American people, obviously, if they see something that is **suspicious**, **something out of the norm that looks suspicious**, they ought to take comfort in knowing our government is doing everything we possibly can.

We are getting back to normal. We're doing so with a new sense of awareness. And the warning that went out today helped heighten that sense of awareness.

> Well, Ann, you know, if you find a person that you've never seen before getting in a crop duster that doesn't belong to you – [laughter] – report it. [Laughter.] **If you see suspicious people lurking** around petrochemical plants, report it to law enforcement. I mean, **people need to be logical**.
>
> And so I would urge my fellow Americans, obviously, **if they see something suspicious, abnormal, something that looks threatening**, report it to local law enforcement. (Bush, 11 October, 2001)

Significantly, there is no real explanation of what might be 'out of the norm' or what might constitute something 'suspicious'; instead, the listeners are told that it should be 'obvious' and are urged to be 'logical', as if this is an entirely reasonable request. This is a way of normalising a terrified society and maintaining a never-ending emotional roller coaster of fear and reassurance. In this manner, the language constructs a ubiquitous and endless emergency in which the state must be relied upon (apart from when it too cowers in a bunker) to safeguard the nation.

'Super-terrorism', rogue states and WMD

A third element of the 'discourse of danger' that is a founding feature of the 'war on terrorism' is its infusion with the apocalyptic language of Armageddon. As mentioned earlier, an important meaning of the September 11, 2001 attacks was their significance as the harbinger of a new age of terror. The discourse goes on to reconstruct them as the start of an age of 'super-terrorism' or 'catastrophic terrorism' where terrorists use weapons of mass destruction to try and kill not just thousands of innocent people, but millions. As Cheney contends, the threat of terrorism is supremely catastrophic:

> The attack on our country forced us to come to grips with the possibility that the next time terrorists strike, they may well be armed with more than just plane tickets and box cutters. The next time they might direct **chemical agents or diseases** at our population, or attempt to **detonate a nuclear weapon** in one of our cities.
>
> **[N]o rational person can doubt** that terrorists would use such weapons of mass murder the moment they are able to do so.
>
> [W]e are dealing with terrorists ... who are willing to sacrifice their own lives in order to **kill millions** of others. (Cheney, 9 April, 2003)

This language is clearly and unambiguously designed to generate maximum fear. The visions presented are apocalyptic, reflecting the most terrifying of Hollywood movies: the detonation of a nuclear bomb in a city, or the release of a deadly chemical or biological agent – resulting in millions dead (it is *The Sum of All Fears*, *12 Monkeys* or *Outbreak*). It is important to note how the discourse employs the vision of a city devastated by a nuclear attack, without openly acknowledging that the source of that vision is the only atomic attack on a city in history (Hiroshima) – committed by America itself. The language constructs a terrifying fear while consigning the source of the fear to historical amnesia. As if this is not enough to induce paralysing terror, Cheney then makes it seem a perfectly sane and reasonable fear to have; any 'rational person' should fear a nuclear holocaust.

This construction of a new world of unimaginable violence (that also seems to echo biblical visions of the last days) is not a one-off example of over-zealous rhetoric; it is actually a common refrain among officials. For example, Paul Wolfowitz reinforces the normalcy of the vision when he states: 'If they had the capability to **kill millions** of innocent civilians, **do any of us believe** they would hesitate to do so?' (Wolfowitz, 4 October, 2001). The form of this language is a rhetorical challenge that traps the listener in its logic because the answer appears self-evident: after all, if terrorists were willing to kill thousands in the WTC attacks, then logically they would kill more than this if they could. The question and its context supply its own unequivocal answer and circumvent the emergence of any alternative possibilities. In this way, it normalises the terror. Donald Rumsfeld reinforces the haunting vision. Although his estimates of the number of casualties are much lower, they are catastrophic nonetheless: 'Let's assume that there's **a nuclear or a chemical or a biological attack** on the United States a year from now. And that involves not thousands, but **tens of thousands** of human beings' (Rumsfeld, 24 October, 2001). Again, there is no reason given why we should contemplate such an attack; the language simply assumes that such an imagining is reasonable. Finally, Powell constructs the vision of a race against time: 'Even as I speak, terrorists are planning appalling crimes and trying to get their hands on weapons of mass destruction' (Powell, 30 April, 2003). This lends an aura of inevitability to the danger: the plans are under way, only the means are missing. In this language we hear an echo of the popular terrorist movie script: the devilish plot is in motion and the heroes are racing against time to save the world.

The official discourse is literally saturated with the language of nuclear, chemical and biological terror. Even without the direct and openly stated visions of horrifying death raining down on American cities, the frequency with which certain kinds of words appear in official speeches would be sufficient to induce terror in itself. For example, apart from the ubiquitous term 'weapons of mass destruction' (made popular in part by its embarrassing absence during the Iraq war in March 2003), all of the following terms appear frequently in official speeches and press conferences: 'weapons of mass terror' (an even more terrifying rhetorical relative of the more commonly known 'weapons of mass destruction'), 'chemical weapons', 'biological weapons', 'nuclear weapons', 'crude nuclear weapons', 'radiological weapons', 'offensive bioweapons', 'chemical warfare agents', 'radiological explosives', 'radiological devices', 'radiological dispersion devices', 'powdered anthrax', 'nerve gas', 'botulinum toxin', 'ricin', 'mustard gas', 'sarin gas', 'smallpox', 'Ebola', 'plague', 'poisons and chemicals', 'dirty bombs', 'toxins', 'increasingly advanced and lethal ballistic and cruise missiles', 'food pathogens' – and many more. Clearly, the intention of the speakers is to construct a consuming fear in their listeners, and given the vast array of such deadly weapons, it seems perfectly reasonable to be afraid.

This discourse is not new. It actually makes use of an academic discourse of 'super-terrorism' or 'catastrophic terrorism' that was popular well before September 11, 2001 (see for example, Carter *et al.* 1998; Falkenrath 2001; Freedman 2002; Laqueur 1999; Schweitzer 1999; Stern 1999). A number of academics and terrorism 'experts' have warned of such attacks using chemical, biological or nuclear weapons for decades, and although the WTC attacks did not involve any weapons of mass destruction, it was still taken as a vindication of their warnings. Obviously, politicians invest their own words with even greater authority if they cite recognised 'experts' and respected academics. However, as we have noted on numerous occasions, an alternative discourse was possible, not least because there is a great deal of controversy over whether terrorists would seriously contemplate the use of such methods. A number of academics have put forward reasons for thinking the vast majority of terrorists are unlikely to ever use such weapons (see Jenkins 1998; Sprinzak 1998; Townshend 2002). Apart from the difficulties of obtaining and using such weapons (they are notoriously unstable and unpredictable), there are real dangers that such attacks would be counter-productive, would undermine support and distort the message and would probably invite massive retaliation. Terrorists are rational actors and are acutely aware of these dangers. We know from interviews with senior al Qaeda figures for example, that they rejected using WMD on September 11, 2001 for precisely these kinds of reasons. From this perspective, it is a massive (and deliberate) over-inflation of the threat. In truth, even nation-states with all their resources would find it extremely difficult to achieve what these terrorists are supposed to be capable of (the only country to have ever detonated an atomic weapon in a city – the United States at Hiroshima – failed to kill 'millions.')

In a discursive variation, this threat of 'super-terrorism' is from a very early stage conflated with and discursively linked to the threat of 'weapons of mass destruction' and the 'rogue states' who might give them to the terrorists. According to the language of officials, 'rogue states' are apparently eager to assist terrorists in killing millions of Americans. As Colin Powell puts it, the threat lies in the 'potentially catastrophic **combination of a rogue regime, weapons of mass destruction and terrorists**' (Powell, 30 April, 2003). This unholy trinity offers an even more terrifying spectre than simply 'super-terrorism', because now we see that terrorists are no longer alone (they are no longer tiny groups of dissidents scattered across the world), but they have the resources and capabilities of states with which to enact their evil purposes. One of the most powerful articulations of this construction comes in Bush's State of the Union address where he first mentions the 'axis of evil' (which is the embodiment of the alliance between terrorists and 'rogue regimes'):

> States like these, and their terrorist allies, constitute an axis of evil, arming to threaten the peace of the world. By seeking **weapons of mass destruction**, these regimes pose a grave and growing danger. **They could provide these arms to terrorists**, giving them the means to match their hatred.

> Thousands of dangerous killers, schooled in the methods of murder, often **supported by outlaw regimes**, are now spread throughout the world like ticking time bombs, set to go off without warning.

> [W]e must prevent the **terrorists and regimes** who seek chemical, biological or nuclear weapons from threatening the United States and the world.

> I will not wait on events, while dangers gather. I will not stand by, as peril draws closer and closer. **The United States of America will not permit the world's most dangerous regimes to threaten us with the world's most destructive weapons**. (Bush, 29 January, 2002)

Bush begins by constructing an alliance between terrorists and certain regimes that appears natural and unquestionable. He states categorically that he knows that there are thousands of terrorists supported by 'outlaw regimes' (the use of frontier imagery) spread throughout the world and that terrorists and regimes are actively seeking weapons of mass destruction. This is simply a fact. Interestingly, and as if we wouldn't notice, by the end of the speech the initial terrorist part of the construction is left out and forgotten; what we are left with is 'the world's most dangerous regimes' threatening to deploy 'the world's most dangerous weapons'. The logic of the language has brought us to exactly the place Bush intended: in order to deal with the threat of 'catastrophic terrorism', we must act against 'rogue regimes' – especially those in the 'axis of evil'. Then, employing Churchillian rhetoric, Bush asserts his determination to meet the danger.

In another example of the association that is carefully and deliberately constructed between terrorists and certain 'rogue regimes', Cheney contends that:

> Containment does not work against **a rogue state** that possesses weapons of mass destruction and chooses to secretly deliver them to **its terrorist allies.**

To meet the **unprecedented dangers posed by rogue states with weapons of mass destruction, and terrorist networks with global reach**, our administration has taken urgent and, at times, unprecedented action.

It is **this alliance between terrorist networks seeking weapons of mass destruction and rogue states** developing or already possessing these weapons that constitutes the gravest current threat to America's national security. Therefore, a vital element of our strategy against terror must be to break **the alliance between terrorist organizations and terrorist-sponsoring states**. The chemical and biological weapons that Saddam Hussein is known to have produced are the very instruments that terrorists are seeking in order to inflict devastating harm on the people of this country, in Europe, and in the Middle East. (Cheney, 9 April, 2003)

Again, the grammar removes any doubt that such alliances exist between terrorists and 'rogue states'. Instead, the language simply assumes that such unions exist and as such, constitute a 'new' kind of threat that 'old' strategies like containment will not counter; in fact, Cheney explicitly states that 'unprecedented' actions will need to be undertaken. In short, even though the logic of the construction is clumsy and unconvincing (Saddam is known to have produced chemical and biological weapons; the terrorists want those weapons; therefore, Saddam and the terrorists are in an alliance), its effect is to close the circle that links them together.

This language was not inevitable or natural. Instead of constructing this diabolical alliance of terrorists and 'rogue states' the Bush administration could have chosen to publicise the conclusions of the Gilmore Commission in 1999, a Clinton-appointed advisory panel that was assembled to investigate the threat of weapons of mass destruction falling into the hands of terrorists. Its final report concluded that 'rogue states would hesitate to entrust such weapons to terrorists because of the likelihood that such a group's actions might be unpredictable even to the point of using the weapon against its sponsor', and they would be reluctant to use such weapons themselves due to 'the prospect of significant reprisals' (quoted in Hiro 2002: 391). This is a perspective shared by no small number of scholars: it is too risky for any state to entrust unaccountable groups of dissidents and terrorists with such weapons. Condoleeza Rice, a key figure in the Bush administration, appears to have shared this view: in 2000 she wrote that there was no need to panic about rogue states because 'if they do acquire WMD – their weapons will be unusable because any attempt to use them will bring national obliteration' (quoted in Callinicos 2003: 44).

The rhetorical strategy of making terrorists and 'rogue states' synonymous is an ingenious discursive slight of hand that provides the authorities with valuable resources. In the first instance, it allows America to retarget its military from a war against a tiny group of individual dissidents scattered across the globe (an unwinnable and unglamorous war) to a number of territorially defined states who also happen to be the target of American foreign policy. In effect, it transforms the 'war against terrorism' from a largely hidden and unspectacular intelligence gathering and criminal apprehension programme, to a flag-waving public display of awesome military firepower that rebuilds the American military's dented self-confidence. In the words of Vice President Cheney, 'To the extent we define our task broadly, including those who support terrorism, then we get at states. And its easier to find them than it is to find Bin Laden' (quoted in Kampfner 2003: 156). Of greater concern, it simultaneously assists the pursuit of geo-strategic objectives in crucial regions such as the Middle East under the banner of counter-terrorism (see Boggs 2003; Callinicos 2003; Mahajan 2003). The invasion and occupation of Iraq to prevent the imminent threat posed by Saddam's weapons of mass destruction for example, resulted in the achievement of a number of other key foreign policy objectives: a greater military presence in the Middle East, the establishment of another client regime in the region, access to a significant source of future oil supplies, the option of relocating America's permanent military bases in Saudi Arabia to Iraq and a greater ability to apply pressure on Iran. In sum, constructing a massive threat of 'super-terrorists' allied to 'rogue regimes' has a great many advantages; there is political capital to be gained from social fear and moral panic.

The dangerous terrorist enemy

As if the new world of terror created by the authorities was not enough to spread panic throughout the community, officials then go to great lengths to explain how these same terrorists (who are eager to kill millions of innocent civilians and who possess weapons of mass destruction or who have allied with states that possess such weapons) are actually highly sophisticated, cunning and extremely dangerous killers. In a series of constructions which sit uneasily with their simultaneous depiction as cowards, crazed fanatics, evildoers and faceless villains, the terrorists are made out to be formidable and frightening foes. In part, the notion of the dangerous terrorist enemy is related to the discursive construction of the terrorist identity examined in the last chapter; fear is a direct consequence of creating an evil, savage and inhuman 'other'. The discursive process is aided by the fact that psychologically there is a reflexive fear of those who are different and unfamiliar. In other words, by deliberately creating a terrorist 'other' who was entirely 'alien', the authorities set in motion a moral panic about those in the community who look like the archetypical terrorist. Simultaneously, it is an overt attempt to amplify the threat and exaggerate the dangerousness of the enemy, thus allowing the authorities to claim even greater powers in their pursuit of them.

There would be no advantage for officials to admit that terrorists are normally rather incompetent and no match for the resources, training and expertise of counter-terrorist units, particularly those of the world's most powerful states; or that they were rather ordinary people just like everyone else. Instead, the authorities make terrorists out to be incredibly sophisticated and fearsome agents – super-terrorists, as it were. For example, John Ashcroft stated that, 'The highly coordinated attacks of September 11 make it clear that terrorism is the activity of **expertly organized, highly coordinated** and **well financed** organizations and networks' (Ashcroft, 24 September, 2001). In the same speech, Ashcroft suggests that these terrorists 'can kill thousands of Americans in a single day' (as if they are that skilled and can do it anytime they choose), they can mount 'sophisticated terrorists operations' and they have the 'capacity to inflict damage on the citizens and facilities' of the United States. Bush echoes this assessment on a number of occasions: 'Our enemies are **resourceful,** and they are **incredibly ruthless**' (Bush, 29 November, 2001); 'Our enemies operate by **highly sophisticated methods and technologies**, using the latest means of communication and the new weapon of bioterrorism' (Bush, 27 October, 2001); 'They are **devious** and **ruthless**' (Bush, 24 November, 2001). Rumsfeld similarly describes them as '**very tough** people' who have 'made careers out of fighting'; they are 'not going to roll over' (Rumsfeld, 24 October, 2001). In each case, the object is to construct a formidable enemy who is so fearsome that only an extraordinary effort will defeat them. Again, it is a common strategy: we know that during the cold war, American intelligence deliberately overestimated Soviet capabilities in order to maintain an extremely high level of threat that justified massive defence spending. The CIA also exaggerated the threat posed by Iraq in the run-up to both the 1991 and 2003 Gulf Wars. Obviously, more measured and realistic assessments of the enemy do not provide the same opportunities for governments.

There is a second aspect to the construction of the danger terrorists pose. Officials stress that in addition to their undoubted skills and abilities, the terrorists are also a vast army of agents spread right across the globe – much like the huge network of Soviet agents that operated around the world during the cold war. Soon after September 11, 2001, for example, Bush revealed: '**There are thousands of these terrorists in more than 60 countries**. They are recruited from their own nations and neighborhoods and brought to camps in places like Afghanistan, where they are trained in the tactics of terror. They are sent back to their homes or sent to hide in countries around the world to plot evil and destruction' (Bush, 20 September, 2001). Given the proximity to the attacks, this was a terrifying scenario: after all, if only nineteen hijackers could cause such massive destruction, how much more death and mayhem could 'thousands' of ruthless terrorists cause? A short time later, Bush raises the level of threat even higher by suggesting that 'There are al Qaeda organizations in, roughly, **68 countries**' (Bush, 11 October, 2001). Similarly, Colin Powell and Donald Rumsfeld attest:

We're talking **several thousand**, maybe **many thousands**. [...] **They're everywhere**. They're in Europe, they're in America. You can find connections to them all around. And we have to get them all, or else we will always have a degree of uncertainty and a degree of insecurity within not only American society but within societies all over the world. (Powell, 23 September, 2001)

It is a network that are **across the globe** ... He's got a whole bunch of lieutenants that have been trained and they've got bank accounts all over and they've got **cells in 50 or 60 countries**. (Rumsfeld, 24 October, 2001)

Deputy US Treasury Secretary, Kenneth Dam, reinforces this message, even though his estimate is lower. He suggests that 'our best information tells us that **al-Qa'ida has cells in more than 40 countries**' (Dam, 22 October, 2001).

In one of the more detailed articulations of the threat posed by these ubiquitous terrorists, Bush constructs a narrative which could have come directly from the pages of a popular spy novel, such as Nelson DeMille's *The Charm School*:

Most of the 19 men who hijacked planes on September the 11th were trained in Afghanistan's camps, and so were **tens of thousands of others**. **Thousands of dangerous killers**, schooled in the methods of murder, often supported by outlaw regimes, are now spread throughout the world **like ticking time bombs**, set to go off without warning. [...] **A terrorist underworld** – including groups like Hamas, Hezbollah, Islamic Jihad, Jaish-i-Mohammed – operates in remote jungles and deserts, and hides in the centers of large cities. (Bush, 29 January, 2002)

Here we have a series of images straight out of popular fiction: 'ticking time bombs' (they were called 'sleepers' during the cold war) just waiting for that phone call to activate them; tens of thousands of agents 'schooled in the methods of murder'; and a vast 'terrorist underworld' of secret codes, tradecraft, plots and conspiracies that stretches right around the world. We should also note that the number of these schooled killers keeps inflating: first there were 'thousands', then 'many thousands', and by 2002 there are 'tens of thousands' spread around the globe. Finally, as if this were not enough in itself, Rumsfeld goes on to suggest that '**terrorists are thriving**' because the proliferation of new global technologies has combined with the network of killers to create an environment where it is quite easy to massacre large numbers of people. That is, 'the willingness to kill large numbers of human beings regardless of their religion or their race or their sex' has combined with 'the availability of these kinds of technologies that enable you to do large numbers of people simultaneously' (Rumsfeld, 24 October, 2001). Put another way, this is an extreme emergency because not only are there tens of thousands of well-trained terrorists 'everywhere', but the open and technologically advanced global system means they can kill large numbers of people with the greatest of ease.

110

In sum, while the numbers of terrorists who threaten us do not always add up, the message clearly does: there are countless thousands of sophisticated, skilled and highly dangerous terrorists spread out across the world just waiting and plotting to kill. With this information, it is perfectly reasonable and rational to be fearful. Curiously, in the 1970s and 1980s, western security agencies created and encouraged a popular mythology surrounding Ilich Ramirez Sanchez, a.k.a. 'Carlos the Jackal' (the name itself is an integral part of the myth), which suggested he was a kind of super-terrorist of exceptional cunning and skills who was personally involved in virtually every major terrorist incident in western Europe at this time. Many works of popular fiction and movies were modelled on his story, such as Robert Ludlum's *The Bourne Identity* and Nelson DeMille's *The Lion's Game*. In reality, as investigator David Yallop discovered, Carlos was actually rather incompetent and relied on good fortune and the incompetence of the security services for many of his escapes and successful operations (Yallop 1993). The case of the Unabomber is similarly instructive: despite the fact his 'embarrassingly ineffectual' letter bombs resulted in only three fatalities over nearly two decades of trying (hardly even comparable with some convenience store robberies), law-enforcement officials (and the media) constructed him as a major terrorist of mythical proportions and spent over $50 million trying to apprehend him (Zulaika and Douglass 1996: 92–4). At the same time, these discursive constructions of mythical individual super-terrorists were sometimes subsumed into a much larger myth of a global Soviet conspiracy during the cold war, where all international terrorism was directed by Moscow and communist agents lurked everywhere waiting for an opportunity to strike. Carlos the Jackal was popularly believed to have been trained in Moscow, for example. Claire Sterling's book *The Terror Network* (1981) was the formative work in the promulgation of this myth, and was highly praised by Ronald Reagan, Alexander Haig, William Casey and other senior American officials. It was only later that it was discovered that Sterling's work was based on deliberate CIA disinformation (Zulaika and Douglass 1996: 14).

Today, as we can see in the language of American officials, a similar myth is currently being constructed around Islamic terrorism: every terrorist attack is said to be the work of al Qaeda; they are thought to be operating at will in virtually every country; they are highly trained and highly sophisticated; they are, according to the authorities, the super-terrorists of the terrorist underworld. The purpose of this myth is to maintain a certain level of social fear and to justify the government's extraordinary measures. Following the Madrid bombings in March 2004, for example, David Blunkett, the British Home Secretary, stated that the attacks demonstrated that the norms of prosecution and punishment no longer applied (*Independent*, 13 March, 2004). On television, Jack Straw, the British Foreign Secretary, argued that the Madrid attacks proved restrictions on civil liberties were necessary for the security of civilised societies. The construction of such myths is also a way for the authorities to cover their own inadequacies and explain their failures; if the terrorists succeed it is because they are incredibly good; if the authorities succeed in stopping them or capturing them it is because the authorities are even better (it is never that the terrorists are fairly incompetent).

The enemy within

As if the threat could not be greater (tens of thousands of highly trained killers lurking everywhere, plotting to deploy weapons of mass destruction in our cities in an insane attempt to kill millions of us and end our way of life), the final curtain of fear is drawn across our terrified imaginations: the threat is not confined to enemies outside the borders of the community, it is already inside – it resides within. As Bush put it, there is a need to 'give law enforcement the additional tools it needs to track down **terror here at home**' (Bush, 20 September, 2001). This language is designed to reinforce the idea that 'the home', a place of comfort and security, has been invaded and infected by the scourge of terrorism. John Ashcroft constructs it even more forcefully:

> The men and women of justice and law enforcement are called on to combat a terrorist threat that is both immediate and vast; **a threat that resides here, at home**, but whose supporters, patrons and sympathizers form a multinational network of evil. The attacks of September 11 were acts of terrorism against America orchestrated and carried out by individuals **living within our borders**. Today's terrorists enjoy the benefits of our free society even as they commit themselves to our destruction. **They live in our communities** – plotting, planning and waiting to kill Americans again. [...] Yet, terrorists – people who were either involved with, associated with or are seeking to take advantage of the September 11 attacks – are now **poisoning our communities with Anthrax**. (Ashcroft, 25 October, 2001)

Again, there is a reference to the 'home' being violated. This is deliberately emotive language, as the threat to the home touches upon some of our deepest cultural insecurities. This language also puts the notion of threat into the mode of disease – terrorism as a cancer or plague – which poisons the body from within. The notion of 'poisoning our communities' is a powerful metaphor invoking very deep cultural fears about the role of poison. In the same speech, Ashcroft articulates the implications of constructing this dangerous 'enemy within':

> To date, our anti-terrorism offensive has arrested or detained nearly 1,000 individuals as part of the September 11 terrorism investigation. Those who violated the law remain in custody. Taking suspected terrorists in violation of the law **off the streets and keeping them locked up** is **our clear strategy to prevent terrorism within our borders**. [...] The federal government cannot fight this reign of terror alone. **Every American must help us defend our nation against this enemy**. (Ashcroft, 25 October, 2001)

There are two clear logics here. First, the 'enemy within' (anyone suspected of being linked to terrorism) must be quarantined and isolated from the general population – taken off the streets and locked up – and second, every true American must join the fight to secure the '*home*land'. In this way, the language normalises both the preventive detention of thousands of suspected Muslims and the creation of informant-based systems like the Responsible Cooperators Program and the Terrorism Information and Prevention System Program (TIPS).

In short, just like the American 'red scares' of the past, the discourse of danger is deployed to create social fear, enforce social discipline, mute dissent and increase the powers of the national security state. Writing a dangerous enemy that lives among the community makes it easier to make policies that serve a wider range of goals than just counter-terrorism. As John Ashcroft put it, 'we seek new laws against **America's enemies, foreign and domestic**' (Ashcroft, 24 September, 2001). Lastly, the language is designed to bring the war home, or, as Bush puts it: 'And make no mistake about it, we've got a war **here** just like we've got a war **abroad**' (Bush, 29 November, 2001). This is part of the attempt to maintain the supreme emergency domestically, to create a war-time atmosphere in the American heartland. It is designed to make every individual feel and act as if they themselves were fighting the war in some way.

The political functions of fear

As Chapter 1 explained, discourses are more than just words or texts; they are also actions and material practices which act as symbols and message transmitters. To put it another way, actions can communicate or 'speak' in a similar manner to spoken or written language. In many cases, actions speak more powerfully than words. In constructing the 'war on terrorism', American officials engaged in a constant display of actions designed to reinforce their words of doom. This is why the site of every speech was chosen so carefully (the Great Wall of China as the site of a major speech about defending civilisation), and the symbols of American unity and power were so carefully manipulated (the flag and the presidential seal prominently displayed near podiums). In constructing the discourse of danger, the American government (and other governments around the world) engaged in a series of powerful discursive actions designed to reinforce the message behind the words. For example, during times of national alert, it is well known that Vice President Dick Cheney was always taken to a secure bunker so the continuity of government could be maintained in case of an attack on the president. This kind of action sends a powerful subliminal message that the government really believes it is in danger of being decapitated, and that even the most powerful people in the country are not safe from terrorists.

Other powerful discursive actions we have seen include: the grounding of passenger flights to America; the placement of armed sky marshals on passenger planes; the flying of jet fighters over major cities; the massive steel and concrete barricades erected around public buildings; military operations where tanks and other heavy equipment are displayed around airports or at other public venues; large-scale public health exercises that simulate a WMD attack on an urban area; massive public safety campaigns for trains; government websites that encourage the building of sealed rooms and the hoarding of supplies; and the institutionalisation of a national terrorist warning system based on the colours red, orange, yellow, blue and green (where red signifies extreme risk of terrorist attack and green signifies low risk). These are very powerful acts that reinforce the seriousness of the threat and send an unambiguous message: if the government scrambles jet fighters over New York or practices treating thousands of WMD victims, then the threat must indeed be 'real' (no government would expend these kinds of resources on a 'fake' or imaginary threat). The use of the colour coded warning system is particularly insidious, because the subliminal message is reinforced at every intersection, reflected in the glow of the traffic lights. If the message is not plain in the words of the authorities, it is glaringly obvious in the actions of the government.

The construction of social fear in American political life is not unusual, even if current levels are as high as they have probably ever been. The construction of fear is a frequently employed strategy of social control for most states. And as we have seen, officials deliberately tap into existing cultural anxieties surrounding infection, poison, anarchy, 'wild men' and weapons of mass destruction, and then reinforce these anxieties through conspicuous public actions – like scrambling jet fighters. Historically, the American government has relied on the discourse of threat and danger on numerous occasions to maintain the integrity of the American nation or 'imagined community'. In the early days of settlement, government officials created the first of what would be a number of 'red scares'. In this script, Native Americans – 'red' Indians – threatened the spread of progressive civilisation along the Western frontier; they had to be exterminated or quarantined in reservations. A second 'red scare' was invoked during the widespread industrial unrest that overtook American industry from the 1890s to the early 1920s; in this case, the infamous 1919–20 Palmer Raids were used to arrest and deport thousands of foreigners suspected of being radicals. The most recent 'red scare' began in the 1950s, when communism was constructed as a catastrophic threat to the American way of life. The McCarthy hearings epitomised the extent of the hysterical fear of the 'enemy within'. Of course, in between the red scares, the two world wars allowed fears of the 'enemy living among us' to encompass people of German, Italian and Japanese extraction: 'Loose Lips Sink Ships' was the Advertising Council's warning in the 1940s (Snow 2003: 93). Since the end of the cold war, American officials have constructed a variety of new dangers: the threat of 'rogue states' like Libya, Panama, Iran, North Korea and Iraq; the threats posed by the drug trade; illegal immigrants from

Haiti or Latin America; and the proliferation of weapons of mass destruction. The discourse of the dangers of (Islamic) terrorism – which we may well call the 'green scare' – is only the latest in a long line of social fears and moral panics that are scripted for the purposes of maintaining inside/outside, self/other boundaries. These discourses are employed continually to 'write' American identity and to enforce a disciplined unity on a sometimes unruly and (dis)United States.

I am not arguing that states do not have a responsibility to warn their citizens about public dangers; they clearly do. However, they also have a responsibility to be truthful and realistic about the actual extent of the risk, and to avoid creating unnecessary anxiety or potentially damaging moral panics. The problem is that there is a great deal to be gained from the manipulation of public fear and it can yield political capital not always available during times of peace and stability. There is a great temptation to deliberately encourage public anxiety for political ends. In a way, threat and danger is actually a foundational feature of modern political life. That is, from one perspective the state itself can be seen as a kind of 'protection racket' based on the fear of disorder and random violence (see Tilly 1985); the 'social contract' upon which the state rests can be considered the institutionalisation of this fear. Under the terms of the contract, we give our loyalty to the sovereign authority of the state in exchange for safety from the forces of anarchy. Thus, like a modern-day gangster, the state has continually to provoke and allay our anxieties to maintain a relationship of dependence: were it not for the state's protection, we are continuously reminded, society would inevitably and quickly return to a 'state of nature' where criminals, hooligans, deviants, foreigners and terrorists would run rampant – it would be a permanent condition of 'war of all against all', as Thomas Hobbes put it. The fee for protection, on the other hand, is a daily surrendering to the state's sovereign power: paying taxes, obeying the law, acquiescing to governmental decisions, participating in state programmes. From this viewpoint, the maintenance of a condition of insecurity is simply a part of the normal functioning of domestic political life.

Of course, as I have already noted, the feeling of threat and danger has another vital political function, namely, constructing and sustaining collective identity. It is well known that individuals unify in the face of an external danger in a kind of instinctual psychological reflex. For sizeable and diverse collectivities such as states therefore, the existence of abiding and multiple exogenous threats is indispensable for supporting the unity of the 'imagined community' that is the nation-state. Extremely large and diverse states in particular, such as India or America, contain a multitude of social cleavages and sectional differences. In such cases, national cohesion and the avoidance of internal conflict is contingent on the maintenance of an overarching, but ultimately artificial, sense of collective identity – which in turn, is reliant on the existence of external, or, foreign threats. While many scholars believe that the international system is by definition dangerous and threatening – providing all states with a pre-existing and permanent external danger – others have shown how state practices actually constitute or create this situation of anarchy through their interaction (see Wendt 1992). External threats do not necessarily exist independently of states; rather, states deliberately construct them for the purposes of disciplining the domestic sphere. Creating and maintaining a perennial 'discourse of danger' therefore, is a key function of foreign policy, designed to enforce inside/outside, self/other boundaries and thereby construct or 'write' collective identity (Campbell 1998). Typically, states construct external threats by positing a rival state (the 'evil' Soviet empire, for example), an opposing ideology (fascism, communism or Islamic fundamentalism) or 'national security' issues such as weapons proliferation, rogue states, illicit drugs and terrorism.

Apart from the maintenance of the social contract and the enforcement of collective identity, there are a number of other reasons officials value the creation of social anxiety and moral panics. In the first place, it can be an effective means of delegitimising dissent and muting criticism. In an atmosphere of national peril, the appeal for unity takes on a much greater moral force and voicing disagreement can be seen as an act of disloyalty or of sowing the seeds of discord. It is a common belief that in times of national danger, there is a need to 'pull together' and maintain a unity of purpose. In many cases, the creation of widespread moral panics can lead to ordinary citizens acting as the primary agents of censure themselves, both in terms of self-censorship (choosing to withhold their own doubts and disagreements in public discourse) and the censorship of others (expressing disapproval when confronted with dissenting or 'disloyal' opinions in others). There have been countless cases of this phenomenon in America since the 'war on terrorism' began, from the sacking of injudicious talk show hosts, to the public burning of *Dixie Chicks* CDs and the banning of 'unpatriotic' t-shirts worn by high-school students.

Related to this, there are a great many vested interests among government agencies in maintaining a sense of national peril; the security agencies in particular – police, FBI, CIA, NSA, Department of Homeland Security, MI5 and MI6 in Britain – receive increased resources and enjoy an elevated status in times of national danger. As Senator Arthur Vandeburg advised President Truman, if you really want all the weapons and taxes to pay for a long war against communism, then you had better 'scare hell out of the American people' (quoted in Sardar and Davies 2002: 183–4). In the 'war on terrorism', all of the national security institutions – the military, law-enforcement agencies, emergency response agencies and intelligence organisations – have received massive extra funding directly because of the fear of terrorist attacks. In America, more than half of the federal budget for FY 2004 was devoted to national defence, with the Pentagon receiving $399 billion and spending on homeland security more than doubling from $18 billion to $38 billion (Hartung 2003). With agencies like the

CIA costing around $30 billion per year, the sums involved are truly vast. In Britain, MI5 has recently been given a 50 per cent increase in its budget to £300 million per year and is set to increase its personnel numbers to the highest level since World War II (Evans 2004). In addition to these public bodies, there are also private-sector interests in the maintenance of social fear; private security providers have benefited greatly from the state of anxiety about terrorism and the sector is thriving with sales of security equipment topping $50 billion per annum in the last few years (see Zulaika and Douglass 1996: 9). There are direct material benefits for a great many government actors – as well as prestige and standing – in maintaining an elevated level of public fear.

Another function of social fear is the distraction of the public from more complex and pressing social ills. As Glassner (1999) has shown, some fears are better than others for politicians, because some fears – such as the fear of being without health care or employment – are not amenable to quick-fix solutions and carry the risk of policy failure. The fear of terrorism on the other hand, is perfect for the authorities because it is ubiquitous, catastrophic, opaque (reliant on government control of secret information) and rooted in deep cultural anxieties. Moreover, there is little risk for the authorities of being seen to fail; every terrorist attack can simply be construed as another reason to expend even greater resources in dealing with the threat – rather than as a failure of current policies. As a consequence, more pressing and more complex threats to individual safety, such as crime, gun control, poverty, workplace safety and health (to name a few), can remain relatively neglected while the government spends hundreds of billions of dollars on the more pressing threat of terrorism. A suffocating smokescreen of fear is required for this strategy to work successfully. When it does, it also allows for the diversion of scarce resources into ideologically driven political projects, such as national missile defence, military expansion and cutting welfare programmes.

Lastly, fear creates calls for retaliation and punishment. Studies have shown that the more fearful people are of crime, for example, the more punitive they require the authorities to be towards criminals (Glassner 1999: 72). This reflects the psychological observation that fear often gives rise to anger and hatred when people begin to resent being made to feel afraid. This atmosphere of retribution gives the authorities greater freedom to use coercive and repressive strategies and to exercise 'raw power'. This is the principle currently at work in the construction of the 'war on terrorism': create enough fear and anxiety about the threat posed by terrorism and people will fully support a massive campaign of punitive violence against terrorists and the states that support them. They will also accept limitations on their own human rights and civil liberties. In part, the Iraqi prisoner abuse scandal was caused by the dread of the terrifying terrorist 'other'; being the object of such fear (and hatred) led directly to harsher treatment. It is also the reason there has been a massive increase in the incidence of hate crimes against Muslims and people of Arab appearance in America and Britain; the moral panic constructed by the authorities has turned Muslims into the feared (and hated) 'other'.

Fear and a sense of threat is an essential element in constructing large-scale political violence whenever it occurs, but particularly in the case of war which requires widespread social support. In the first instance, the notion of the 'supreme emergency' justifies war-based violence in a legal and ethical sense. That is, the construction of the 'supreme emergency' is a way of creating a just cause for a defensive war – nations can defend themselves if they feel the threat is so severe that it endangers the existence of the state itself. Even more crucially, creating a sense of threat and danger is the primary means (along with dehumanising the enemy as we saw in Chapter 3) of getting people to participate or acquiesce in large-scale violence. This process of threat creation has been a particularly noticeable feature of every civil war in the last few decades. In the Balkans, Slobodan Milosevic convinced the Serbian people that their culture, their way of life and their very existence was under threat from Croats and Bosnians; this led many to join the war to defend the Serb nation and many more to acquiesce or support it tacitly. Similarly, the Hutu-dominated Rwandan government was able to convince a large proportion of the Hutu population in 1994 that the Tutsi-dominated RPF was coming to slaughter them all; in the climate of fear and intimidation that followed, 800,000 people were slaughtered in 100 days, many by ordinary people (rather than military personnel). In effect, the fear and sense of threat generated in these societies was sufficient to motivate ordinary people to engage in or support pre-emptive military attacks on their perceived enemies. A similar process has occurred in the 'war on terrorism': the construction of fear and a powerful sense of threat have justified pre-emptive attacks on Afghanistan and Iraq, being widely supported by a terrified population.

Conclusion

The net result of the present discourse of danger so carefully constructed by the authorities is a people living in a state of 'ontological hysteria' – a nation constantly anticipating the next attack, just 'waiting for terror' (Zulaika and Douglass 1996). This is the 'reality effect' of the language: it is people who feel anxious whenever they have to fly anywhere or whenever they ascend a skyscraper to go to work; it is people who feel afraid crossing Times Square or mixing with crowds, or who rank terrorism as the number one threat to their personal safety; it is the thousands of Americans who built themselves tape-sealed rooms stocked with provisions, water and gas masks for a prolonged siege by terrorists (on the advice of federal agencies); it is the thousands who died whilst driving to their destinations when they became too fearful to fly, and the hundreds who died in firearm accidents when they bought a gun following the terrorist attacks.

Another reality effect can be seen in the actions of the authorities (and the almost total acceptance of those actions by the public, the media and even by opposition politicians): two major wars fought in two years (followed by extremely costly ongoing 'security operations'), the arrest of several thousand suspects in America and around the world and vast sums spent unquestioningly (even by the opposition Democrats) on domestic security, border control and the expansion of the military. It can be seen in the intrusive and daily disruptions to everyday life: airport security measures, the checking of containers at ports, sky marshals, heightened security at public events, metal detectors, baggage searches and identification checks for virtually every transaction. Only the 'reality' of the threat of terrorism allows such massive interruptions to national life and such colossal spending. As we have seen in this chapter, the manner in which the threat has been discursively constructed – as catastrophic, ubiquitous and ongoing – normalises the entire effort and makes it appear entirely rational and sensible. Most people feel the new measures are a reasonable response to the threat and most accept them without complaint.

The whole situation would be somewhat equivalent to a health authority spending tens of billions of dollars on the prevention of mad cow disease or flesh-eating viruses, instead of the more mundane threats to personal health like influenza, diabetes, tuberculosis, malaria, cancer, heart disease and the like. Just like terrorism, these spectacularly horrific diseases actually kill a tiny number of people per year and pose a minute risk to the health of most people. It seems reasonable to suggest that few citizens would tolerate a government which devoted more than 50 per cent of its health budget to treating diseases that most people will never get while ignoring more common ailments that greatly affect people's quality of life. Another comparison is the risk posed by meteors, which theoretically could kill millions if they hit a large city. The question is: would we be happy for the government to spend hundreds of billions of dollars on a national meteor defence ('NMD') system, especially if it took money away from education, health or welfare services?

In reality, a small fraction of the cost currently spent on the anti-terrorism and national missile defence systems would vastly increase people's safety and well being, especially if it was invested in gun control, public health, auto-safety, crime control and medical research – among others. If an alternative interpretation of the threat emerged to challenge the dominant orthodoxy (that it was vastly overblown, or misdirected, for example), support for the consumption of such massive amounts of resources might be questioned and the present political order could be destabilised. A massive and 'real' threat then, is necessary for the continued viability of the 'war on terrorism'; writing the threat of terrorism is co-constitutive of the practice of counter-terrorism.

As I have outlined in this chapter, the language of threat and danger was not inevitable or simply a neutral or objective evaluation of the threat. Rather, it was the deliberate and systematic construction of a social climate of fear. There were and still are a great many alternatives to the language of threat and danger. Although threat and danger is ultimately a matter of perception and perceptions can vary greatly from person to person, it would still be possible to present a range of perspectives and information which would allow a less hysterical assessment of the situation. For example, the authorities could have tried to reassure the nation that the September 11, 2001 attacks were atypical events, both in terms of the ability of the terrorists to carry them out (the unusual failure of intelligence cooperation), and in terms of the extreme rarity of those kinds of attacks (the exceptionally rare occurrence of mass-casualty terrorism). Officials could have also pointed out all the measures they were taking to ensure security while also stressing that terrorists are tiny groups of people with few resources who have never yet managed to overthrow a democracy or bring down a civilisation. The authorities might have also publicised the findings of their own studies and those of 'experts' that show the likelihood of terrorists obtaining or using weapons of mass destruction to be extremely small. Lastly, the authorities could have tried harder to place the events in context, thereby reassuring people this was not the beginning of a new apocalyptic age of terror (it was part of a long-running cycle of violence and counter-violence), nor was their personal safety at extreme risk from terrorism (the risk of terrorist attack still ranked very low compared with other more 'normal' risks).

Instead, officials in the 'war on terrorism' engaged in the deliberate construction of a world of unimaginable dangers and unspeakable threats. Within the suffocating confines of such an emergency, where Americans measure their daily safety by the colour of a national terrorist alert scale (reflected in the glow of every traffic light), it seems perfectly reasonable for the entire resources of the state to be mobilised in defence of the homeland and for pre-emptive war to be pursued. It also seems reasonable for national unity to be maintained and expressions of dissent curtailed. Once it is accepted that terrorism is really this dangerous, a global 'war against terrorism' on the scale and duration of the cold war appears perfectly reasonable.

5

Writing the good (new) war
on terrorism

B Y THIS STAGE, IT SHOULD BE OBVIOUS that the official language of counter-terrorism implicitly constructs the 'war on terrorism' within the 'virtuous' or 'good war' tradition (see Lawler 2002). Locating the American response to the September 11, 2001 attacks in the bounds of the overarching framework of the World War II meta-narrative for example, and describing it as part of the eternal struggle between good and evil and civilisation and savagery (see Chapter 2), implies that by definition it must be a good and just war. This is a rather opaque construction and the rhetorical connections between the current war and previous 'good wars' America has fought are oblique rather than explicit. An analysis of the language reveals that in addition to these implicit discursive associations, senior officials in the Bush administration framed the counter-terrorism campaign as the quintessential 'good war' from the very beginning, suggesting that it fitted all the criteria of a defensive, legally sanctioned and necessary war of last resort – a truly just war.

There are three notable aspects to this particular rendering of the 'good war on terrorism'. In the first place, following the two world wars, the practice of war was stigmatised as one of the great evils of modern times; its heroic and redemptive qualities had been utterly discredited in the trenches of World War I with its mud and poison gas, and in the World War II concentration camps, the reciprocal firebombing of cities and the atomic terror of Hiroshima. As a consequence, the international society of nations after 1945 developed a series of agreed rules and norms regarding the right and proper conduct of war; states that engaged in war had to clearly and incontrovertibly demonstrate that their war was legally constituted, it was defensive rather than expansionist, it was rightly conducted (with due care for the lives of innocent civilians), it would not cause a greater injustice than the initial harm and it was the last resort after recourse to all avenues of diplomacy had been explored.

As a consequence, the resort to war – even by very powerful states like America – now requires careful and extensive justification to both domestic and international audiences (see Hurrell 2002). Within America itself, war had to be even more vigilantly legitimised following the debacle in Vietnam when the full horror of modern warfare was beamed nightly into American homes in glorious Technicolor. For the 'war on terrorism', this type of justification was actually relatively simple. After all, the discursive foundations had already been well established: the September 11, 2001 attacks had been rhetorically fixed as an illegal (and horrific) act of war that demanded a military response, and the terrorists had been constructed into evil and inhuman killers who would not respond to diplomacy or traditional methods such as deterrence or containment. In effect, the language employed to make sense of the terrorist attacks made a 'war' against terrorism appear inherently virtuous and fully justified. In one sense, it seemed undeniable that if any war was a truly 'just war', this was it (see Falk 2001).

A second reason why administration officials chose to employ an overtly 'good war' or 'just war' narrative lay in the inherent religiosity of American society. Although dismissed as unimportant by many political analysts, protestant Christianity is in fact deeply embedded in American political and cultural life: there are 70 million born-again evangelicals in America, and the 19 million Christian Right voters who purchase books like Pat Robertson's *New World Order* or the Tim LaHaye novels about the end of the world now represent the single most influential voting bloc in the country (Aune 2003: 520). George W. Bush is arguably America's first Christian fundamentalist president and many of his senior officials, notably Attorney General John Ashcroft, share his beliefs. President Bush's political outlook is highly influenced by his faith and he regularly holds prayer meetings in the White House before starting official business. Actually, Christianity has always played an important role in American politics, from the Puritan founding fathers and the revivalism of the nineteenth century to the television evangelists and the Moral Majority of the twentieth century (see Hughes 2003). This marriage of evangelical Christianity and conservative politics – what is sometimes referred to as 'theo-politics' (McDaniel 2003) – means that major policy initiatives are often justified in pseudo-theological or theo-political terms. In this case, tapping into the deep wellspring of American religiosity as a means of solidifying public support, the 'war on terrorism' was imparted with God's blessing by its careful construction as a divinely sanctioned, traditional 'just war'.

Another important feature of the official construction of the '*good* war on terrorism' lies in the ever-growing popularity and increasing commemorations of the last great 'good war' – World War II. From Stud Terkel's Pulitzer Prize winning bestseller '*The Good War*', Tom Brokaw's *The Greatest Generation* and Stephen Ambrose's *D-Day: June 6, 1944* to *Schindler's List*, *Saving Private Ryan*, *Band of Brothers* and *Pearl Harbor* (among others), there has been a massive 'memory boom' in America that has transferred the memories and narratives of the so-called Great War (in the US this refers to World War II) to generations that had not lived through it. In fact, 'by the end of the twentieth century, narratives about "the good war" had come into such prominence in America's media culture that the war, as secondary memory, became fresh again' (Rosenberg 2003: 125). While it is not entirely certain what is driving this World War II memory boom (at least at the cultural level), what is clear is that it is part of a broader political process in which war is being relegitimised as an instrument of foreign policy. War is being given a new aura of respectability in the modern political context; no longer seen as singularly evil, it is now much more widely accepted as a means of enforcing global justice and affecting humanitarianism. The discursive construction of the 'good war on terrorism' has simply tapped into (and reinforced) this cultural-political phenomenon; at the official level, every opportunity is used to paint the counter-terrorism campaign as a moral struggle in the same mould as the (inherently good) World War II – often to the ire of veterans who fought in it.

This kind of justification is in itself not unusual in American foreign policy; virtually every war from World War I to the 1991 Gulf War, the Somali intervention in 1993 and the Kosovo campaign in 1999 has been rhetorically constructed in this way. However, there are some aspects to the current 'war on terrorism' that make its particular linguistic composition rather unique. The main problem for the Bush administration has been that this 'good war' was always inherently unstable (unlike World War II). In practice, its 'good war' credentials soon began to unravel somewhat under the pressure of its internal contradictions and its actual prosecution in Afghanistan, Iraq and beyond. In the first instance, it quickly became obvious that it was a war against an amorphous non-state enemy with no defined territory, no government and no conventional army. It was actually a conceptual contradiction: 'war' in a conventional sense is impossible against a phenomenon like 'terrorism.' It was also a war without any clear end point; if there was no conventional terrorist army to defeat or actual terrorist territory to occupy, could the war ever be over? Aspects of the conduct of the war itself also presented a number of tensions: how could the assassination of foreign heads of state and terrorist suspects in other countries be considered the right conduct of a 'good' war? Were the many thousands of civilian casualties in Afghanistan and Iraq really part of a proportional response? Was the use of cluster bombs, 'daisy cutters' and other indiscriminate weapons justified against an enemy that hid among a civilian population? And how was the status of the 'illegal combatants' held at Guantanamo Bay or the mistreatment of prisoners in Iraq to be reconciled with the 'good war' language of defending freedom and democracy?

These internal tensions and paradoxes meant that the 'good war on terrorism' had to be reflexively remade and reformulated as it went along. In order to deal with the obvious contradictions and the doubts they inevitably raised as to its inherent goodness, alternative discursive strategies were required. The main feature of the reflexive reconstruction was to make out that the war against terrorism was a 'new' and 'different war' unlike any seen before; officials argued that it was the 'first war of the twenty-first century'. This strategy proved very useful for explaining away the contradictions as an unavoidable feature of the necessarily 'new' situation. That is, although it was still a 'good war', it was also a 'new war' with a different set of ethical imperatives and moral boundaries.

In this chapter, I attempt to chart the contours of the discourse of the 'good war on terrorism', both in its initial construction as a 'just war' and its later reflexive reconstruction as a 'new' and 'different war'. The first section focuses on the way that senior policy-makers discursively constructed the 'war on terrorism' as a 'good' war, while the second section turns to an examination of the ways in which the discourse of the 'good war on terrorism' manages its inherent tensions and contradictions.

Constructing a 'good' war on terrorism

The language used by officials to construct a 'good' or 'virtuous' counter-terrorist war is moulded closely on what has become known as traditional just war theory. With its roots in the writings of the early Christian philosopher Augustine and debated by philosophers and jurists for several hundred years, just war doctrine attempts to define the conditions under which war is permissible (*jus ad bellum* or justice in going to war) and the manner in which war is prosecuted (*jus in bello* or justice in the conduct of war). Although it is still an ongoing debate, there is a general consensus that a truly just war must conform to the following conditions: it should have just aims and intentions, such as national self-defence or humanitarian intervention on behalf of others; it should be legally declared by competent authorities and supported by the wider community of civilised nations; it should be rightly conducted with due regard for the safety of non-combatants; it should not create a greater evil than the one it is attempting to redress; it must have a high chance of success within a short period of time so as to minimise the period of human suffering; and it should only be undertaken as a last resort once all other peaceful or non-violent avenues have been exhausted (see Walzer 1992).

As the following sections reveal, the Bush administration discursively constructed the 'war on terrorism' almost exclusively within these just war parameters. In part, this close reading of just war theory is designed to appeal to the Bush administration's conservative Christian supporters who are more likely to endorse a theologically defined just war – as opposed to one solely justified by national security. At the same time, it is moulded on popular 'good guy' versus 'bad guy' binaries, as well as the Pentagon public relations template for 'selling' wars to the public.

Writing a just cause

From the first day President Bush declared a 'war' against the evil of terrorism, senior officials have gone out of their way to emphasise that it is a war with a genuine *casus belli* or just cause. This language attempts to ensure that the war is firmly fixed in the just war paradigm and there is no ambiguity about the real intentions of the interventions in Central Asia and the Middle East. Two main discursive constructions can be observed in the official discourse about the war's cause: first, that it is a legally defined defensive war (in accordance with international law); and second, that it is a war to secure justice and to defend freedom.

In the first instance, it is frequently claimed by officials that the war is being fought solely for defensive purposes; an 'act of war' was committed against America and America has the right to defend itself militarily. The most important effect of this discursive reconstruction of the terrorist attacks was that it allowed the response to be framed in terms of accepted international legal norms about the right conduct of war. Thus, the military attack on Afghanistan in early October 2001 is described as an act of 'self-defence', which is perfectly legal under international law: 'What the United States of America is doing is exactly what I said. It is attempting to **defend the United States** by taking this battle to the terrorists' (Rumsfeld, 7 October, 2001). A few days later, in the most explicit reference to international law, Under Secretary of State Marc Grossman affirmed:

> I believe that Security Council resolution 1368 that was passed on the 12th of September, offers all of **the legal basis** and requirement that we need, in addition to **Article 51** of the United Nations Charter, which is **the right of self-defense**. And **we believe the United States was attacked** on the 11th of September and that **we have a right of self-defense** in this regard. So, sir, I think in terms of **a legal basis** for what we're doing and **the moral basis** for what we're doing ... **the right of self-defense** more than covers this. (Grossman, 19 October, 2001)

Crucially, Grossman takes the justification to an even higher rhetorical realm by stating it is more than simply a legal right of nations; it is also a moral right. Here the language of morality ranks even higher than the language of law.

Donald Rumsfeld repeats a similar construction in reference to the Afghan campaign by appealing to what is now accepted as the universal right of every nation to act in self-defence:

> The only way to deal with the terrorists that has all the advantage of offense is to take the battle to them, and find them, and root them out. And that is **self-defense**. And there is no question but that **any nation on Earth has the right of self-defense**. And we do. [...] if the question is, do we have a **right to defend ourselves** by going

after people who murder thousands of Americans in a preemptive way, **to defend ourselves**, you bet your life we do, and we're doing it. (Rumsfeld, 28 October, 2001)

It is important to note that the choice of legal arguments for attacking Afghanistan was strategically selected: going for legal justification in terms of *self-defence* (Article 51) rather than United Nations Charter Chapter VII action (which authorises military action only under the authority and direction of the UN Security Council) provided a greater freedom to manoeuvre and avoided existing and constraining precedents (Hurrell 2002: 188). In effect, it allowed America to choose when, who and how to attack without having to gain the permission of the Security Council or the consent of the wider international community. The main point is that the entire discursive formation of this argument depends on the initial terrorist attacks being written as 'acts of war'; without this initial linguistic foundation, the argument would be void. There is no legal right to attack another country in response to the commission of a purely criminal act. It would have appeared unreasonable and disproportionate to invade another nation that was simply harbouring wanted criminals; few would have countenanced invading Mexico to capture fugitive bank robbers for example, or invading Libya to capture the Lockerbie bombing suspects.

Later, in June 2002 the Bush administration announced a new national security doctrine of pre-emptive self-defence or 'anticipatory self-defence' – the so-called 'Bush Doctrine'. Enshrined in *The National Security Strategy of the United States of America* of September 2002, this policy stated that America reserved the right to use pre-emptive (in reality, 'preventive') war against any country it suspected of harbouring terrorists or hostile intentions. From one perspective, this novel doctrine was an attempt to draw up a new legal precept which would add another 'just cause' to the existing legally accepted reasons for going to war. It was discursively constructed upon the earlier invocation of America's right of self-defence. In addition, the construction of the 'supreme emergency' in which terrorism is made out to be a real and imminent threat to the very existence of the nation (see Chapter 4) gives logic and validity to the conception of preventive war. The first major use of this doctrine in the 'war on terrorism' was the attack on Iraq in March 2003.

However, the attempt to use just war legal arguments and to create new legal precepts has not been entirely successful for the Bush administration: a great many judicial experts have concluded that the doctrine of 'pre-emptive' (preventive) war rides roughshod over all existing precedents and precepts about the acceptable reasons to go to war, and that the war against Saddam was strictly speaking, illegal under current international law. This has led other observers to conclude that the language of legal self-defence is simply a discursive smoke screen for the pursuit of other more political and geo-strategic goals (see Callinicos 2003; Chomsky 2002; El Fadl 2002; Mahajan 2003). Even in the case of the attack on Afghanistan for example, it is noted that the toppling of the Taliban regime gave America greater access to the Central Asian region and Caspian oil – an outcome replete with geo-strategic advantages and suggestive of less than pure (or just) motives.

A second prominent feature of the language surrounding America's construction of a just cause lies buried in the ubiquitous references to 'justice', 'freedom' and 'liberty'. In official texts, these terms are employed literally hundreds of times to characterise the actions, aims, conduct and outcome of the 'war on terrorism'. Historically, these are seen as constituting proper 'just causes'. In particular, officials consistently stress that the 'war on terrorism' is focused on bringing the terrorists to justice or ensuring that justice is achieved. In most instances, the language is framed in the mythology, folklore, metaphors and linguistic idioms of the American frontier – note the use of *Wanted Dead or Alive* posters, the bounties offered for information in the Rewards for Justice programme, the 'Most Wanted Terrorists' featured on the popular television programme *America's Most Wanted* and Bush's public appearances wearing cowboy boots. In fact, frontier legends and mythology – the story of the Alamo and Custer's Last Stand, for example – are common rhetorical resources in American politics: 'Remember the Alamo' became a battle cry to attack Mexico, which in turn evolved into 'Remember Pearl Harbor' during World War II (see Rosenberg 2003). In this case, the campaign in Afghanistan which was designed to 'smoke them out of their holes' (Bush, 15 September, 2001) fits easily into America's rich mythology of redemptive violence seen in popular representations of the frontier. In a sense, the 'war on terrorism' is representative of *Shane*, *Tombstone, Unforgiven*, the mythic John Wayne or Clint Eastwood exacting revenge, enforcing a kind of natural frontier justice and ridding the west of dangerous villains so decent folk can rest easy.

In perhaps his most famous (and most nonsensical) quote about justice, Bush states assuredly: 'Whether we bring our enemies to **justice**, or bring **justice** to our enemies, **justice will be done**' (Bush, 20 September, 2001). Aside from sounding like a line from a movie, it is also presented as more than simply a goal or a cause or a statement of intent; it is an eschatological or perhaps even an empirical fact. Grammatically, it signals a powerful sense of certainty to the listener. He could have used a more passive form – 'justice may be done' – or a more subjective form – 'I hope that justice will be done'. In a way, Bush is asserting that regardless of any individual actions by the terrorists, the outcome of 'justice' is preordained. It is thus imbued with a kind of metaphysical reality and a sense of historical inevitability. The phrase also contains echoes of frontier justice in the form of a town posse. In the context of the overall speech (see appendix), Bush is saying that America is forming an international posse (coalition) to go and smoke the outlaws out of their holes in Afghanistan.

In other words, the discourse makes it clear that this campaign will be a collective administration of justice, not a solo crusade. The pronoun 'we' is used in nearly every case in reference to the administration of justice. This is partly because justice is a collective act; it is the will of the community, not the decision of lone individuals. In his speech of 11 October, 2001, Bush makes a total of thirteen references to 'justice'. In the initial references to the justice of the campaign against terrorism, Bush also employs the term 'we' numerous times. He is establishing from the very beginning that the quest for justice involves the whole nation, himself included, as well as the great coalition of allies:

> **We're** mounting a sustained campaign to drive the terrorists out of their hidden caves and to bring them to **justice**.

> **We're** angry at the evil that was done to us, yet patient and **just** in our response.

> Their intention was to so frighten our government that **we** wouldn't seek **justice**; that somehow **we** would cower in the face of their threats and not respond abroad or at home.

> [T]he truth of the matter is, in order to fully defend America, **we** must defeat the evildoers where they hide. **We** must round them up, and **we** must **bring them to justice**.

> And slowly, but surely, **we're** smoking al Qaeda out of their caves so **we** can bring them to **justice**. People often ask me, how long will this last? This particular battlefront will last as long as it takes to bring al Qaeda to **justice**.

> **[W]e're** slowly, but surely, with determined fashion, routing that network out and bringing it to **justice**.

> It is important that **we** stay the course, bring these people to **justice** ... (Bush, 11 October, 2001)

In the first part of the speech, Bush is clearly speaking on behalf of the political community. Rhetorically, it is a powerful linguistic act of unification which leaves no room for ambiguity or disagreement: 'we' are mounting a campaign, 'we' are angry, but 'we' are just in our response. A simultaneous meaning is that the 'we' refers to the entire resources of government. Here Bush is suggesting all the branches of the government are working together in a united effort. He also takes the opportunity to stress how much the government is achieving: 'we' are responding; 'we' are smoking them out (the frontier motif); 'we' are routing them out; 'we' are bringing them to justice. Expressed another way, 'we' (the nation) can be assured that 'we' the government is putting its full weight behind this campaign for justice.

Part way through the speech, however, Bush changes his expression and starts to use the personal pronoun, as in: 'People often ask **me**, how long will this last?' This is the signal of a transition in the language to a more personal degree of involvement. In the following quotes from the same speech, Bush uses the term 'I' as a way of stamping his personal involvement in the collective efforts of the people and government; the mixing of 'I' and 'we' in the same sentence rhetorically joins the individual president – with all the power and symbolism of the office – with the (grammatically) united and purposeful nation. These couplings are then followed by singularly personal statements. As the president speaking publicly to the nation, this is another way of adding legitimacy and authority to the campaign for justice:

> [T]he doctrine **I** spelled out to the American people in front of Congress said not only will **we** seek out and bring to **justice** individual terrorists who cause harm to people, who murder people, **we** will also bring to **justice** the host governments that sponsor them, that house them and feed them.

> **I** don't know if he's dead or alive. **I** want him brought to **justice**, however. **We** are following every possible lead to make sure that any al Qaeda member that could be in the United States is brought to **justice**.

> **I** am absolutely determined – absolutely determined – to root terrorism out where it exists and bring them to **justice**.

> [F]irst let **me** reiterate, **my** focus is bringing al Qaeda to **justice** ... (Bush, 11 October, 2001)

Bush's use of the highly personal phrase, 'I am absolutely determined – absolutely determined' invests the quest for justice with the highest authority, as well as a personal affinity. The repetition of the president's 'absolute' determination is designed to instil confidence and reinforce the intent. It echoes an earlier statement: '**we** will go forward to defend freedom and all that is **good and just** in our world' (Bush, 11 September, 2001b). The reference to bin Laden being 'dead or alive' is another frontier idiom, while the linking of goodness and justice here discursively ties the 'good war' and the 'just war' together more explicitly.

As I previously stated, the appeal to the just war paradigm is also achieved discursively through the relating of historical narratives about America's past 'good' wars with the current war. Specifically, the acts of September 11, 2001 are discursively recast in the mould of World War II and in particular, the treacherous attack on Pearl Harbor (see Chapter 2). What makes this analogy so compelling is the failure of the policy of appeasement and the necessity of the use of force to defeat an evil system like fascism (Lewis 2002: 170). The 'war against terrorism' is not just perfectly legal under international law and focused on the defence of justice and liberty, it is an example of a virtuous war against an evil system. In a way, another strand of the just cause – the *casus belli* – is being alluded to here: it is always a right and good cause to fight the tyrannies of fascism, communism, and now, terrorism.

In summary, the language of the 'war on terrorism' clearly locates it in the just war tradition by explicitly stressing its 'just cause' and by explicitly referring to self-defence and the overall goals of pursuing 'justice' and defending 'freedom' and 'liberty'. In this way, the 'good' war against terrorism is constructed through the explicit rhetoric of being a 'just war'. Significantly, the discourse is fairly opaque in spelling out what justice actually is or what it entails in this case – beyond the vague idea that it involves killing or capturing bin Laden and al Qaeda ('those responsible for the attacks'). It could have been far more explicit in this regard. For example, President Bush could have said that justice will be done when bin Laden and his senior officers are made to face charges in a court of law such as the International Criminal Court. The fact that no such specific conception is given of what justice involves provides the American government with a certain level of flexibility. There are elements of several conceptions of justice which can be seen in this language – retributive justice, frontier justice, just war theory. They are then 'cobbled together under the one term to give the impression that we are all fighting for the same cause – that justice requires, if not demands war, enemy, and a little, unavoidable, collateral damage' (McCarthy 2002: 132–3). This is then, a deliberate discursive strategy allowing a diverse range of actions, some completely unconnected with any commonly accepted notions of justice (like the assassination or torture of terrorist 'suspects') to be included in the prosecution of the 'just war'.

A properly constituted war

The 'war on terrorism' is also constructed as a just war by virtue of it being properly constituted, both in terms of the declaration of war by a proper authority and in the composition and legitimacy of the forces. The first point – a declaration of war by a proper authority – presented no difficulties for the Bush administration. It was declared by the president a few days after the terrorist attacks and overwhelmingly supported by Congress (only one Democratic congresswomen, Rep. Barbara Lee, voted against it), as well as by the vast majority of Americans. More problematic has been the claim that it is a war truly supported by international opinion and the wider global society of states. As a consequence, great emphasis has been placed in the official discourse on the notion of a grand coalition of states that is collectively participating in the 'war on terrorism'. In every-day usage by officials, the fact that the forces fighting in both Afghanistan and Iraq are almost without fail referred to as 'Coalition forces' is significant for trying to establish this as a legitimate, internationally sanctioned war, rather than as an act of aggression by a single state and its allies. The media's ubiquitous and uncritical use of the same term reinforces the official construction.

In the following texts, the legitimising support of the world is constantly invoked; a vast international coalition is said to be behind America's campaign and the 'war on terrorism' is less a unilateral effort than an expression of the unity of the world:

> We are receiving expressions of **support from around the world** – and not just rhetorical support, but real support for whatever may lay ahead in this campaign [...] It's a **coalition** that will stay intact, that will be built upon over time. (Bush, 15 September, 2001)

> **More than 40 countries** in the Middle East, Africa, Europe and across Asia have granted air transit or landing rights. Many more have shared intelligence. **We are supported by the collective will of the world**. (Bush, 7 October, 2001)

> **The world stands united in this effort** ... Our partners in this effort represent nations and peoples of **all cultures**, **all religions**, and **all races**. (Rumsfeld, 7 October, 2001)

This is a powerful rhetorical strategy that clearly marks the counter-terrorist campaign as a just war, representing as it does, the will of all cultures, all religions and all races. That is, by virtue of its international backing and cooperation by a large number of nations, the 'war on terrorism' is imbued with a moral purpose much greater than if it had been a unilateral military action.

There are a great many who have questioned the extent to which it is a genuine global coalition, as well as the extent to which these countries have signed up willingly. Even though there are more than forty countries in the 'coalition against terror', they include many small and/or poor countries like Afghanistan, Albania, Azerbaijan, Bulgaria, Colombia, Denmark, Eritrea, Estonia, Ethiopia, Latvia, Macedonia, Nicaragua, The Philippines, Palau, Iceland, Costa Rica, the Marshall Islands, the Solomon Islands, Micronesia, Pakistan, Slovakia and Uzbekistan – among others. It is also well known that many of these countries joined America's coalition after being offered powerful incentives (such as financial or military aid) or following thinly veiled warnings about the consequences of *not* joining the coalition. And of the larger countries within the American-led coalition – such as Australia, Britain, Italy, Poland, Japan, South Korea, Spain – many of them joined even though most of their own citizens were opposed to the war. Perhaps more importantly, the countries which have so far refused to join the coalition include Argentina, Brazil, Canada, China, Egypt, France, Germany, India, Indonesia, Ireland, Mexico, Russia, South Africa, Sweden and Switzerland – along with more than 120 other countries. In an important sense, the language of 'coalition', 'partners' and the support of 'the collective will of the world' is deployed to deflect attention away from the true character of the coalition and to mask the rather limited support it has so far garnered. The language constructs a reality – a legitimacy and moral purpose to the war – that is actually highly contested and somewhat illusory.

Writing just conduct

Another major element in discursively constructing the good and just 'war on terrorism' involves establishing that it is rightly conducted with due regard for the safety of non-combatants; this is the establishment of *jus in bello* – justice in war or right conduct in war. It is one of the most constantly heard refrains in official counter-terrorism texts that extreme care is continually being taken to avoid civilian casualties (or 'collateral damage'), and that the combination of smart weapons and careful targeting actually makes modern warfare relatively bloodless (see Wheeler 2002). This rhetorical strategy has a long genealogy in Western military language, but first came to prominence in the 1991 Gulf War when the first generation of 'smart' weapons began to be used; arguably, it was perfected during the Kosovo campaign in 1999. For example, it has been the practice of government and military officials for some time now to refer to aerial bombing as 'surgical strikes'; this metaphor invokes the discourse and practice of medicine, transforming the dropping of hugely injurious bombs from acts of tremendous destruction and terror into positive acts of healing (see Macallister 2004; Shpiro 2002). The language of 'targets' helps to move the actions of war into the realm of the abstract, thereby objectifying human life and obscuring the human toll (see Neisser 2002). Instead of 'our forces attacked bridges and roads vital for everyday economic life' or 'we attacked young conscripts from poor families', it is expressed as 'we struck **military targets**' or 'we attacked **strategic targets**'. Similarly, the term 'collateral damage', which is frequently used as a euphemism for civilian dead and wounded, is part of a large and sophisticated technical-military language that is deployed by military public relations experts to 'sterilize the horrors of war' (see Louw 2003: 220). As I have previously mentioned, it is also part of a wider effort to relegitimise war by remaking it appear clean, redemptive and therapeutic – instead of cruel, destructive and horrifying.

Actually, the internationally agreed norm of non-combatant immunity has deep roots in western and non-western moral thought and international humanitarian law (see Wheeler 2002), making it an ideal narrative for officials to draw upon. The day after the initiation of 'strikes' against Afghanistan for example, Donald Rumsfeld took pains to emphasise the careful and legitimate targeting and the use of the almost magically guided munitions which protect human life: 'So to summarize, **every target was a military target**. The reports indicating that there were attacks on Kabul are incorrect. The attacks were on the **military targets** surrounding the city' (Rumsfeld, 8 October, 2001). The strategy here is to fix the legitimate credentials of the campaign by emphasising that no civilians are ever deliberately targeted and that only 'legitimate' military targets are attacked. In other words, any civilian deaths could be justified because they would be an *unintended* consequence of attacks against legitimate targets. Linguistically, it is important to note the way in which the primary noun stands for the process: 'The **attacks** were on the military targets' instead of, for example, '**we were attacking** military targets'. This linguistic form reduces human agency, depersonalises the process and makes the attacks appear like a natural phenomenon – something which happened without a responsible agent.

In addition to this subtle message there is also the claim that special guided munitions allow for such precision that the war can be conducted with almost absolute safety for civilians and non-combatants; these weapons are a way of protecting the innocent. This message is repeated numerous times by officials:

> [T]he United States of America is very careful about collateral damage. We have weapons that are undoubtedly **more accurate and more precise** than probably any country on earth, and we are careful about what we do. (Rumsfeld, 28 October, 2001)

> Afghanistan proved that **expensive precision weapons defeat the enemy and spare innocent lives**, and we need more of them. (Bush, 29 January, 2002)

> The new technologies of war help to protect our soldiers, and as importantly, **help protect innocent life**. You see, new technologies allow us to redefine war on our terms, which makes it more likely the world will be **more free and more peaceful**. (Bush, 2 May, 2003)

In this case, we also note the way in which the modality of the statements is always categorical and truth-based, in the sense that the speakers commit themselves completely to the statement. For example, the form, 'expensive precision weapons defeat the enemy and spare innocent lives' presents the knowledge claim as true and incontrovertible. Crucially, it transforms the weapons into active agents of good – these weapons actually spare lives. In one sense, this language deflects and obscures the reality that weapons can only ever destroy lives, that killing and maiming human beings is their entire *raison d'être*. Bush could have said, 'expensive precision weapons often, but not always,' spare innocent lives' as a more neutral mode of speech. In addition, it is expressed in an objective rather than subjective modality: the structure is 'The new technologies … help protect innocent life', rather than a subjective form like, 'We think the new technologies will help to protect innocent lives.' The use of categorical, objective modalities both reflects and reinforces the authority of the speakers (Jorgensen and Phillips 2002: 84). In other words, there is a consistent attempt to emphasise the care that is being taken by the authorities and the unintentional nature of any civilian casualties. This is an explicit attempt to fix the conduct of the war within the precepts of just war doctrine.

The problem is there will always be civilian casualties in war. Even the most advanced precision weapons cannot avoid the unintentional killing of the innocent; a modern 2,000lb bomb for example, is highly destructive and will likely cause death and injury for hundreds of yards around the target site. Military and political officials have consistently misrepresented how accurate and selective the new weaponry is and there is something of a myth surrounding their effectiveness (see Wheeler 2002); it is well known that a fairly high percentage of precision-guided munitions fall outside their target zone due to failures in guidance systems. In either event, a large percentage of the bombs still used in modern warfare are not guided or electronically targeted. The result is that just as in the past, tens of thousands of civilians are invariably killed and wounded whenever a major war occurs – as the Afghan and Iraqi campaigns attest.

How does the official discourse reconcile this anomaly with just war precepts? There are a number of important features to note. In the first place, officials suggest we can not always be clear about who is responsible for those deaths; therefore, we should avoid assigning responsibility until we have all the facts. In an extraordinary text, Donald Rumsfeld lists four justifications for civilian deaths, all of which assist in absolving American forces of responsibility. Confronting the question of civilian casualties head-on, Rumsfeld says: 'Now the truth ultimately will come out. Will there be some bumpy times between now and then? You bet. And will there be some people who are killed, who ought not to have been, killed in this conflict? There will be.' He then goes on to list the qualifying justifications one after the other in the same paragraph:

> Some will be killed through errant weapons, none of which are 100 percent in terms of their performance, just like our cars aren't. And we know that.

> The numbers of people on the ground firing up at our aircraft, that ordnance comes down and hits people as well and kills people.

> The opposition forces are shooting at the Taliban forces and people are going to get killed there. So it is not readily apparent when somebody's dead as to exactly where the ordnance came from.

> I know for a fact that we are just being enormously careful. We are doing everything humanly possible to try to avoid collateral damage. We're focusing everything on military targets. (Rumsfeld, 24 October, 2001)

Rumsfeld is arguing that errant weapons, defenders firing at aircraft and the Northern Alliance shooting at the Taliban will all be responsible for civilian casualties. The crucial point is that America is trying to be careful and doing 'everything humanly possible' to avoid civilian deaths (collateral damage); and everything is being focused on 'military targets'.

Another strategy to deflect responsibility away from the American military is to refer to the deaths of innocent civilians in the September 11, 2001 attacks (see Chapter 2). In essence, the dead civilians in Afghanistan and Iraq are justified by reference to the dead civilians in New York and Washington; the US could not be blamed because the responsibility rested solely on those who had initiated war on September 11, 2001 (see Wheeler 2002). Donald Rumsfeld uses this rhetorical strategy on more than one occasion: 'There are going to be loss of life – there already have been. It started on **September 11th** in this building. And there are going to be more' (Rumsfeld, 24 October, 2001). A few days later, he repeats the same message: 'We would all like it to end as soon as possible', he states. 'The problem you're facing is that thousands of Americans and, indeed, people from another 50 or 60 countries were killed in the United States on **September 11th**. [...] **The problem in the world is not the United States of America; the problem is terrorists**' (Rumsfeld, 28 October, 2001). There is an explicit effort here to push the responsibility for innocent deaths onto the terrorists: it is they who are morally responsible for the civilian deaths in Afghanistan because they started it and if they hadn't attacked the US there would be no war in Afghanistan. In fact, the entire problem lies outside of the responsibility of the United States; it is not America that is at fault, it is the terrorists.

Finally, as Under Secretary of State Marc Grossman expresses it: 'I believe, sir, that when there is a fair and accurate representation when this campaign is over, we will find that the number of civilian casualties actually has been very, very low' (Grossman, 19 October, 2001). Secretary of Defense Donald Rumsfeld goes even further: 'I can't imagine there's been a conflict in history where there has been less collateral damage, less unintended consequences' (quoted in Wheeler 2002: 210). According to officials, the whole debate is somewhat moot because so few civilians will be, or have been killed. A war with so few civilian deaths makes it a truly 'good war' by definition. Of course, the current policy of the American military is never to discuss actual numbers of dead or wounded enemy soldiers or civilians, so what constitutes 'very, very low' casualties is never open to interrogation.

At one level, this official construction of a rightly conducted war is part of the well-known 'villain/victim' narrative that the Pentagon has tried to enforce on the public not only in the Afghan and Iraqi campaigns but in virtually every war since Vietnam: not only would the war against terrorism destroy bin Laden and the evil terrorists, but in the process Afghans would be liberated from the backward (uncivilised) and inhuman Taliban regime (see Louw 2003: 222). This 'villain/victim' template is now an established feature of the Pentagon's media management strategy in times of war. It relies on the notion that wars should have a clear and simple narrative which identifies a 'bad guy' (the villain) to be dealt with, as well as a captive and oppressed population (the victims) to be saved by the well-intentioned hero (the United States military). This narrative structure was clearly employed in both the Afghan and Iraq wars. In both cases, the 'war on terrorism' was discursively constructed as a 'good war' by virtue of the notion that its military goals were partly humanitarian; they were saving the victims of oppression. For example, on the eve of the first military strikes on Afghanistan, a major effort by all senior officials was put into emphasising the humanitarian goals of the military action. It was stressed over and over again that the military were engaged in a dual role of humanitarian aid delivery and military action: 'At the same time, the oppressed people of Afghanistan will know the generosity of America and our allies. As we strike military targets, **we'll also drop food, medicine and supplies** to the starving and suffering men and women and children of Afghanistan' (Bush, 7 October, 2001). This text emphasises both that the Afghan people are starving (and therefore it is imperative that they are fed), and that military action is being accompanied by efforts to feed the hungry. It is a powerful and active linguistic construction that clearly connects the events with the responsible agent in order to fix their humanitarian intentions: '*we'll* also drop food and medicine'. The oppressive nature of the Taliban regime is highlighted (the villains), implying that the liberation of the Afghan people (the victims) will itself be a humanitarian act, not simply a political or strategic achievement.

In sum, this is an explicitly consequentialist moral justification for the war in Afghanistan: the ultimate outcome or consequence of the campaign is constructed as being so good and fulfilling so many humanitarian imperatives that it is by definition a good war, even if there were many civilian casualties along the way (which according to officials there were not):

> In a short period of time, most of the country now is in the hands of our allies and friends. We've rescued the humanitarian aid workers. We've destroyed the Taliban military. They're in total confusion. The government that used to hate women, and not educate its children, and disrupt humanitarian supplies, and destroy religious symbols of other religions is now in rout. (Bush, 29 November, 2001)

This is another powerful rhetorical construction, and similar arguments are made in relation to the campaign against Iraq. In fact, the claims are even greater here; the war in Iraq not only allowed for humanitarian aid delivery, but it also averted an environmental catastrophe and a large-scale humanitarian crisis, safeguarded a vital resource and by implication, 'liberated' an oppressed people:

> In the current conflict, forces sent in early protected the 600 oil fields in southern Iraq, **prevented an environmental catastrophe**, and **safeguarded a resource** that's vital for the future of the people of Iraq.

> But so far, in Operation Iraqi Freedom, **we've averted a large-scale humanitarian crisis**. U.S. and Royal Marines succeeded in taking the Al Faw Peninsula and **cleared a path for humanitarian aid**. And today, even as fighting continues, **coalition forces are bringing food and water and medical supplies to liberated Iraqis**. (Cheney, 9 April, 2003)

The language suggests that even though civilians may have been killed in the liberation of Afghanistan and Iraq, on balance, the citizens of these countries are better off than they would have been without military intervention. Therefore, the war is morally justified through a post-hoc evaluation of its outcome.

Traditional just war doctrine makes it clear that such consequentialist or post-hoc purposes are illegitimate. Instead, a clear motive for going to war must exist before war is undertaken, and it must fall within prescribed (good) intentions such as self-defence from imminent threat or humanitarian intervention. Good intentions lie at the heart of just war theory and unintended consequences – no matter how fortuitous – cannot be employed after the fact to justify attacking another nation (see Walzer 1992). In part, the controversy surrounding the prosecution of the 2003 Iraq war lies in its unclear intentions: was Iraq attacked because it posed an imminent threat? Or because the Iraqi regime had ties to terrorists planning to attack America? Or was it attacked to liberate the Iraqi people from Saddam's tyrannical rule? The fact that all three justifications were used at different times and that the first two justifications were subsequently proven to be false somewhat damaged the administration's claim to just war status.

Writing a winnable war

As I stated earlier, one of the central tenets of just war doctrine is that any war undertaken must have a reasonable chance of success in order to minimise human suffering. From the very beginning of the 'war on terrorism' – on the first day, in fact – the war was constructed as ultimately winnable. President Bush stated on September 11, 2001, 'we stand together to **win** the war against terrorism' (Bush, 11 September, 2001b). This theme of victory over terrorism is constantly reiterated. In virtually every case it is stated grammatically as a certain fact: '**we will win this conflict** by the patient accumulation of successes' (Bush, 7 October, 2001); 'We will fight for as long as it takes, and **we will prevail**' (Bush, 24 November, 2001); 'And on the home front, terrorist violence must be prevented, and must be defeated. And **it will be**' (Bush, 29 November, 2001). When asked about the length of the war – a direct reference to the chances of winning in a reasonable period of time – Bush replied: 'People often ask me, how long will this last? This particular battlefront will last as long as it takes to bring al Qaeda to justice. It may happen a month from now; it may take a year or two. **But we will prevail**' (Bush, 11 October, 2001). Again, there is no question about the outcome, even if the timeframe is a little vague, and the language is categorical. In this case, the certainty of victory rhetorically overwhelms the uncertainty over the length of the campaign; the end result – winning – is more important than the time it takes to get there.

In another powerful statement, Bush implies that the day of victory is assured and the only doubt lies in when it is to be realized. He suggests that with greater effort, it could even be hastened: 'By waging this fight together, we will **speed the day of final victory**' (Bush, 31 May, 2003). Such pronouncements by the president, the most potent symbol of American power, imbue it with rhetorical force and give it the status of certain knowledge. By invoking the collective term 'we' – 'we will win', 'we will prevail', 'we will speed the day' – Bush is not only signalling his personal involvement, but also the collective involvement of the government, its agencies, resources and allies. In another grammatical strategy, victory over terrorism is constructed as being certain regardless of the actions of the terrorists. There is little they can do to prevent the final victory of America: 'They will try to hide, they will try to avoid the United States ... we will do whatever it takes to smoke them out and get them running, and **we'll get them**' (Bush, 15 September, 2001). In respect of the perpetrators of the terrorist attacks and in a personal reference to bin Laden, Bush defends the inevitability of the outcome: 'In terms of Mr bin Laden himself, we'll get him running. We'll smoke him out of his cave, and **we'll get him eventually**' (Bush, 11 October, 2001). Again, the collective 'we' signifies the power behind the statement.

In the following text, Vice President Cheney once again enlists historical narratives of the defeat of communism during the cold war to demonstrate the certainty of victory over terrorism:

> Your faith in freedom's ultimate triumph was vindicated when **the Berlin Wall was toppled**, when **an evil empire vanished** from the face of the earth. Today, freedom has a new set of totalitarian enemies. Once again we're called on to defend the safety of our people and the hopes of all mankind. And once again, **your faith in freedom's triumph will be vindicated**. (Cheney, 1 May, 2003)

Fundamentally, the ultimate victory over the evil of terrorism is no less certain than the victory over the evil of communism. In part, this ubiquitous triumphalism is simply an element of the psychology of war: every nation goes into war believing it can win and reinforcing the belief in victory is how the authorities try to sustain morale. However, in the context of all the other discursive strategies – establishing a just cause, constructing just prosecution, claiming international support – it is also clearly part of the attempt to place it in the just war framework.

In reality, there is no possible way to win the 'war on terrorism'; it is simply the wrong metaphor. Conceptually, winning a war against terrorism would be akin to winning a war against insurgent warfare; this is because terrorism is a strategy of political violence which will always appeal to certain kinds of actors (states, dissidents, guerrillas, revolutionaries) or be advantageous in some situations (a people under a brutal occupation by a superior military power). As a retired American general wryly noted: 'Terrorism is not an enemy. It cannot be defeated. It's a tactic. It's about as sensible to say we are going to declare war on night attacks and expect we're going to win that war. We're not going to win the war on terrorism' (quoted in Snow 2003: 82). Even with a more sympathetic reading of the notion of victory in this war, the chances of winning a war against terrorism are about the same as winning wars against poverty, drugs or crime. It seems highly unlikely (and history has shown) that such complex social problems can ever be fully eradicated, and in most cases, applying a military solution has little chance of success. In truth, the language of victory is a type of discursive curtain that works to obscure the real difficulties of dealing with a challenge like terrorism.

Writing a war of last resort

Another aspect of the discourse which constructs it as a good and just war is its characterisation as a war of last resort. Just war theory insists that states should only go to war if all other peaceful or diplomatic alternatives have been attempted and there is absolutely no other option. As shown previously, there is a constant attempt to paint the 'war on terrorism' as the only possible course of action and the only way to defeat this kind of evil. Within western political discourse, there is a very powerful narrative about certain kinds of states and actors that cannot be dealt with on normal diplomatic terms: fascism, communism, rogue states and now terrorists (see Hurrell 2002: 195). According to this narrative, these kinds of actors are purely evil, unreasonable and irrational and can only be restrained through the threat or deployment of massive counter-violence. In particular, the main 'lesson' of World War II is that diplomacy ('appeasement') does not work against evil opponents such as Hitler – which is why Saddam was so often compared with Hitler.

In the official counter-terrorism discourse, there are two main discursive strategies that tap into this particular mythology. First, there is an insistence that the 'war on terrorism' is the 'only way' to fight this kind of enemy; there is no peaceful or diplomatic alternative and there is no other choice:

> [T]here can be no peace in a world of sudden terror. In the face of today's new threat, **the only way** to pursue peace is to pursue those who threaten it. (Bush, 7 October, 2001).

> **[T]he only way** to deal with these terrorist threats is to go at them where they exist. You cannot defend at every place at every time against every conceivable, imaginable,

even unimaginable terrorist attack. And **the only way** to deal with it is to take the battle to where they are ... (Rumsfeld, 7 October, 2001)

This language implies that the United States has no other choice but to pursue the terrorists in a violent counter-terrorist campaign. As Colin Powell expresses it, 'war has been declared upon us by the al-Qaida organization, and **we have no choice** but to fight that war with the kind of campaign that the President has put together' (Powell, 21 October, 2001). In part, this is related to the meta-narratives of World War II, the cold war and civilisation versus barbarism (see Chapter 2); the moral of these mythologies is that there is no other way to relate to certain kinds of enemies and that in those cases, violence was not only necessary but also redemptive. As 'the only option', the counter-terrorist war is by implication a war of last resort and thus, a just war.

A second and related strategy is to insist that the reason this is the only way to conduct the campaign against terrorism is because the normal methods employed in the past will not work. Partly, this is because the nature of the enemy is different – no less evil, but qualitatively different. On another level, this is a discursive strategy aimed at ruling out or disqualifying alternative counter-terrorist approaches before they can even be suggested. In the following texts, the vice president and president both insist that non-violent statecraft and law enforcement will not work against terrorists and terror states; for them, direct military force is the only method that will work:

> Those who hate all civilization and culture and progress, those who embrace death to cause the death of the innocent, **cannot be ignored, cannot be appeased. They must be fought**. (Bush, 20 October, 2001).

> If we are to protect the American people and defend civilization against determined enemies, we cannot always rely on the old Cold War remedies of **containment** and **deterrence**. **Containment does not work against a rogue state** that possesses weapons of mass destruction and chooses to secretly deliver them to its terrorist allies. **Deterrence does not work** when we are dealing with terrorists who have no country to defend, who revel in violence, and who are willing to sacrifice their own lives in order to kill millions of others. (Cheney, 9 April, 2003)

> For my country, the events of September the 11th were as decisive as the attack on Pearl Harbor and the treachery of another September in 1939. And the lesson of all those events is the same: aggression and evil intent must not be ignored or appeased; they must be opposed early and decisively. [...] **Some challenges of terrorism, however, cannot be met with law enforcement alone. They must be met with direct military action**. (Bush, 31 May, 2003)

In each case, there is the appeal to long-established good war narratives and the 'lessons of history'. This is a common rhetorical ploy for politicians; it involves reinterpreting current events through the lens of traditional meta-narratives to draw appropriate 'lessons'. In this case, the lessons are that, like Hitler and Nazism, the only way to defeat terrorism is through the application of overwhelming military force.

Once this discursive foundation has been laid, the assumption that the enemy is so intransigent that it cannot be negotiated with in good faith is then proved true by an ingenious diplomatic sleight of hand: demands are made that no sovereign nation could possibly accept and when these demands are rejected this is taken as proof of the enemy's intractability. In this way, officials can then claim that force is genuinely the last resort – and the war is a just war. This was the diplomatic path seen in both the Afghanistan and Iraq campaigns (see Mahajan 2002, 2003); it reflects a pattern set in the first Gulf War in 1991 and in Kosovo in 1999. In the lead up to the Afghanistan campaign, American diplomacy deliberately prevented a secret deal with the Taliban regime to hand over Osama bin Laden. One study of this episode surmised: 'And so we are left with the conclusion that the United States deliberately made sure that bin Laden could not be turned over through diplomatic channels, through negotiation, because that would' deprive them of their primary *casus belli*' (Mahajan 2002: 30).

In any case, terrorist experts agree there are a large number of alternative approaches to counter-terrorism and that coercive or force-based approaches are only one of many possible responses. More critically, they are not necessarily the most successful approaches. Gus Martin outlines a wide range of strategies for dealing with terrorism: use of force, such as punitive strikes, pre-emptive strikes, repression and suppression campaigns; operations other than war, such as covert operations (infiltration, disinformation and cyberwar), intelligence gathering, enhanced public security and economic sanctions; conciliatory options, such as diplomacy and negotiation, conflict resolution, social reform, restitution and policy concessions; and legalistic responses, such as law enforcement and criminal investigation cooperation through interagency cooperation and international tribunals (Martin 2003: 346–7). In short, war is never the only option or last resort for dealing with terrorism; there are alternatives, many of which have a far better record of success historically than war-based approaches. In order to forestall the consideration of these more complex and challenging methods, officials go to great lengths to construct the 'war on terrorism' as the only remaining alternative.

Divine calling and historic responsibility

Apart from its deliberate conflation with just war theory, the 'war on terrorism' is also written as an inherently 'good war' by virtue of being a divine calling and an historic responsibility that only America can fulfil. We have already seen an oblique appeal to 'good war' status through the meta-narratives of World War II, good versus evil and civilisation versus barbarism (see Chapter 2); fighting against totalitarianism, evil and barbarism clearly implies that America is fighting a 'good' war. However, as the following analysis demonstrates, the official discourse explicitly associates the 'war on terrorism' with a sense of divine calling and historic responsibility, which is a far more direct appeal to good war status. In large part, this language taps into the deeply held (and deeply religious) American myths of manifest destiny, Nature's Nation, God's Chosen Nation and 'American exceptionalism' (Hughes 2003). These beliefs are embedded in American political life and are discursively reflected in the Great Seal of the United States; in this potent symbol, God's eye looks down on the new order being built while the Latin inscription simply states: '*annuit coeptis*' – 'he (God) has favoured our undertaking'.

In the first instance, the war is imbued with a sense of theological calling and divine sanction through the ubiquitous use of religious terminology (the distinctly Christian language of evil, for example) and the constant appeal to universal (God-given) values (freedom, democracy, liberty) (see Lincoln 2002). The repeated (and often retracted) references to the counter-terrorist war as a 'crusade', which was for a short time called 'Infinite Justice', discursively renders it a religious war – even a holy war (Morris 2002: 152). The writing of a good (and holy) 'war on terrorism' actually began just a few days after the terrorist attacks, on September 14, 2001. This date was declared a National Day of Prayer and Remembrance by the president and a service of remembrance for the victims was held at the National Cathedral in Washington – a national symbolic site where government, religion, culture and the military coalesce (Silberstein 2002: 40). Here, in a powerful rhetorical turning point, the potent symbolism of the location and the ritualism of the service combined with the words of respected religious leaders and the president to construct a thoroughly religious conception of the war. After the military's presentation of the colours, all of the religious dignitaries – Dean Baxter, Reverend Caldwell, Imam Dr Siddiqi and the Reverend Dr Billy Graham – echoed Bush's language of 'evil' in their prayers for the nation. Dr Graham went on implicitly to sanction Bush's 'war on terrorism' by stating: 'We're facing a new kind of enemy. We're involved in a new kind of warfare' (quoted in Silberstein 2002: 49).

Finally, it was time for the president to speak. Bush started by remembering the victims: 'So many have suffered so great a loss [...] We will read all these names. We will linger over them, and learn their stories, and many Americans will weep.' Following this discursive act of commemoration and the personalising of suffering, Bush donned a more pastoral role, assuring the nation that the universe has a moral design, that their prayers were heard and understood and that God was with them:

God's signs are not always the ones we look for. We learn in tragedy that his purposes are not always our own. Yet the prayers of private suffering, whether in our homes or in this great cathedral, are known and heard, and understood.

This world He created is of moral design. Grief and tragedy and hatred are only for a time. Goodness, remembrance, and love have no end. And the Lord of life holds all who die, and all who mourn.

The most crucial point in the speech came when Bush said, 'War has been waged against us by stealth and deceit and murder' and as a consequence, America's 'responsibility to history is already clear: to answer these attacks and **rid the world of evil**'. In the context of the site of the speech (the National Cathedral), the occasion (A National Day of Prayer) and the military ritualism (the presentation of the colours), this was a powerful call to arms. It was a call to divinely sanctioned war – a crusade against evil. As explained in Chapter 3, Bush's conception of evil is inherently Christian, implying the need for purification and eradication while obstructing any possibility of compromise.

Bush ended his address by invoking God's blessing on the nation and asking God to watch over and guide America in its task. He fortifies the appeal by quoting from scripture:

On this national day of prayer and remembrance, we ask almighty God to watch over our nation, and grant us patience and resolve in all that is to come. We pray that He will comfort and console those who now walk in sorrow. We thank Him for each life we now must mourn, and the promise of a life to come.

As we have been assured, neither death nor life, nor angels nor principalities nor powers, nor things present nor things to come, nor height nor depth, can separate us from God's love. May He bless the souls of the departed. May He comfort our own. And may He always guide our country.

God bless America. (Bush, 14 September, 2001)

The discursive act of divine sanction for a kind of holy war against evil was then subtly reinforced by the singing of the final hymn, 'Battle Hymn of the Republic'. The opening stanza potently underlines Bush's central message:

Mine eyes have seen the glory of the coming of the Lord,
He is trampling out the vintage where the grapes of wrath are stored,
He hath loos'd the fateful lightening of His terrible swift sword,
His truth is marching on.

In a sense, Bush was claiming the mantle of God's sword; America would march out to bring God's swift justice to the evildoers. Through the combination of language, religious symbolism, ritual and claims to authority, Bush appealed directly to the beliefs of millions of American evangelical Christians and invested the 'war on terrorism' with transcendent meaning and a divine sanction.

There are a great many other examples of this kind of discursive rendering of the holy 'war on terrorism'. For example, in another speech Bush clearly implies not just that America is the only nation which can achieve universal human freedom, but that in this endeavour God is clearly on America's side: 'The advance of human freedom – the great achievement of our time, and **the great hope of every time** – now **depends on us**. [...] Freedom and fear, justice and cruelty, have always been at war, and we know that **God is not neutral between them**' (Bush, 20 September, 2001). Similarly, in the following example reference is made to God's gift of freedom, to the Scriptures and to the sacred ideals America as a nation holds:

> [W]e accept the **duty**, as old as the **Scriptures**, to comfort the afflicted and to feed the hungry.
>
> These two commitments define your mission – and they define **America's role in history**. We understand that strength is necessary to confound the designs of evil men.
>
> We will use the great power of America to serve **the great ideals of America**. And by these efforts we will build a lasting, democratic peace – for ourselves, and **for all humanity**.
>
> May **God** continue to bless the United States of America. (Bush, 21 May, 2003)

Actually, this text contains a mix of appeals: to the Scriptures, to God, to America's role in history, to universal values and to duty. It is a powerful hybrid combination that clearly marks the war on terrorism as a 'good' war and claims for itself a transcendent status. This kind of language taps into the deep religiosity of American society and the deeply held belief in American exceptionalism. Secretary of State Madeline Albright expressed the contemporary version of this myth when she referred to America as 'the indispensable nation'. Hughes argues that the label 'American exceptionalism' actually obscures the profoundly religious origins of the chosenness vision: 'It is one thing to claim that America is exceptional in its own eyes. It is something else to claim that America is exceptional because God chose America and its people for a special mission in the world' (Hughes 2003: 19). Perhaps what is most ironic is that Bush's call to holy war is a direct echo of bin Laden's call to jihad; each demonises the other as the ultimate expression of evil and reasons that eradication is the only option (see Lincoln 2002: 20–32).

A second related appeal in the official discourse is to an historic 'calling' or responsibility which only America can fulfil. Like the 'indispensable' role of America in defeating nazism in World War II and communism in the cold war, the 'war on terrorism' is painted as a moral obligation for the world's remaining superpower which cannot be shirked. Such a view of history taps into popular myths about America's role in the world seen in movies like *U-571* where, in a rescripting of history, an American submarine captures a German enigma code machine and turns the tide of the sea war (actually it was a British submarine). Even science fiction movies such as *Independence Day*, *Deep Impact* or *Armageddon* express the view that America is the one nation which can save the world from catastrophe.

The official discourse begins by insisting the world is poised at a unique juncture in history and now is the time to act: '**It is now our time to act** ... And so we're going to slowly, but surely, tighten the net on terrorists, wherever they live. And **it's essential to do so now**. **It's essential to do so now**' (Bush, 11 October, 2001). Here Bush is saying that this moment is 'our time', the time 'we' have chosen to act. It is not only the correct or propitious time to act, but it is 'our' time to act – it is our responsibility. His repetition of the phrase 'it's essential to do so now' powerfully reinforces this construction. He reiterates the same message a few days later: '**Now is the time to act** boldly, to build and defend an age of liberty' (Bush, 20 October, 2001). Coupled with this is an attempt to construct the present historical juncture as unique and special: 'This is **a unique moment in our country's history** – it truly is – and the American people are rising to meet it' (Bush, 2 May, 2003). Grammatically, this implies the listeners are privileged to be a part of something special.

The discourse takes the idea of the timing of the war even further, suggesting America has in fact, been given a specific responsibility by History – the great march of time and events – to lead this campaign against evil: '[O]ur **responsibility to history** is already clear: to answer these attacks and rid the world of evil. [...] [T]he commitment of our fathers is now **the calling of our time**' (Bush, 14 September, 2001). The theme of 'responsibility to history' is again extended by Dick Cheney's formulation:

> The government of the United States has a moral duty to confront those threats, and to do whatever it takes to defeat them. And as the leading power, we have a further responsibility to help keep the peace of the world and to prevent terrorists and their sponsors from plunging the world into horrific violence. [...] [I]n the final analysis, history will judge us. (Cheney, 9 April, 2003)

Here, the responsibility to history has been transformed into a 'moral duty', which is even more forceful. Not only this, but history will judge America if it fails to fulfil its moral duty. In part, this duty flows from the natural responsibility placed on the world's leading power. In other words, there is no one else to do it; America must take final responsibility. This is a powerful discursive construction which actually places the decision to launch the 'war on terrorism' outside of the American government itself, and in a sense, absolves it of responsibility. It is not just a strategic decision, but an historic calling, a duty, a moral responsibility which mere humans cannot alter. The reference to America's status as the world's leading power is an echo of Albright's conception of the United States as the 'indispensable nation'.

The 'war on terrorism' then, is not just a quest for justice or a security interest, it is a moral responsibility, an obligation – a 'calling': 'The advance of freedom is more than an interest we pursue. It is a **calling** we follow' (Bush, 21 May, 2003). This is a forceful rhetorical construction which firmly fixes the war on terrorism as a 'good war'. After all, how can it be anything but a 'good war' if it is sanctioned by History and if it is a moral obligation, a solemn duty, a responsibility and 'the' calling of the twenty-first century? As one commentator notes, 'The word "calling", with its theological overtones as well as its Weberian connotations, attaches a redemptive cast to counterterrorism' (Troyer 2002). In fact, it could also be argued that the 'calling' of the 'good war on terrorism' is a direct outcome of the earlier discursive foundation laid by the circular ontology of the 'evil' discourse:

> [B]ecause 'terrorists' are evil, America is good and virtuous; the 'Axis of Evil' implicitly positions the US and its allies as the 'Axis of Good'. But this is not simply a binary opposition: the ontological element, the nature of American being, makes America *only* good and virtuous. It is a small step then to assume that you are chosen both by God and history. (Sardar and Davies, 2002: 198; original emphasis)

In summary, the counter-terrorist war is constructed as a 'good war' by virtue of it being a properly constituted and properly prosecuted just war, as well as a divinely sanctioned and historically called war. The official discourse leaves no doubt that America has no other option – it is duty bound – to once again save the world from evil enemies, just as it did in the (good) Second World War.

A reflexive 'new' war

Despite its powerful discursive construction as a quintessential good and just war, there were a number of obvious contradictions and tensions which cast a great deal of doubt on how 'good' the 'war on terrorism' really was. In particular, the war lacked a clearly identifiable (state) enemy, it had little prospect of a clear victory, it appeared that it might last for decades, there were many thousands of civilian casualties in Afghanistan and Iraq and the extra-judicial assassination and use of torture against suspected terrorists looked more like a 'dirty war' than a 'good war'. At the very least, the use of the term 'war' posed serious problems because of its inherent meanings, both legal and practical. War is properly understood as a state of open and declared military conflict between nations and there has evolved a set of internationally accepted rules and conventions to

146

regulate its conduct. To designate a campaign against terrorism as a 'war' therefore, is first and foremost a contradiction in terms: war cannot be properly declared except against another recognised state. Certainly, war cannot be declared against a kind of military tactic – terror or terrorism – as the phrase 'war on terrorism' implies. In addition, and more importantly, to construct the campaign as a war actually confers an appearance of legitimacy on the enemy, dignifies the original attacks as acts of war and suggests that America will be bound by the accepted laws of war (see Card 2003: 165). There was thus a major contradiction involved in using international law to justify attacking Afghanistan and Iraq, but then denying its applicability and undermining the very same international law by abrogating the Geneva Conventions for prisoners captured in Afghanistan and Iraq. The promulgation of the pre-emptive (preventive) war doctrine also contradicted established international law, which again undermined America's claim to be prosecuting a traditional just war.

It is possible to see two main reflexive strategies in the official discourse which attempt to deal with these tensions. In the first instance, the contradictions are resolved by refocusing the 'war on terrorism' on so-called rogue states, or the states comprising the 'axis of evil', who, it is argued, will give weapons of mass destruction to terrorists. The rhetorical strategy employed here is to transform the object of the war from a non-state enemy who cannot legally or practically be declared war on, to a state enemy who can. This rhetorical transformation was complete when Bush asserted that 'Afghanistan is the first overseas front in this war against terror' (Bush, 29 November, 2001). Strategically, this rhetorical transformation also facilitates the conduct of a right 'war' against terrorism. Just war requires the proper declaration of a state of war by appropriate authorities, plus due notification to opponents. A war against terrorist cells makes this problematic; refocusing on particular states resolves this contradiction. This particular grammatical reworking functions therefore, as a reflexive means of resolving the contradictions involved in declaring war on 'terrorism'.

The second, and most ingenious rhetorical strategy, has been to reconstruct the 'war on terrorism' as a special kind of 'new' war, a 'different' war, an 'exceptional war'. In fact, there are literally hundreds of instances in official texts where the 'war on terrorism' is described in terms of its 'new' features and characteristics. This transformation began with the depiction of the September 11, 2001 attacks as an 'exceptional event' and the start of a whole new era of terror. Attorney General John Ashcroft has been pivotal in this rhetorical construction, arguing for example, that there is a '**new** terrorist threat to Americans' which poses 'a **new** challenge for law enforcement'. He goes on to argue that this new threat requires '**new** laws against America's enemies', as well as '**new** leaders – and **new** role models' (Ashcroft, 24 September, 2001). In another major speech, Ashcroft states that after the '**new** attacks', the war represents 'a **new** offensive against terrorism' which involves '**new** weapons', '**new** powers' and '**new** tools' of law enforcement (including a special '**new** subpoena power'). It is, he says, a '**new** era in America's fight against terrorism' (Ashcroft, 25 October, 2001).

Rhetorically reconstructing the war in this manner facilitates the resolution of its more obvious contradictions by appealing to the unprecedented nature of the situation. In a way, it is a reassertion of the 'supreme emergency' facing the nation which by itself may justify almost any countermeasure. Many of the texts also emphasise how the current war is different to the wars of the past and how we are now living in a wholly different kind of world. For example:

> All of this was brought upon us in a single day – and night fell on **a different world** [...] Americans should not expect one battle, but **a lengthy campaign, unlike any other we have seen**. (Bush, 20 September, 2001)

> I've therefore characterized this conflict, this campaign, this so-called war, as being **notably different** from others. (Rumsfeld, 7 October, 2001)

> [T]his **new war** will be a conflict 'without battlefields and beachheads,' in short, an **unconventional war**. [...] [T]he war on terrorism is a **new** endeavor. (Dam, 22 October, 2001)

This is a deliberate and reflexive rhetorical strategy which begins with the construction of the September 11, 2001 attacks as a 'new' kind of warfare by a 'new' kind of enemy. The existence of so many novel features inevitably implies that we now inhabit a 'new' and 'different' world. Logically following from this, there is a need for a 'new' kind of defensive war which we would expect to be different from the old kind of war. As a consequence, we should not expect that the old moralities or modalities of war necessarily apply. By remaking the 'war on terrorism' as the '*new* war on terrorism', the discourse resolves two obvious problems. First, the difficulty of conferring legitimacy and legal status on the enemy is resolved by making them a 'new kind of enemy', one which does not need to be a recognised state or accorded the respect usually given to the opposition in war; new types of enemies can be treated in new ways. Second, because it is a new kind of war, it means the long-accepted rules of war no longer apply; a new war requires new rules of conduct.

In perhaps his most detailed exposition of the 'new' war, Bush states:

> And the world has come together to fight **a new and different war**, the first, and we hope the only one of the 21st century.

> [W]e're engaged in **a different type of war**; one that will use conventional forces, but one in which we've got to fight on all fronts.

148

[T]his is **an unconventional war**. It's **a different kind of war**. It's not the kind of war we're used to in America.

This is **a different kind of war** that requires a **different type of approach** and **different type of mentality**.

It is important that we stay the course, bring these people to justice, to show – and show others how to fight **the new wars of the 21st century**.

All of us in government are having to adjust our way of thinking about **the new war**.

I think the American people do understand that after September 11th, that we're facing **a different world**. (Bush, 11 October, 2001).

This construction provides policy-makers with a great deal of flexibility in dealing with the inherent tensions of the discourse: anything which does not fit the traditional conception of the 'good war' can be explained away as a necessity of the 'different kind of war' now being fought. This is partly how Bush justifies the creation of a new category of legal subjects in the war on terrorism. A 'new war' can obviously have new kinds of combatants without any major contradiction: 'Non-citizens, non-U.S. citizens who plan and/or commit mass murder are **more than criminal suspects**. They are **unlawful combatants** who seek to destroy our country and our way of life' (Bush, 29 November, 2001). On the rhetorical foundation of the '*new* war on terrorism', the contradictions involved in denying enemy soldiers any rights under the Geneva Conventions or the criminal justice system are reconciled. It is a powerful rhetorical strategy that can be reflexively and flexibly employed to justify and explain almost any aspect which may not fit the normal construction of the 'good war' – including the institutionalisation of torture during interrogation and the extra-legal killing of terrorist suspects on foreign soil.

Critically, the discourse surrounding the 'new' war America is fighting both reflects and appeals to the deeply embedded myths surrounding the establishment of the republic. It intersects with the notion of America as Nature's Nation and God's chosen people – a 'new' nation facing 'new' challenges in the world. This sense of being disconnected from history (and therefore able to write its own history) is powerfully echoed in American place names: New England, New York, New Hampshire, New Jersey, New Orleans, New Haven, New Mexico, New Iberia, New Albany, New Boston. The diplomatic language directed at 'old' Europe in the lead-up to the Iraq invasion reinforces this sense of difference, simultaneously chastising Europeans for being mired in the sordid details of history and slow to follow America's lead in the new war. The linguistic binary opposition between new and old infers that America's 'new' war is progressive and entrepreneurial, while 'old' Europe's caution is reactionary and backward-thinking.

A related construction of the 'new' war implies that because it is a different kind of war to those of the past, it may take a great many years to complete; it might even be a war without end. This is certainly the case if, as Bush states, the war 'will not end until every terrorist group of global reach has been found, stopped and defeated' (Bush, 20 September, 2001). Even if it was practically possible to do so, such a task would likely take decades. Donald Rumsfeld states that it will by necessity be a multi-pronged campaign over a long timeframe: 'this effort will continue in a variety of different ways over a sustained period of time', and 'we intend to pursue it until such time as we're satisfied that those terrorist networks don't exist. That they have been destroyed' (Rumsfeld, 7 October, 2001). Ashcroft makes a similar point: 'this is a long-range effort to fight terrorism' and 'we're going to be in this for the long haul' (Ashcroft, 29 November, 2001). The 'war on terrorism' is also rhetorically likened to the cold war in terms of its aims and long-term effort. This is a strategy of using historical analogy which both hints at the long time frame necessary to prosecute the war and provides the meta-narrative of the cold war as a medium through which it can be understood. Rumsfeld suggests that:

> [T]hese strikes are part of a much larger effort against worldwide terrorism, one that will be **sustained** and which is **wide-ranging**. It will likely be **sustained** for a period of **years**, **not weeks or months**. This campaign **will be waged much like the Cold War**, in the sense that it will involve many fronts over a period of time and will require continuous pressure by a large number of countries around the globe. (Rumsfeld, 8 October, 2001)

Actually, another veteran of the cold war, Vice President Cheney, takes this particular construction to its logical conclusion. He states that the new war would be different from previous wars, 'in the sense that **it may never end**. At least, not in our lifetime' (quoted in Mahajan 2003: 42). This is clearly a problem for the discursive construction of the 'good war', because a 'good war' should always have a clear endpoint and take the shortest time possible to avoid prolonged suffering. The contradiction is resolved by stating it will be a *different* war; this war is so new and so dissimilar to previous conflicts that it may not end in the way wars normally end. This strategy, as with the other discursive strategies I have discussed, permits a flexible defence of the primary construction of the 'good war on terrorism' in spite of its inherent contradictions and tensions.

Conclusion

The notion of the 'good war' is one of the most powerfully and carefully made constructions of the entire discourse of the 'war on terrorism'. It is the culmination and the very purpose of the discourse in the first place: to create a war nobody could object to on the grounds that it was immoral or unjust, and to enlist widespread public support (especially the support of conservative Christians) for whatever actions the American government decided was necessary in its promulgation. The main strategy for ensuring widespread social acceptance was to construct and essentialise the war in such a way that it would be seen to be a 'good war' in every possible sense: in terms of its legality, its conduct, its just cause, its necessity, its divine sanction, its duty to the world and in a long-term historical sense, as one of the many good wars which have been fought by America. The political rhetoric about America's good war is not necessarily new or unusual, in the sense that every war is normally justified in these terms; even warlords claim to fight for human rights or to prevent genocide against their followers. However, American self-perceptions preclude the conduct of war for any reason other than a truly just cause. For this reason, the public justification of the counter-terrorist campaign took on added significance.

As senior administration officials found, the task of creating a 'good war' is not nearly so straightforward, especially when it is a 'war' against an –ism: a war on terrorism. The conduct of war, moreover, is always messy and with contemporary weapons there is always a great deal of very public and horrific human suffering. To get around this, the most ingenious discursive strategy was employed: reconstruct the war not only as a 'good' and 'just' war, but also as a 'new' and 'different war'. The combination of these two discursive constructs into a novel kind of 'good but different war' allows for the public justification of elements that do not normally fit into a 'good war' framework, thereby maintaining stability in the overall meaning structure. Now, the more traditional aspects of the 'war on terrorism' can be defended as part of the 'good war' – attacking evil regimes – while the unusual aspects which do not fit this conception – assassinating suspects, denying Afghan fighters legal rights as prisoners of war, employing torture on suspects – can be defended as being part of the 'new war': they are regrettable but unavoidable in the 'new' type of warfare.

The power of this 'good (new) war' construction lies in the fact that from within the confines of the discourse itself – the structures and forms of language employed by officials – it is virtually impossible to deny the legitimacy of the war or to suggest any kind of non-military alternative. Even if the Bush-led 'war on terrorism' is sometimes poorly executed, it is extremely difficult to argue against the rightness and justice of the overall counter-terrorist war. To do so would require deconstructing every one of the discursive strategies I have examined in this chapter. Crucially, from within the discourse it would be extremely difficult to take even a *neutral* standpoint on the war. To attempt such an act of rebellion would be to suggest it was not a just, right and virtuous war; it would also be to suggest that we should not follow history's calling, that civilisation is not worth defending against evil and that we should not respond to the catastrophic threat posed by rogue states and their terrorist allies. In essence, the language, in the

151

way it is deployed by officials, is almost impossible to resist. It forces the listener either to simply accept it as an inherently and axiomatic good war, or to take what appears to be an absurd stance which says that pursuing justice and fulfilling one's historic responsibility is wrong. This is how discourses function; they structure thought in a specified direction by making some positions appear as commonsense and others as absurd or nonsensical.

As I have reiterated throughout this book, this language was not natural or inevitable; nor is it politically neutral or objective. Rather, it is deliberately constructed to reinforce administration policies and to 'manufacture consent' among the public for a massive campaign of violent counter-terrorism. As always, other narratives were available: an international campaign against global violence (of all types) could have been constructed; the language of Martin Luther King's Christian pacifism could have been drawn upon instead of that of militant evangelical Christianity; or a law-enforcement frame could have been employed instead of the just war conception.

Unfortunately, the onset of the 'war on terrorism' has come at a moment when a broader relegitimisation of war as an instrument of foreign policy is already well under way. Due to the rise of humanitarian war doctrines in the 1990s in particular, war as an activity is no longer viewed as being inherently evil; the notion of the 'good war' has come out of the closet. This climate has allowed the Bush administration to wrap the counter-terrorist war in a cloak of respectability. At the same time, and much more ominously, it has also allowed for the return of the national security state (seen most prominently during the superpower conflict) and the largest rearmament since the height of the cold war – processes which would have been difficult to legitimise in the pre-September 11, 2001 world. Writing the 'good (new) war on terrorism' has not only facilitated a counter-terrorist campaign of both international and domestic dimensions, it has also assisted an intense and ongoing process of global militarisation. As a consequence, the omens suggest we will be fighting the good 'war on terrorism' for many decades to come.

6

Language and power:
reproducing the discourse

S O FAR I HAVE EXAMINED the primary narratives at the heart of the 'war on terrorism' – the way in which language constructs the events of September 11, 2001, and the way it creates identities, threats and the counter-terrorist war. In this sense, I have been examining the constituent parts that taken together make up the whole. In order to take the analysis to the next level, I will now consider the discourse as a totality; I will look at the forest rather than just individual trees. When examining a discourse *in toto* there are a number of important questions to consider: What are its main features and what makes the discourse distinctive or unique? How does it compare with previous discourses of counter-terrorism or other political discourses? And what can this macro analysis tell us about the way the discourse functions politically? Not surprisingly, the 'war on terrorism' as a political discourse has both unique and generic characteristics, as well as continuities and discontinuities from previous counter-terrorism approaches. While it functions like many other political discourses in some respects, it is also quite distinctive in others.

Apart from the objective appraisal of its most interesting features, there is another more fundamental and important question about the nature of the discourse: how successful has it been so far, and how powerful is it really? In other words, we need to examine whether the architects of the discourse have achieved their goals of legitimising and entrenching their specific approach to counter-terrorism while at the same time marginalising and excluding alternative discourses. Although it is not easy to measure, there are good reasons for believing that the 'war on terrorism' has been extremely successful in this regard, and that it now stands as the dominant foreign policy approach in American politics. At one level, the power of the discourse is due to its internal construction; it is a coherent, appealing and reassuring narrative for Americans which restores the confidence and sense of purpose which was so severely undermined by the terrorist attacks. On another level, political discourses only rise to prominence in this way when other social actors – the media, in particular, but also institutions like universities, churches and foundations – reproduce and amplify the language across the wider society. This is exactly what happened in the years following September 11, 2001; the media, together with other important actors, reproduced the official discourse in a relatively unmediated fashion, while at the same time silencing and marginalising alternative narratives. Without such faithful reproduction, it seems likely that the 'war on terrorism' would have remained a marginal foreign policy discourse largely ignored by the wider public – as happens with most foreign policy discourses in America.

The characteristics of the counter-terrorism discourse

There are a number of significant and interesting aspects to the discourse which help to illuminate the way in which it functions. Some of its features are novel and new, while others exhibit similarities with earlier political discourses. In the first instance, when we look at the overall body of the language we note that it draws upon a great many existing narratives and myths common to American political and cultural discourse. It also employs a number of framing devices and rhetorical modes which are common to American politics. This is a way of saying that the discourse is characterised by *hybridity* and *intertextuality*; its whole is a kind of discursive amalgam or hybrid which weaves together a range of other discourses, myths and narratives – it draws on other 'texts' in society. As each chapter has shown, the language of the 'war on terrorism' taps into a plethora of narratives and tropes: long-established discourses of threat and danger, such as 'red scares', 'war on drugs' and the 'enemy within'; existing foreign policy narratives of 'rogue states', 'outlaw' regimes and the dangers posed by weapons of mass destruction; religious myths and narratives of God's Chosen Nation and Manifest Destiny; nationalist myths of American exceptionalism and American innocence; 'good war' narratives surrounding World War II and the cold war; imperial narratives of civilisation versus barbarism; and popular Manichean narratives of good versus evil. Actually, the discourse is quite impressive for the ease with which it weaves these sometimes disparate narratives into one almost seamless story of America's historic good fight against terrorism/barbarism/evil – how it powerfully combines and distils so many different American myths and stories into a new super-narrative.

Given the great many narrative forms and modes and its complex textuality, the discourse is surprisingly disciplined and consistent. In my examination of over 300 pages of speeches by dozens of different speakers, from the president to ambassadors, and covering more than two years, I found virtually no instances of deviation from the primary narratives; the words used were almost identical, the grammatical structures the same and the meanings remained consistent. Every speaker told the same story in a similar way, and frequently used exactly the same words. This lends a great deal of coherence to the overall narrative, which in turn reinforces its believability and influence among its listeners. Apart from its consistent and coherent story however, it is also a very appealing and reassuring discourse in that it reinforces the belief that Americans are a special nation, that they are essentially good people whatever others may think and they have a unique role to play in the world. This confidence and self-belief was sorely dented by the terrorist attacks, and in one sense, the discourse is an attempt to rebuild America's self-image.

Related to its intertextuality, the *genealogy* of the discourse shows clear lines of continuity with earlier responses by American governments to national crises and security threats. For example, the current Bush-initiated 'war on terrorism' follows closely the discursive form of the preceding 'wars on terrorism' declared by the Reagan and Clinton administrations. In succession, each president discursively constructed terrorism as the greatest threat to American and international security and then attacked 'rogue states' in the Middle East as a response: Libya was attacked in Reagan's war on terrorism, Sudan and Afghanistan in Clinton's and Afghanistan and Iraq in Bush's. More significantly, Reagan used almost identical language to that of the Bush administration, speaking of 'the **evil scourge** of terrorism' which was a plague spread by the 'depraved opponents of **civilization** itself'; Reagan's Secretary of State, George Shultz, said that terrorism was 'a return to **barbarism** in the modern age' (quoted in Chomsky 2003). A few other examples of the genealogical origins of Bush's language include:

> I will direct the resources of my administration against **this scourge of civilization** and toward expansion of our cooperation with other nations combating terrorism in its main forms. (Reagan, 19 October, 1980)

> Those who directed this atrocity must be dealt **justice**. They will be. (Reagan, 27 October, 1983)

> The American people are not – I repeat, not – going to tolerate intimidation, terror and outright **acts of war** against this nation and its people. And we're especially not going to tolerate these attacks from **outlaw states** run by the strangest collection of misfits, loony toons and squalid criminals since the advent of **the Third Reich**. (Reagan, 8 July, 1985)

> The magnitude of **the threat posed by terrorism is so great** that we cannot afford to confront it with half-hearted and poorly organized measures. (Shultz, 25 October, 1982)

> From a practical standpoint, a purely passive defense does not provide enough of a deterrent to terrorists and the states that sponsor terrorism. **Terrorism is a form of warfare**, and history has taught us that to deter war, one must be able to strike back or act pre-emptively. (Shultz, 24 June, 1984). (All quotations taken from Wills 2003: 2, 4, 85, 135)

Similarly, in dealing with the communist threat, Reagan (like Bush) demonised his opponents, calling the Soviet Union the '**evil** empire'. There are also a great many examples of a similar use of language by the Clinton administration during the second 'war on terrorism' (see Hiro 2002: 275–6). In other words, American administrations use comparable language, which in turn constructs analogous policies. Such discursive continuities can also be seen in the 'war on drugs' initiated in the 1990s; it too involved declaring that the drug trade was a 'clear and present danger' to American security and then engaging in military action in Central America. Far from unique then, the discourse of the 'war on terrorism' follows long-established interpretive tendencies; the tendency to militarise foreign policy responses, a fear of internal subversion, a sense of endangerment towards 'the other' and the demonising of opponents (Campbell 2002; see also Zulaika 2003; Zulaika and Douglass 1996).

At one level, there is little that is new or unique about the language of the 'war on terrorism'; it is simply the manner in which American governments have always spoken about and responded to severe crises – it is a reflex, ingrained over time and institutionalised through practice. It could also be argued that most states respond in this mode when they are threatened, especially large and powerful states. In effect, one of the reasons the discourse has been so uncritically accepted (particularly by the political classes within America) is because it is founded on the logic of previous American responses to similar crises; it is a familiar and reassuring discourse – to both the public and to policy-makers.

It is clear from previous chapters that the discourse is also highly *reflexive*; that is, it has to continuously reconstruct and reinvent earlier discursive formations in order to maintain coherence in the face of internal and external contradictions and challenges. Once the authorities declared the WTC attacks to be an 'act of war' and that a 'war' against terrorism would follow, they had to go back and reflexively recast the war as a 'new' and 'different' kind of war in order to avoid the suggestion that the terrorists might be legitimate soldiers or warriors, or that they might have a legitimate political cause. In order to overcome the problem of having a 'war' against a terrorist foe, a whole new linguistic term and legal-military category had to be invented: 'enemy combatant'. Similarly, the 'war' against the abstract noun 'terrorism' proved to be equally problematic. Importantly, it is also a war against a military tactic or strategy (terrorism is a *method* more than an ideology; it is a *means* to achieving certain political ends) – which makes it akin to a 'war against insurgency' or a 'war against deterrence'; clearly, this is absurd. In order to rectify this contradiction, as well as the problem of a 'war' against individuals and tiny groups scattered across the globe, the authorities had to reflexively remake the 'war on terrorism' into a war against 'outlaw nations and their terrorist allies'. In short, the discourse does not remain static; rather, it has to evolve and constantly reinvent itself to cope with its inherent instabilities and contradictions, while attempting to maintain its central formations.

Another prominent characteristic of the discourse is its *opacity*, or lack of transparency. Many of the key terms and phrases are never properly defined or explained, which results in their meanings having to be assumed or inferred through the context in which they occur. As Suman Gupta notes, it is a discourse of 'indistinct, hazy, decontextualised – and let's face it, deeply worrying – abstractions' (Gupta 2002: 22–3). For example, there is no clear explanation of what actually constitutes 'evil' or what the ethical boundaries of 'good' behaviour are: does it include bombing a wedding party in Afghanistan, or the use of cluster bombs in urban areas, for example? Or does it only apply to the actions of specifically designated 'terrorists'? Similarly, there is no clear definition anywhere in the discourse of 'terrorism' itself, except the implication that it defines the nature of the enemy. Other important concepts used by officials – freedom, civilisation, victory – remain equally opaque. Moreover, they raise important questions which are never answered: How does bringing 'freedom' to other nations tally with support for brutal dictators, such as the Saudi or Uzbek regimes? In what sense does the treatment of terrorist suspects at Guantanamo or Abu Ghraib fit into 'civilised' behaviour? What measure will be used to determine 'victory' over terrorism? It is not simply that these concepts are inherently difficult to define or explain. Rather, it is that keeping them deliberately undefined – keeping them opaque – allows the speakers to use them in politically defined ways and for specific purposes, such as denigrating or delegitimising particular opponents.

One of the most obvious characteristics of the 'war on terrorism' is its extremely *gendered* language and its reflections of traditional patriarchal male-female roles. It is actually an overwhelmingly masculine narrative full of stereotypical masculine heroes (firefighters and police officers, soldiers/warriors, the courageous president), equally stereotypical female victims (the oppressed women of Afghanistan, Private Jessica Lynch, the '*Home*land') and an accompanying set of traditional masculine behaviours and images (missions to smoke bin Laden out of his cave, Wanted Dead or Alive posters, macho warriors battling a savage enemy). It is not simply that the discourse reflects primarily masculine values, but also that women have been rendered largely invisible in both the media (except as victims), and more importantly, in the decision-making arena since September 11, 2001. Some scholars have argued that US foreign policy and political culture is deeply and inherently masculinised, and the militarised approach to the 'war on terrorism' is simply a reflection of this dominant trait. That is, the reflexive need to appear 'tough' in the face of any crisis or challenge makes a war-like response appear natural and normal, and privileges the use of military force as a foreign policy tool – while simultaneously silencing women's voices and restricting their access to political influence (see Enloe 2002).

The gendered language of the counter-terrorism discourse however, is more than simply an unconscious reflection of dominant cultural attitudes; rather, as with other aspects of the discourse, it has an important political function – it 'serves to legitimate certain activities and ways of thinking over others' (Tickner 2002: 336).

In a related sense, the discourse is also notable for its *ideological* character, if we understand ideology to be 'meaning in the service of power' (Fairclough 1995: 14), or as constructions of meaning that contribute to the production, reproduction and transformation of relations of domination in society (Jorgensen and Phillips 2002: 75; Fairclough 1992: 87). Far from being a neutral reflection of international realities, or the objective and dispassionate discussion of competing policy alternatives, the 'war on terrorism' is both embedded within and attempts to advance, an ideological position and a set of ideological policies. For example, Chapter 2 explored how the discourse is welded to a neo-liberal version of globalisation: the terrorist attacks, officials argue, threaten the positive gains of globalisation and thus must be opposed. This is an attempt to protect the existing relations of domination inherent in the global capitalist order over which America presides. Similarly, the gendered nature of the 'war on terrorism' is an attempt to reproduce and sustain the patriarchal structures of society. Overall, we could argue that the discourse seeks to maintain and continually reproduce the power of the (highly gendered) 'military-industrial' complex which is so central to the American political-economy.

Lastly, and from a negative perspective, the discourse is notable for its *silences* and gaps – for what it omits. As mentioned in Chapter 1, what is missing from a discourse can often be more revealing than that which is included. In this discourse there are a number of glaring omissions – apart from the missing stories about the dead and injured civilians in Afghanistan and Iraq. First, there is little mention of history or context – except to invoke the analogies of the 'good wars' against fascism and communism. Some of the histories which are missing from the story of America's 'war against terrorism' include: the record of American involvement in the politics of the Middle East – its support for Israel, its military bases in the Arabian Peninsula, its alliances with despotic regimes, its murky dealings with the Taliban and the Mujahaddin before them, its oil politics; the history and context of al Qaeda's decade-long struggle against American policy in the region; the global context of state failure and breakdown, arms trading (America being the world's largest dealer of weapons) and increasing levels of violence and disorder; and the histories and lessons of other nations' struggles against terrorism, such as Israel, Northern Ireland, Italy, Germany, Spain, Sri Lanka and Chechnya – to name a few. Instead, the discourse assumes a 'ground zero' or 'year zero' attitude, as if it were the start of a new phase of history, rather than its continuation (or repetition).

There is also a missing political dimension; the war is defined as a struggle between 'good' and 'evil' rather than as a contest over policies or global military, political and economic structures. What we never seem to hear are the political motives of the protagonists – either the terrorists' or the counter-terrorists'. Lastly, there is an absence of discussion regarding the possible range of counter-terrorist policies available to governments, particularly non-war-based methods. Instead of acknowledging that there are a great many models and paradigms for dealing with terrorism – legal and policing-based approaches, diplomatic and political approaches, conciliatory approaches, long-term structural approaches – it is axiomatically assumed that military and repressive approaches are the only rational and realistic options. These silences are not merely accidental omissions; they are deliberate exclusions, designed to ensure that no challenge is made to the dominant narrative.

The power of the discourse

Perhaps the most important characteristic of the discourse, at least for the purposes of this book, relates to the success of the discursive project: to what extent have the architects of the discourse succeeded in their aims? Providing a complete answer to this question would entail an extremely complex and involved study which would ultimately remain contestable and highly subjective. Although it may be a simplification, I want to suggest that the success of a discourse can be measured by the extent to which it allows the authorities to enact their policies with significant support (or at least without significant opposition), and the extent to which alternative narratives and approaches are marginalised and silenced in the public arena. At a deeper level, a discourse can be considered successful when its words, language, assumptions and viewpoints are adopted and employed uncritically in political discourse by opposition politicians, the media, social institutions (like churches, schools, universities, associations, pressure groups) and ordinary citizens. While no discourse can ever be completely hegemonic or totalising – there will always be other competing discourses and arenas of contestation – a political discourse can be considered successful to the extent it becomes institutionalised and normalised within and across a range of important political and social institutions.

Employing these crude terms, it seems reasonable to argue that the discourse has been extremely successful. This is partly what makes it unique: the extent to which it has marginalised alternative discourses and established itself as the main language of counter-terrorism – even for opponents of the administration. In the first place, the Bush administration has enacted virtually all its intended policies with extraordinary levels of support from both the opposition Democrats and the wider public; from the USA Patriot Act (which the Senate approved 98 to 1 and the House of Representatives approved 369 to 66), to the war against Afghanistan, budget increases for the military, national missile defence and the treatment of terrorist suspects, the administration has been surprisingly unhindered in its ability to achieve its purposes. And it has done so with extremely high public approval ratings. Even when the administration has enacted measures which clearly endanger individual civil liberties and personal freedoms (so deeply cherished by Americans), there has been relatively little protest from the public. It is only really the Iraq war and to a lesser extent, the military tribunals at Camp Delta that have provoked any serious criticism or debate. However, even this disapproval has been unable significantly to alter the overall thrust of administration policies.

An indication of the extent to which the discourse has been accepted and absorbed – even by political opponents of the administration – can be seen in the way Democratic presidential nominee Senator John Kerry employs the same kinds of discursive constructions as administration officials. For example, an examination of Kerry's key foreign policy speeches reveals that he too assumes the existence and aptness of a 'global **war on terrorism**'; 'we're in a time of **war**', he confidently states. He also speaks about 'a **new threat**' posed by a '**new** ideology of **hatred**' from 'those practitioners who would **pervert** Islam's true message'; it is, he says, a 'mortal challenge' and 'a common **threat to the global system**'. Like Bush, Kerry also locates the current conflict within the meta-narratives of Pearl Harbor and World War II, the cold war, civilisation versus barbarism and the threat posed by terrorism to 'the benefits of **globalization**'; and like Bush, he also believes that 'this is no ordinary time' (it is an historic calling), and that '**winning** the War on Terror' is imminently possible. More detailed examples of his statements on terrorism reveal the extent to which the official discourse has penetrated Kerry's language:

> [I]t's clear that we need more than a one-dimensional war on terror. Of course we need to hunt down and destroy those who are **plotting mass murder** against Americans and **innocent** people from Africa to Asia to Europe. We must **drain the swamps** of terrorists [...]

> [There is] a global consensus that **weapons of mass destruction** under the control of terrorists represent the **most serious threat** to international security today, and warrants an urgent and global response. (Kerry, January 23, 2003)

> The war on terrorism is not just an American cause; it is a global conflict against **a hidden and deadly enemy** with many faces in many places. (Kerry, December 3, 2003)

> [T]oday the agents of terrorism work and **lurk** in the shadows of **60 nations on every continent** ...

> The War on Terror is ... a clash of **civilization** against chaos; of the best hopes of humanity against dogmatic fears of progress and the future.

[W]e must act immediately to prevent terrorists from acquiring **nuclear**, **chemical**, **or biological weapons**.

The safety of our people, the security of our country, **the memory** of our brothers and sisters, mothers and fathers, neighbors and **heroes** we lost on **September 11th** call on us to **win this war** we did not seek.

[T]oday, the **Cold War** is memory, not reality. I believe we can bring a real victory in the War on Terror. (Kerry, February 27, 2004)

In essence, we can see virtually all the primary discursive constructions of the 'war on terrorism' within these statements: the memory and victim-hood of the grievous September 11, 2001 attacks; the demonisation of the enemy terrorists (they breed in 'swamps'); the innocent and heroic Americans who need protecting; the threat and danger posed by the combination of terrorists and weapons of mass destruction; the historic calling to fight this just war; and the certainty of victory. The fact that an avowed opponent of the Bush administration would employ the very same language is testament to the power and success of the discourse.

This relates to a second measure of the success of a discourse: the extent to which alternative narratives and discourses have been marginalised and silenced in public debates. It is widely agreed by observers that alternative and critical voices are rarely heard in the political arena in America, and virtually all of the debate is confined to contestations over tactics and strategies, rather than over substantive or foundational issues. In this case, for example, while there may be doubts expressed about whether attacking Iraq was a justifiable part of the campaign against terrorism, or whether this strategy has backfired, there is little or no debate about the broader contours of the 'war on terrorism' itself – whether a 'war' is necessary, effective or practical in the first place, whether terrorists should be treated in the same way other criminals are treated, or if the threat of terrorism has been exaggerated.

Another measure of success relates to the extent to which the language, concepts, assumptions and privileged knowledge of the discourse becomes institutionalised and normalised in the operation and practices of institutions. In this regard, it seems obvious that the discourse has already been highly successful; after all, it is now embedded into a number of major pieces of legislation (such as the USA Patriot Act), into policy documents (such as *The National Security Strategy of the United States* document of September 2002 and *The National Strategy for Combating Terrorism* of February 2003), and within the standard operating procedures and guiding principles of security organisations from the CIA to the Department of Homeland Security and the Coastguard. Over time, as was observed during the cold war, the language and assumptions of the

161

discourse become a normal part of daily practice, and are then reproduced through institutional memory and workplace habit. In this way, practice reinforces meaning and vice versa; the language and institutions soon become co-constitutive of the reality of the war against terrorism. As will be discussed below, the discourse has also been inculcated and absorbed into other social institutions, especially the mainstream media. To the degree in which this process is already well under way, it seems likely that the 'war on terrorism' – as a framework for American foreign and domestic policy – is here to stay for some time.

A final measure of the success of the discourse is the extent to which the language is adopted and uncritically accepted by groups and individuals in society. This is almost impossible to measure and assess accurately – in the absence of interviewing every person in the country. Nonetheless, we can infer that the discourse has been largely successful in this regard, if we accept the evidence of crude indicators such as opinion polls; it seems unlikely the American public would give Bush such high approval ratings if they felt he was constantly lying or misrepresenting the facts or was leading the country into disaster. The extraordinarily high levels of approval for Bush's leadership over the initial two years (at times above 90 per cent), and support for the wars against Afghanistan (up to 90 per cent support) and to a lesser extent, Iraq (over 50 per cent for the first year at least), indicates that Americans generally believe the discourse; that is, they accept the administration's interpretation of the WTC attacks and the necessity for a 'war' against terrorism. Most Americans believe the wars against Afghanistan and Iraq have aided the 'war on terrorism' and have made Americans safer (Younge 2003). It appears the public also accepts the administration's construction of the threat and danger: polls have found anxiety regarding a possible terrorist attack remains at very high levels, despite the time since the attacks (see Kern *et al.* 2003: 290; Nacos 2002: 61). Related to this, more than 70 per cent of Americans have said they are willing to give up some freedoms during the 'war on terrorism', even if it would last for decades (quoted in Hertsgaard 2002: 49).

Other poll evidence suggests that Americans have taken to heart the dangers posed by the 'enemy within': 82 per cent support increased government power to detain immigrants, even legal ones, and nearly a third (31 per cent) believe that Arab Americans should be detained in camps (*ibid.*). In terms of the discourse of identity, a survey of American opinion leaders after the attacks by the Pew Research Centre found that 52 per cent agreed 'America does a lot of good in the world' (*ibid.*: 8). Additionally, another Pew elite opinion survey found that when asked whether American policies might be a major cause of the terrorist attacks, less than 20 per cent agreed (Hiro 2002: 417). At a more fundamental level, the discourse successfully depoliticised the administration's approach to counter-terrorism: polls showed that while Americans remained politically divided on other issues, most did not view national security and defence as a political or partisan matter (Schechter 2003: xli). In effect, the discourse has effectively placed the 'war on terrorism' beyond politics or debate for most people in America.

Importantly, we know that administration officials are fully aware of how powerful language can be because they deliberately (and cynically) manipulated the public into believing Saddam was involved in the September 11, 2001 attacks. Despite the absence of any evidence showing that Iraq was connected to the attacks, in press conferences and speeches officials implied, gently suggested and regularly gave the impression there was a connection between Iraq and al Qaeda. As a direct consequence of this deliberate (mis)use of the language of inference, a Pew Research Centre poll in October 2002 found that 66 per cent of Americans believed Saddam was involved in the terrorist attacks, while 79 per cent thought that Iraq possessed or was close to possessing, nuclear weapons (quoted in Rampton and Stauber 2003: 78–9). These misconceptions persisted throughout the following months. In early March 2003, a Gallop poll found 88 per cent of Americans thought Saddam was involved in supporting terrorist groups who planned to attack the United States, and 51 per cent still thought he was directly implicated in the September 11, 2001 attacks (quoted in Kern *et al.* 2003: 302). More significantly, nearly all those who thought Saddam was involved in the WTC attacks supported the war to remove him from power. This is direct testament to the success and power of the discursive strategies employed by the administration; as media commentators noted, 'Simply by mentioning Iraq and al Qaeda together in the same sentence, over and over, the message got through' (Rampton and Stauber 2003: 96). It is also an indication of the media's complicity with the administration that, unlike the press in Britain which took a more critical view, it did not vigorously challenge the official line or attempt to rectify these misconceptions.

The power of the discourse and its successful inculcation into American foreign and domestic policy is a function of several factors. First, it is in large part due to the ingenuity and shrewdness of the discourse itself – its careful composition, its appeal to popular and deeply embedded myths and narratives, its reassuring tone, its use of clever rhetorical strategies and forms and its choreographed discursive and symbolic accompanying actions. Second, it is the result of the sheer volume of the discourse; administration officials have given thousands of speeches, interviews and broadcasts about the 'war on terrorism', averaging around ten per day over the entire period since September 11, 2001. For example, in the twenty-six days from September 11 to October 6 President Bush alone gave more than fifty public statements on the 'war on terrorism', most with extensive media coverage; and in the following two months from October 7 to December 7, he made seventy-six public statements, using opportunities such as the visit to an elementary school or the joint appearance with President Putin of Russia to relay his message (Nacos 2002: 148–9). This amounts to a kind of rhetorical or discursive blitz on the public; it is the commonly used strategy of 'manipulation by inundation'. Michael Deaver, a media adviser to President Reagan, recalls that in order to establish the White House version of reality and to overwhelm all other competing messages, officials had to repeat the same statements over and over again: 'It used to drive the President crazy, because the repetition was so important. He'd get on that airplane and look at that speech and say, "Mike, I'm not going to give this same speech on education again, am I?" I said, "Yeah, trust me, it's going to work." And it did' (quoted in Livingston 1994: 89). The Bush administration operated on the same assumption that if you say something loud enough and long enough, the public will eventually accept it as the truth.

More important than either of these two factors however, is the role of social institutions such as the media, academic institutions, foundations and think-tanks and religious groups, in transmitting, reproducing and amplifying the discourse; without the intervention of these actors, officials would have little hope of even being heard. The media in particular has played a decisive role in transmitting the words of officials to the wider public. Normally, discourses are heavily mediated by social actors; that is, they are interpreted, absorbed, reconstituted and then reproduced in a new form to other listeners. Along the way, meanings are often altered or lost, and the discourse assumes new forms and takes on novel elements. This is not surprising, because humans are subjective creatures, and words and language must be deciphered and decoded before they can be passed on. Most observers however, agree that the media, since September 11, 2001 at least, has transmitted the main messages of the administration in a relatively unmediated and uncritical fashion. Some would go so far as to suggest the American media has almost without exception fallen in behind the government's war plans and acted virtually as a mouthpiece for the administration (see Hertsgaard 2002; Schechter 2003; Solomon 2002, 2003). Similarly, a great many academics, think-tanks and foundations, religious leaders and other important social actors, have reproduced and amplified the administration's message to their listeners. Outside of America, the leaders of some of America's closest allies such as Tony Blair and John Howard have also transmitted the discourse to their own citizens (and to international media who have then retransmitted it back to the American public); they too have reproduced the language in a largely unmediated form, often using identical words and phrases. It is this continual reproduction and amplification of the discourse that in large part explains why it has proved so successful.

Media reproduction of the 'war on terrorism'

The role of the media is critical to the success of any political discourse because in modern societies it is the main transmission belt or conduit between politics and society. There are few alternatives to communicating political messages to the public at large; therefore, for any political discourse to be successful, politicians have to go through the media. At the same time, in today's mass societies people are almost entirely dependent on the media for information about public affairs and rely heavily on media sources for cues on how to understand and interpret that information (Nacos and Torres-Reyna 2003: 135). It is well-known that television is the primary source of information for most Americans. In addition, due to the nature of the medium itself, the media plays a key role in 'framing' public communication about national events. Given the infinite amount of information in the world and the myriad ways of describing events, choices have to be made about what to focus on and how best to communicate it. Thus,

> The idea of 'news frames' refers to interpretive structures that journalists use to set particular events within their broader context. News frames bundle key concepts, stock phrases, and iconic images to reinforce certain common ways of interpreting developments. The essence of framing is selection to prioritise some facts, images, or developments over others, thereby unconsciously promoting one particular interpretation of events. (Norris *et al.* 2003: 10–11).

The framing of news in turn gives the media an agenda-setting role (determining the most important issues), a priming role (signalling and preparing the public to receive messages about those issues) and an evaluative role (offering or implying solutions).

The role of the media is never more important than during times of national crisis. There are two main reasons for this. First, the media looks primarily to political leaders for cues about how to interpret and explain national events and it offers officials almost unlimited access to communicate with the public. The frames employed by the media to transmit messages from politicians are thus critical. Second, in times of crisis the public relies heavily on the media for information and explanation, and the way in which the media frames such events will therefore have a powerful effect on the public's subsequent understanding, perception and knowledge. It is because the media plays such a crucial role that it is always in danger of being manipulated by political actors who will use it to try to 'manufacture consent' for particular policies (see Herman and Chomsky 1988).

When it comes to violent political events, particularly terrorism, the power to shape the public's outlook rests almost solely with governments because it is to government officials that reporters tend to defer to explain wars, terrorism, hijacks, political killings, coups and the like. Livingston argues:

> The power to shape perceptions of violent events and their principal actors (both perpetrators and victims) usually rests not with the terrorists but with government officials. Who the terrorists are in the first place is a question largely determined by

these officials. Those who have routine access to the mass media, those to whom reporters turn when the dust settles and the shooting stops, have the ability to shape coverage and perceptions. (Livingston 1994: 178)

Presidential speeches in particular draw news coverage from all the major television networks and newspapers and are then transmitted widely to the public. In this sense, senior politicians are 'opinion leaders' in times of crisis; they shape the terms of the debate and set the parameters of discussion. Studies back the view that the media takes its cues from officials in framing and describing violent events, often using the exact same words (Carruthers 2000: 191). For example, in 1998 the media watchdog group Fairness and Accuracy in Reporting (FAIR) criticised the news media for reporting the killing of Dr. Barnett Slepian by anti-abortionist extremists as murder (rather than terrorism), while at the very same time describing an arson attack by extreme environmentalists in Colorado as an act of terrorism (rather than protest or vandalism). The news media appeared to take its cue directly from President Clinton who declared, 'I am outraged by the murder of Dr. Bennett Slepian in his home last night ...'. CBS opened its broadcast that night by reporting, 'President Clinton says he is outraged by the murder of a Buffalo, New York, area doctor who performs abortions' (quoted in Nacos 2002: 96).

There is no question that following September 11, 2001 the mainstream American media (and large parts of the mainstream media in other countries) continued in this semantically complicit mode and framed the attacks and the military response to the attacks in a manner which both reflected and supported the language and actions of the Bush administration. Some observers have even gone so far as to say that 'the American press proved an eager amplifier of the government's message' (Hertsgaard 2002: 85; see also Nacos 2002: 159–60). As Rupert Murdoch stated on behalf of Fox television, 'We'll do whatever is our patriotic duty'; CNN made a similar promise: 'In deciding what to air, CNN will consider guidance from the appropriate authorities' (quoted in Solomon 2003: 246). Even some of the nation's most influential journalists openly pledged their allegiance: CBS *Evening News* anchor Dan Rather publicly stated on a late-night television show, 'George Bush is the president ... [If] he wants me to line up, just tell me where' (Hertsgaard 2002: 85).

Apart from these visible expressions of support, there is other evidence that the media was complicit in reproducing the official discourse. First, it is notable that the media immediately followed the administration's lead in imposing a war-based frame on its coverage of events and used the same language as officials in its stories: cable TV networks employed ubiquitous on-screen banners which proclaimed 'America's New War' or 'War Against Terrorism'; in the month following the terror attacks, ABC News broadcast 86 stories employing the terms 'war' and 'terrorism', and there were 96 such segments from CBS News, 133 from

NBC News, 316 from CNN, and 166 on National Public Radio; and in the print media, the Lexis-Nexis archive published 5,814 articles that mentioned the two terms (Nacos 2002: 146). And, following the official discourse (see Chapter 2), in the month leading up to October 23, 2001, the *New York Times*, the *Washington Post*, the *Chicago Tribune* and the *Los Angeles Times*, published a total of 754 articles which referred to World War II or nazi Germany in connection with the 'war on terrorism' (Lewis 2002: 169). Related to this, the TV networks in particular also adopted an overarching narrative style scripted in the mode of a popular war movie that reinforced the 'good war' message: on CNN for example, banners sequentially told the story of 'America under Attack', 'America Strikes Back', 'America's New War' and 'America Recovers'. The 'war on terrorism' was in one sense, 'written' by the networks as a Hollywood blockbuster – an immediate sequel to 2001's widely anticipated *Pearl Harbor*.

Second, there is agreement among observers and scholars that the media also displayed a tendency to transmit the words of officials in a relatively unmediated and unimpeded fashion, at least in the immediate post-attack period. For example, studies show that the press relied overwhelmingly on official sources for their information (up to 75 per cent), and in the weeks following the attacks, only 25 per cent of media content was analysis, opinion or speculation (Schechter 2003: 56–7). There was little attempt to interpret or explain what officials said; instead, the media tended to reproduce and transmit the words of officials directly. This pattern has since been maintained: an analysis of 414 stories about Iraq aired on the ABC, CBS and NBC networks between September 2002 and February 2003 found that all but thirty-four stories originated from three government agencies – the so-called 'golden triangle' of The White House, the Pentagon and the State Department (Snow 2003: 46). In addition, important or symbolic speeches such as the president's State of the Union Addresses and commemoration ceremonies for the victims were broadcast live to the nation and often watched by tens of millions of Americans; 80 million Americans, for example, watched President Bush's Address to Congress and the Nation on September 20, 2001. Overall, administration officials were given a great many opportunities to speak directly to the public, without any interference or mediation by the media.

Third, studies show that in the mainstream media critical voices and alternative viewpoints were largely excluded and marginalised. For example, one major study of TV, magazines and newspapers showed that in the immediate post-September 11 period, stories which were critical of the administration made up only around 10 per cent of media coverage; in addition, nearly two-thirds of all press coverage was predominantly pro-American policy (Schechter 2003: 56–65; Hertsgaard 2002: 103). Crucially, most editorials were sympathetic to, if not directly supportive of the administration's position. It was not uncommon to see op-ed pieces in newspapers such as the *New York Times* which directly reproduced the language of officials. Thomas Friedman's columns for example, at times reproduced the official discourse almost verbatim: 'this attack was the **Pearl Harbor** of World War III'; 'This is a **cancer**'; 'a **tumor** like Osama bin Laden can grow in its midst and then **metastasize** into the world and threaten us'; 'Their terrorism is driven by pure **hatred**'; 'we must now fight a war against terrorists who are **crazy** and **evil**'; 'we will do whatever it takes to defend **our way of life**'; 'You, bin Laden, are nothing but a hijacker – **a hijacker of Islam**'; 'America is under attack. We're fighting for **our self-defense**. We are fighting to maintain the free and open society that is the basis of all **that is good in America**'; 'we see the war in Afghanistan as **a just war** to end terrorism. [...] For us, this is **good versus evil**' (Friedman 2002: 33–69). This kind of mimicry of the official discourse with its direct reproduction of the main narratives and discursive constructions was and still is regularly observable in American newspapers (see Hanson 2002; Kern *et al.* 2003).

In many instances, even the existence of opposition to administration policies was barely acknowledged: major newspapers had only small inside articles on anti-war activities, and between September 15 and December 15, 2001, domestic anti-war protests were mentioned only once by ABC News and NBC News, twice by CNN and three times by CBS News (Nacos 2002: 159). In a more sinister development, studies have since revealed that sectors of the media consistently misrepresented opinion poll data in order to maintain the impression that the war against Afghanistan was more widely supported than it actually was (see Miller 2002). In essence, those who dissented from the mainstream view and opposed the military response to the terror attacks gained very little access to media forums; alternative discourses were effectively excluded and silenced. At times, peace groups were refused commercial airtime on the major networks even when they attempted to buy it (Rampton and Stauber 2003: 172). In other words, the media was (and still is) crucial for both transmitting and reproducing the discourse in a relatively unmediated fashion, for symbolically and discursively reinforcing the administration's language and for preventing alternative discourses from being heard. Given such open collaboration between America's political elite and the press, it is not surprising that the language, assumptions, perceptions and knowledge of the 'war on terrorism' gained such widespread currency so swiftly and became embedded into domestic and foreign policy.

The reasons for such acquiescence by the media lie in a number of important developments. First, it is due to well-established newsgathering processes in the reporting of terrorism and foreign policy stories in general. As mentioned above, and confirmed by a great many studies, the media most often allows official sources to make the decisions about what should be called 'terrorism' in the first place – as opposed to 'hijackings' or 'bombings', for example (Livingston 1994: 65–80). Perhaps more importantly, standard operating procedures for reporters assume that official sources are legitimate, credible and reliable, and that the media principle of 'objective reporting' requires consulting government officials.

For their part, government sources are often the most ready and willing to provide regular, scheduled and often pre-packaged flows of information. Obviously, their position as dominant news sources allows officials to influence greatly the subsequent form of stories about terrorism. Some have argued that there exists a 'mediaocracy' where 'the media is no longer a separate fourth estate functioning as an independent watchdog, but, rather it is an active participant in the policy debate', where 'government and media tend to synergize and interact with shared assumptions and common messages, particularly on national security' (Schechter 2003: xxvii).

The docility of the media is also partly the result of structural changes within the industry itself, particularly accelerating corporate consolidation. Ten corporations now control more than half of America's media outlets, most importantly, every news organisation that reaches a mass audience – this includes newspapers, radio and television stations, magazines, books, music and the internet. The consequence of this monopolisation is that the media tends to be supportive of the prevailing political and economic system and the foreign and domestic policies flowing from it. Reporters and editors tend to produce news that conforms to the views of their corporate owners (not surprising considering that corporations like General Electric, a leading Pentagon contractor, also owns NBC). In addition, the profit motive now dominates media organisations to a degree never seen before, making news a kind of commodity. The commodification of news can greatly affect the newsgathering process – the fear of libel or opposition from advertisers can kill certain kinds of stories, the pressure for profits has seen cutbacks in newsrooms and the scaling back of foreign bureaus – and programming decisions – 'info-tainment' and 'terror-tainment' are more profitable than straight news or in-depth reporting. These processes have undoubtedly had a chilling effect and have undermined the media's critical edge and independence. Externally, the rise of global and instant communication and the need for cost-cutting in an increasingly competitive market has dramatically increased the speed of the news cycle, which in turn has greatly reduced the lead-in time for stories. Operationally, this has further increased media reliance on official sources; it is much quicker and cheaper to call an administration press officer for information than to research a story from scratch – especially in the case of foreign news.

Overall, the effect of these processes is to make the media highly susceptible to being 'managed' by powerful official sources. This is exactly what occurred after the terror attacks when the media acted more like stenographers to power than a Fourth Estate watchdog (Hertsgaard 2002: 93; McChesney 2002: 135). For its part, the Bush administration has employed a mix of overt as well as more calculating and underhanded attempts at media enlistment and censorship; only a few of the many instances of such behaviour can be mentioned here. In the initial phase of the 'war on terrorism', it is well known that in November 2001,

White House advisers met with the heads of Viacom, Disney, MGM, Fox, Warner Bros and Paramount to discuss how the Hollywood machine could be retrofitted for more explicit propaganda purposes (Lewis *et al.* 2002: 126). During the military campaigns, the Pentagon's refusal to allow reporters to accompany troops in Afghanistan, and the practice of embedding reporters in the Iraq operation, was a blatant attempt to censor information reported during the fighting. When a *Washington Post* war correspondent tried to investigate civilian casualties in a village in Afghanistan, he was prevented at gunpoint by American troops from reaching the site (Hertsgaard 2002: 103). And, in early October 2001, Condoleeza Rice asked the media not to show unedited videos by bin Laden, ostensibly because they could have contained coded messages to his followers; two weeks earlier though, the administration had encouraged the showing of a bin Laden video that displayed his prior knowledge of the September 11, 2001 attacks (Nacos 2002: 152). The extent to which the media meekly deferred to administration control can be seen in the glaring failure to mount a significant protest at government interference and press restrictions. It can also be seen in the shameful failure to challenge the USA Patriot Act, despite its clear dangers to American freedoms; a survey by FAIR showed that NBC and CBS did not run a single story on the potential impact of the act on civil liberties in the lead-up to its adoption (Maxwell 2002: 247; see also Hertsgaard 2002).

In addition to the overt efforts to control reporting, there were also a number of indirect methods for enforcing media discipline. In December 2001, Attorney General John Ashcroft directed remarks towards critics who questioned his proposed restrictions on civil liberties: 'Your tactics only aid terrorists – for they erode our national unity and diminish our resolve. They give ammunition to America's enemies, and pause to America's friends' (quoted in Rampton and Stauber 2003: 167). These warnings echoed those of White House press secretary Ari Fleischer, who told journalists that they 'need to watch what they say, what they do.' Combined with conservative media pundits who suggested that the media was willing to compromise national security, a climate of intimidation increased the pressure on the mainstream media to mute any criticism of American policies. Other veiled warnings came in the form of threats to cut reporters out of the loop and deny them access to officials. Added together, these actions provided powerful incentives to report favourably on the conduct of the 'war on terrorism'. Actually, this situation was not necessarily unique to the post-September 11, 2001 period. Earlier governments, particularly the Reagan administration, had used identical tactics in their dealings with the media (see Livingston 1994; Rampton and Stauber 2003), and in 1950, President Truman appealed to newspaper editors to enlist in the struggle against communism and back the cold war with a 'campaign for truth' (see Schechter 2003: 131–2).

At the same time, the media responded to the crisis (and to government attempts at manipulation) with a great deal of patriotism, self-censorship, oversensitivity to public opinion and deference to authority (see Louw 2003). Examples of such behaviour were legion; as before, only a few can be mentioned here. In displays of unbridled patriotism, television networks prominently displayed American flags in their framing banners; news anchors and correspondents wore pins of the flag or red, white and blue ribbons on their lapels; and promos for news programmes featured photos of soldiers accompanied by renditions of 'The Star-Spangled Banner'. In an example of self-censorship, Walter Isaacson, the chairman of CNN, issued a memo to his American staff not to mention civilian casualties in Afghanistan without also recalling American terror victims, for fear of appearing unpatriotic (Schechter 2003: xlii). A separate memo from the network's head of standards and practices, Rick Davis, actually suggested the kinds of language CNN anchors could use: 'We must keep in mind, after seeing reports like this from Taliban-controlled areas, that these U.S. military actions are in response to a terrorist attack that killed close to 5,000 innocent people in the U.S.', or 'The Pentagon has repeatedly stressed that it is trying to minimise civilian casualties in Afghanistan, even as the Taliban regime continues to harbour terrorists who are connected to the September 11 attacks that claimed thousands of innocent lives in the U.S.' The memo went on to say that 'Even though it may start to sounding rote, it is important that we make this point each time' (quoted in Solomon 2003: 252). Note also how the language reproduces the official discourse; it speaks of the 'innocent' Americans killed (the myth of innocence) and the military's efforts to 'minimise civilian casualties' (the just war injunction of proportionality).

Other examples of this kind of self-censorship include the overnight dismissal of two newspaper columnists who had questioned why President Bush did not return to Washington during the crisis on September 11, 2001, and the public apology by television personality Bill Maher, after he commented that if the terrorists were anything, they were not cowards (Hertsgaard 2002: 46). There were also instances of advertisers pulling advertisements from programmes which contained what were perceived to be unpatriotic and insensitive comments; this sent shockwaves through the television industry and immediately had a chilling effect on expressing views that were not in accord with the official line. On the radio, a number of Clear Channel stations pulled the *Dixie Chicks* from their play lists after the lead singer made a disparaging remark about George Bush at a London concert, and then fired two disc jockeys when they defied the ban (Rampton and Stauber 2003: 170). Such actions – in addition to the heavy-handed efforts of the administration – sent a powerful message to everyone in the mainstream media that anything less than total adherence to the official line would be met with professional and public ostracism.

None of this is meant to imply that there were no examples of critical journalism in America, or that media reproduction of the discourse has been uniformly maintained; clearly, there were examples and by late-2004 the media appeared to be a little less deferential towards the administration. Additionally, there is a vibrant alternative media in America that retains a healthy scepticism, independence and critical attitude towards officialdom. In the immediate aftermath of the terrorist attacks however, the media played a mainly supportive role in entrenching the rhetoric of the 'war on terrorism' in public discourse. For the reasons explained above – the historic ties between the political establishment and the media, patterns of media ownership, journalistic investigative procedures – it is unlikely that any serious deviation from the central narratives will take place in the near future. Even if debates arise in the media over the tactics of the war (whether it was right to attack Iraq; whether more should have been done to counter the threat from al Qaeda), it is doubtful that the more fundamental issues about the 'war on terrorism' will become the focus of a full public debate.

The role of other social actors

Although the media clearly played the most important role in disseminating the administration's discourse, other important social actors have also contributed to the discursive reproduction of the 'war on terrorism'. In this section, I want briefly to look at the roles of the academy, think-tanks and foundations and religious groups. Each of these actors is an authoritative discursive site in society: the academy, for example, has an important function in explaining and interpreting politics to students, as well as (sometimes) acting as critic to society; think-tanks and foundations seek to educate the public and influence policy; and religion plays an important role in mediating between the dictates of individual conscience and the demands of civic duty. Thus, when academics or church leaders make statements that reproduce or support the 'war on terrorism', it lends legitimacy and force to the words of officials. If there was space, we could also examine the role of schools, popular fiction, the new media and foreign leaders such as Tony Blair, in spreading and disseminating the discourse. Suffice it to say that a great many social actors and institutions have deliberately or inadvertently amplified the discourse, thereby contributing to its power and success. In part, this is due to the inbuilt nature of discourses: as the language becomes absorbed and accepted by listeners, they unconsciously begin to reproduce it themselves.

Since the terrorist attacks in September 2001, a great many academics have publicly stated their support of the Bush administration and have used their position to reproduce and disseminate the official discourse to their own audiences. Whether it is deliberate – due to ideological agreement with the official policies and/or a desire to support the administration – or inadvertent – due to uncritical absorption of the language – there is no doubt that support for the discourse from such authoritative sources greatly helps in its promotion. An example of an overt attempt was *What We're Fighting For: A Letter from America*, issued in February 2002 under the auspices of the Institute for American Values and signed by sixty prominent scholars. In the report, the authors endorse the administration's counter-terrorist policies and in the process, reproduce a great deal of the official discourse itself. For example, the document is replete with references to the 'slaughter of **innocent** persons', the threat to 'our entire **way of living**', the 'unmitigated global **evil**' of terrorism, the '**acts of war**' on September 11, 2001, the '**just war**' being waged against the terrorists, and the '**universal** moral truths' that 'are in fact the shared inheritance of humankind' which America is purportedly defending. Its concluding paragraphs even more explicitly reflect the official discourse:

> [T]here are times when the first and most important reply to **evil** is to stop it. There are times when waging war is not only morally permitted, but morally necessary, as a response to calamitous acts of violence, **hatred**, and injustice. This is one of those times.

> [T]he mass murders of September 11 demonstrated, arguably for the first time, that this movement now possesses not only the openly stated desire, but also the capacity and expertise – including possible access to, and willingness to use, **chemical, biological and nuclear weapons** – to wreak massive, horrific devastation on its intended targets. Those who slaughtered more than 3,000 persons on September 11 and who, by their own admission, want nothing more than to do it again, constitute **a clear and present danger** to all people of good will **everywhere in the world**, not just the United States. Such acts are a pure example of naked aggression against **innocent** human life, **a world-threatening evil** that clearly **requires the use of force** to remove it. Organized killers with global reach now **threaten all of us**. In the name of **universal human morality**, and fully conscious of the restrictions and requirements of a **just war**, we support our government's, and our society's, decision to use force of arms against them. (Institute for American Values 2002)

In effect, the language employed by these academics reproduces the primary narratives of good versus evil, the hatred of the terrorists, innocent Americans, the universal values that America is protecting, the catastrophic threat and danger posed by terrorism and the necessity for a just war against them.

A great many other academics have also reproduced the discourse in their own works, often deliberately, but sometimes unconsciously. There is not the space to provide more than a few short examples here. Professor Richard Falk, a highly regarded scholar of international law and, paradoxically, a long-standing opponent of previous US military actions, has argued that the 'war on terrorism' is 'the first truly **just war** since **World War II**' (Falk 2001), in part because 'the United States had **little choice** but to respond in a **war** mode' as 'Osama bin Laden and al-Qaeda **cannot be deterred**' (Falk 2002: 326, 330). This language reproduces several of the primary motifs of the discourse: its just war status, the

World War II 'good war' narrative and the just war argument of last resort. It is reproduced again in the same 2002 volume in a chapter entitled 'How to fight a just war', in which Jean Elshtain argues that the reason why America has launched a war against terrorism has 'nothing to do with American mega-lomania, or errant nationalism, or narrow pride. It has to do with **a just response to aggression** and **the responsibility** that **a great nation** with a preponderance of power, but one nonetheless vulnerable for all that, must feel toward her own citizens, first, but toward the possibility of a measure of peace **for all humankind** as well' (Elshtain 2002: 269). In an echo of the official discourse, it is argued that the terrorist attacks were an act of war, the response is a good and just war and America has an historic calling to save the world. A final example of an academic reproduction of the discourse comes from Professor Richard Betts, director of the Institute of War and Peace Studies at Columbia University. His 2002 article speaks about the '**irrational evil** of terrorism' and how the attack on Afghanistan 'constitutes retaliation, punishing the Taliban for shielding al Qaeda and sending a warning to other potential state sponsors. It is also **active defense**, whittling down the ranks of potential perpetrators by killing and capturing members of the Islamist international brigades committed to jihad against the United States' (Betts 2002: 24, 32). This echoes the good versus evil narrative, as well as the just war construction that the 'war on terrorism' is at heart an act of self-defence.

Another important group of social and political actors who have deliberately and successfully reproduced the official discourse in the public domain has been the well-funded and overlapping network of conservative think-tanks and foundations, such as the Heritage Foundation, the Project for the New American Century (PNAC), the American Enterprise Institute for Public Policy Research, the Council on Foreign Relations and the RAND Corporation, among many others. These groups publish books, magazines and websites, e-mail bulletins to thousands of supporters, hold conferences and public seminars, testify before Congress, offer expert consultation to government committees, lobby officials and are highly professional in ensuring that their leading 'experts' appear with great regularity on television and in print. For example, in the year up to August 2002, the neoconservative Washington Institute for Near East Policy had fourteen op-ed articles printed in the most prominent American newspapers including the *New York Times*, the *Washington Post*, the *Wall Street Journal*, the *Los Angeles Times* and *New Republic* (see Parmar forthcoming). Considering that some of the key architects of the 'war on terrorism' belong to this network of foundations – Paul Wolfowitz, Donald Rumsfeld, and Dick Cheney, for example, are all founding members of PNAC – it is not surprising that they actively amplify the discourse. A visit to any of their websites provides numerous examples of the reproduction and amplification of the official discourse. Apart from actively promoting the discourse, a number of these institutions have also taken on a more sinister role as the gatekeepers of the administration's counter-terrorism approach. The group Americans for Victory Over Terrorism, for example, is committed to monitoring and publicly exposing academics, reporters and politicians who deviate from the primary narratives – to rooting out the 'enemy within' (defined as those who oppose the administration's anti-terrorism strategy). Similarly, the Middle East Forum targets universities to correct 'inaccurate Middle Eastern curricula in American education' by uncovering 'biases' and 'basic errors' by 'irresponsible' professors (ibid.).

The most well-known attack against perceived opponents of the 'war on terrorism' came from the American Council of Trustees and Alumni (ACTA), an education watchdog committee formed by Lynne Cheney, the wife of Vice President Dick Cheney. ACTA published a report in November 2001 entitled *Defending Civilisation: How our Universities are Failing America.* The report listed what it claimed were over 100 examples of a 'blame America first' attitude, and in a throwback to McCarthyism it also included a blacklist of the guilty academics in an appendix. It went on to argue that 'Rarely did professors publicly mention **heroism**, rarely did they discuss the difference between **good and evil**, the nature of Western political order or the virtue of a **free** society. Their public messages were short on **patriotism** and long on self-flagellation' (quoted in Silberstein 2002: 138). The universities were thus the 'weak link' in America's response to terror. The report stated that the war on terrorism is also the defence of civilisation, and that 'when a nation's intellectuals are unwilling to defend its civilization, they give aid and comfort to its adversaries' (quoted in Silberstein 2002: 140). The dominant narratives of the 'war on terrorism' are amplified and reproduced even as alternative perspectives are attacked.

As I previously noted, America is an extremely religious country and has a sizeable Christian constituency; it is not uncommon to see politicians employing religious narratives to appeal to the religious vote, and there are strong political ties between the religious right and the neo-conservative movement. George Bush and John Ashcroft, among others in the administration, openly declare that they are 'born-again' Christians. Given the infusion of religious motifs and narratives within the discourse itself, it is unsurprising that some church leaders have eagerly embraced the language of counter-terrorism. As above, there is only the space for a few examples of religious amplification of the official discourse. In early 2002, *Christianity Today*, a leading American evangelical magazine, published a report about a meeting of the Society of Christian Ethics. The language used in the article is revealing:

> The consensus of 350 professional ethicists at an international conference was that the conflict fits the **just war** principles articulated by Augustine ...
>
> Daniel Lee, professor of ethics at Augustana College in Illinois, said that ... bombing Taliban and Al Qaeda forces is justified on the moral grounds of **self-**

defense. Destroying the Taliban is the lesser of two **evils**, he said, adding, 'Should **Hitler** have been allowed to overrun Europe?'

U.S. methods fit the **just war** principle of discrimination, said John Kelsay, professor of ethics at Florida State University in Tallahassee ... Kelsay said **the U.S. has used smart bombs and avoided targeting civilians**. (Religion News Service 2002)

As might be expected, Christian leaders were often preoccupied with the just war status of the 'war on terrorism'; similar debates were also widespread in religious circles in the run-up to the Iraq war. On the whole, conservative sections of the church amplified the administration's characterisation of the good and just war against terrorism. Even in this brief report, there is reference to both traditional just war theory (proportionality and self-defence as defining criteria) and the 'good war' narrative of the fight against Hitler.

Another example comes from Richard Land, president of the Southern Baptist Convention's Ethics & Religious Liberty Commission and presidential appointee to the US Commission on International Religious Freedom. In a widely reported article, Land speaks about 'the **act of war** that was perpetrated on the United States on Sept. 11'. He then goes on to reproduce many of the primary constructions of the official discourse:

> One of the many examples of the moral difference between the United States and its allies, i.e. **the civilized world**, and our opponents, the forces of **barbarism and terror**, is that we are taking great pains **to minimize civilian, noncombatant casualties** and **we are targeting only legitimate military targets**.

> When all the diplomatic efforts to secure **justice** fail, **the only way** to safeguard our nation is to strike at the source of this **evil**.

> The allied military response that began Oct. 7 was **a defensive action**. [...] We must remove their safe havens and camps that allow them to strike at a time of their choosing against **innocent men, women and children**. If you want to get rid of **the malaria of international terrorism**, you just can't swat mosquitoes; you have to **drain the swamp**. (Land 2001)

This article is interesting in that Land succeeds in reproducing several of the main discursive constructions of the official discourse: the meta-narratives of civilization versus barbarism and good versus evil; the just war doctrines of proportionality and self-defence; the myth of American innocence; and the essentialising of the inhuman terrorists in their malarial swamp. The use of this kind of language is fairly widespread, especially in conservative Christian circles. Pat Robertson, a key figure in the Christian Coalition and one-time presidential candidate, speaks publicly about the need to 'bring to **justice** known terrorist operatives'; the fact that America is 'at **war**'; the threat of '**biological**, **nuclear and chemical warfare**'; the need for the '**united** action of all of us'; and the certainty that America is 'going to win the battle against terror' (Robertson, March 25, 2002).

In religious societies like America, churches and church leaders are authoritative social actors. They act as mediators between the political and personal sphere, providing trustworthy interpretations of national events and guidance about correct political beliefs. In turn, adherents attach great significance to the words of their spiritual leaders. The success of the 'war on terrorism' therefore, is in part due to its reproduction and amplification by many of America's important religious figures. The fact that the discourse originates from a Christian president and a conservative Christian world-view, and that it is permeated by religious narratives and motifs, makes its amplification that much more uncontested and straightforward.

It is important to note that we could also have examined the written materials used in schools to explain the 'war on terrorism', or the language of talk-back radio hosts, military recruitment campaigns, city councillors, business leaders, judges or any other influential or authoritative source. As with the actors examined here, there is little doubt that we would probably find that the discourse of the 'war on terrorism' has been accepted, absorbed and reproduced by a significant proportion of those actors too. None of this is meant to imply that any of the groups speaks with a single voice or that there is no resistance to the 'war on terrorism'. There are a great many academics and schoolteachers, think-tanks and foundations, religious leaders and other prominent individuals who actively oppose the 'war on terrorism' and who are working to challenge the official discourse; I have quoted many of them in this book. My argument is simply that there are likely as many, if not more, authoritative groups and individuals who actively promote and reproduce the discourse, and that in combination with politicians and the collaboration of the media, this discourse of counter-terrorism has become the dominant national security narrative in American political life today. My concern is that the daily reproduction and institutionalisation of the discourse will make it very difficult to dislodge for some time to come.

Conclusion

In this book, I have tried to show that the discourse of the 'war on terrorism' operates on many levels. At its most basic level, the language used by officials is an attempt to convince the public that a 'war' against all forms of terrorism is necessary, reasonable, inherently good and winnable. The four primary messages it seeks to convey are: the September 11, 2001 attacks were an act of war; the terrorists are inhuman barbarians who deserve to be eradicated from civilised society; the threat posed by terrorism is catastrophic and it is only rational to respond with all due force; and the American-led war against terrorism is by definition a good and just war. In this most rudimentary sense, the language accompanying the 'war on terrorism' is a public relations or propaganda exercise; it is designed to 'sell' the policies of counter-terrorism. In this regard, there is no doubt that it has been highly successful – at least within American society, the primary target audience. By any measure, it is a consistent, reassuring and appealing message which clearly resonates with a traumatised and uncertain society.

At a much deeper level, it is at the same time a highly complex and intertwined set of narratives and rhetorical strategies that aims to reinforce the authority of the state and reify its disciplinary practices. Its objective is to establish what counts as real knowledge, to set the limits of common sense, to demarcate the terms of the debate, and to exclude alternative paradigms and approaches. In this sense, it is more than just the attempt to 'spin' government policy for public consumption; it is actually an exercise of power through the deployment of language. And in this too, the American government has succeeded beyond its wildest expectations; not only does the public support the administration's version of reality, but so do the Democrats, the mainstream media and a great many other important social actors. As a consequence, the administration has been able to construct and institutionalise an approach to counter-terrorism with substantive political support and without any significant opposition. As with the cold war paradigm, the 'war on terrorism' will most likely endure for decades, especially if it is continually reproduced and amplified across society by a significant portion of authoritative social actors.

This understanding of the counter-terrorism discourse – as a political act, not just a rhetorical act – has important implications for society at large and for democratic politics in particular. It means that the space for discussion has been marked out and restricted before it even begins; that there are things that cannot be spoken, words that cannot be uttered; and that there is only really one conclusion to be drawn. Within the confines of the discourse, for example, it makes no sense to discuss the lessons of earlier struggles against terrorism by other democratic states, because this is a 'new' war against a 'new' enemy using 'new' weapons. Nor is it possible to suggest that political dialogue might be an option, or that 'war' might not be the best way to deal with terrorism, or that the treatment of terrorist suspects is unethical, or that the threat is vastly overblown, or that winning is not even possible in a conflict of this kind. Within the logic of the discourse, using its language and its inbuilt assumptions, such statements are non sequiturs – they are nonsensical fictions. Employing the language of counter-terrorism, only one conclusion appears logical, reasonable and commonsensical: we need to fight a global war against terrorism. The success of the discourse therefore, can be measured by the absence of informed, rigorous and vibrant debate about terrorism and the response of the democratic state; it can be measured by the diminution of real politics; it can be measured by the degree to which individuals can think in a language other than the language of the 'war on terrorism'. The mental straightjacket that has been engendered by the discourse must be countered, and the political space to question and challenge the discourse must be recaptured. Resisting the discourse is not an act of disloyalty; it is an act of political self-determination; and it is absolutely necessary if we are to avoid another stupefying period of fear and violence like the cold war.

Conclusion:
politics, violence and resistance

> When some men suffer unjustly ... it is the fate of those who witness their suffering to suffer the shame of it. (J.M. Coetzee, *Waiting for the Barbarians*)

I EMBARKED ON THIS BOOK as a study into the causes of political violence. I wanted to understand how societies such as America and Britain, which pride themselves on their liberal democratic cultures, could in the space of less than two years actively support or at least acquiesce to a massive campaign of counter-terrorist violence involving destructive military assaults on two of the world's poorest countries, political assassinations, aid and support to dictators, the torture of prisoners and the systematic violation and erosion of deeply cherished civic rights. What could induce ordinary citizens to participate – at least tacitly – in such sustained and pervasive violence which has by now killed tens of thousands of other ordinary people in Afghanistan, Iraq and elsewhere? Research undertaken into the causes of internal wars (another kind of political violence) in countries such as Rwanda and Bosnia, pointed towards the pivotal role played by language in the construction of political violence, in particular the war-based discourses of national leaders (see Jackson forthcoming). My initial aim was to see if similar processes were occurring in America as those that had occurred in the lead-up to the Balkans conflict; to see if the causes of the Rwandan genocide were in any way comparable with the causes of the 'war on terrorism'.

The simple but disturbing answer was positive: the causes are broadly similar. Through a careful analysis of the official language of counter-terrorism, I discovered that the discursive strategies employed by the American and British administrations to construct the 'war on terrorism' were the same as those used by leaders and political entrepreneurs in these other conflicts. As Charles Townshend has expressed it, constructing political violence of any kind – war, revolution, ethnic cleansing, terrorism or counter-terrorism – involves a distinct process:

> In the modern world, certainly, the ethical mechanism by which ordinary people have been able to set aside pity and remorse in order to kill other ordinary people has been *symbolic generalisation* – the smothering of the victims' individual human qualities by their collective identity (whether religion, class, race, or ethnicity). Far from being at all monstrous (in the sense of unusual), this kind of stereotyping powered most, if not all, of the wars, genocide, and violent revolutionary struggles of the twentieth century and remains the common currency of nationalist discourse and the motor of ethnic cleansing. (Townshend 2002: 16; my emphasis)

In each instance of 'symbolic generalisation', including the 'war on terrorism', the same discursive practices can be observed: the creation of a sense of exceptional grievance and victim-hood; the demonisation and dehumanisation of an enemy 'other'; the manufacture of a catastrophic threat and danger which demands immediate and forceful action; and the justification and legitimisation of pre-emptive (or preventive) counter-violence. When these messages are repeated endlessly through the media, in university lecture halls and churches, through laws, by institutional practices and in daily conversations – when society is saturated with the same words over and over – ordinary people are persuaded to go to war and to stand by when human rights are abused. The 'war on terrorism', like other kinds of political violence, is not a natural or normal response to objective conditions or events; nor is it simply an inevitable response to the actions of others. It is rather, a totalising discourse which has been deliberately, and in some senses, artificially, created to make people who would otherwise be circumscribed by normal social codes of non-violence, tolerance and human rights, complicit or even willing participants in a massive project of counter-terrorist violence. It is a political and social construction, an edifice built on language and discursive practice.

The current prominence of the 'war on terrorism' – its domination of public political discourse – poses three grave dangers to the functioning of political life and democratic society. At the most fundamental level, the construction of large-scale political violence of any kind entails the destruction of the moral consensus and the collapse of the moral community – and its replacement with discourses of victim-hood, hatred of the 'other', fear and counter-violence. Once a society embraces these new political narratives, once it venerates its grievances and truly hates and fears an enemy 'other', public and political morality is quickly lost in the maze of national security expediencies. There is no starker illustration of western society's current moral vacuity than the serious public debate about torturing terrorist suspects – not to mention its all-too-common practice by America and its allies. This is the moral mathematics of Hiroshima, where '9-11' (the new 'ground zero') represents Pearl Harbor. In this calcuation, if the torture/nuclear incineration of thousands of evil terrorists/treacherous Japanese will save American lives by preventing another 9-11/Pearl Harbor, then it is acceptable behaviour. As Slavenka Drakulic expresses it, 'once the concept of "otherness" takes root, the unimaginable becomes possible' (Drakulic quoted in Neuffer 2001:32). The once unimaginable has in fact, become normal in our society and we see it all around: in the failure to demand investigation into documented war crimes and atrocities committed by Coalition forces in Afghanistan and Iraq; in the silence over the gross mistreatment of terrorist suspects, especially the legal minors (children) or those who are interrogated and tortured for years and then released without charge; in the broadening victimisation and discrimination against the Muslim/Arab 'other' by the authorities and society at large; in the often inhuman treatment of immigrants and asylum seekers; in the lack of protest at the policies of assassination and extra-judicial killing, or the brutality of the occupation of Iraq; and in the widespread acquiescence to the insidious erosion of long-held political and civil rights domestically.

The simple reason for this tacit complicity in the construction of military and structural violence is that these kinds of all encompassing and smothering discourses destabilise the moral community and replace non-violent political interaction with suspicion, fear, hatred, chauvinism and an impulse to defend violently the 'imagined community'. In addition, they automatically foreclose certain kinds of thought, simply because the language with which to frame doubts or question official justifications no longer exists or is inaccessible. While some individuals may initially feel unease at pictures of abused and humiliated 'terrorist' suspects at Camp X-Ray, of tortured Iraqi prisoners or dead Afghan civilians, they have no language or frame of reference in which to articulate those doubts. As time goes by, and when the discourse has been effectively absorbed by society, they may jettison such feelings altogether and consider the harsh treatment of suspects or the 'collateral damage' from bombing campaigns to be both justified and morally acceptable. Certainly, this process of destabilising the moral codes of individuals has already taken place among many in the armed forces. The pictures of abused Iraqi prisoners in April 2004 which sent shockwaves around the world were in this regard, not unexpected; they were the direct consequence of a discourse that constructs the enemy 'other' as inhuman and evil. Most Americans still feel the 'war on terrorism' is going well; meanwhile, the moral uncertainty they feel is the direct result of the discourse of counter-terrorism.

This is also an example of the well-known mimetic nature of violence – the instinctual psychological tendency to respond to an act of violence with identical or greater violence, to mimic the attacker – which has been a feature of virtually every war and counter-terrorist campaign. Townshend argues that, 'Probably the biggest hazard inherent in reactions to terrorism is the impulse towards imitation' (Townshend 2002: 114). History is replete with examples of just such mimetic counter-terrorist violence: Israel's targeted killings and assassinations mimic Palestinian attacks; in Northern Ireland the British security services mimicked the IRA when it too began killing members of the para-militaries; the 'dirty wars' by the Argentine and Spanish governments mimicked those of their opponents; and during Reagan's war against terrorism, CIA officers in Beirut tortured suspects to death during interrogation and then sponsored a car bomb aimed at Sheik Fadlallah in revenge for the Marine barracks bombing – it missed the Sheik but killed 92 bystanders and injured more than 250 others (Wills 2003: 56, 87). Within the atmosphere created by the present discourse of counter-terrorism it passes almost unnoticed that both sides (the American administration and al Qaeda) are employing exactly the same discursive strategies – both appeal to victim-hood and grievance, both enlist religion as supreme justification, both frame the struggle as one of good versus evil, both demonise and dehumanise the other and both claim the mantle of a just/holy war/jihad. The result of this discursive mirroring is predictable: the killing of civilians without pity or remorse, whether by suicide bombers hoping to force the American military out of Iraq and Saudi Arabia or by US helicopter gunships attacking insurgents on the streets of Fallujah.

There is no escape from the fact that in America and Britain discrimination and the abuse of human rights has now been normalised and is considered an inevitable if regrettable part of the counter-terrorist effort, including judicial abuse, torture and war crimes; we are now firmly ensconced in a '*dirty* war on terrorism' both at home and abroad. This is a perilous position for a society supposedly built on the belief in human dignity, human rights and democratic participation. It implies that we have retreated from a universal and cosmopolitan vision of society to a particularistic, tribal vision; that we have bankrupted our moral vision of universal human rights and social inclusion in favour of a dubious sense of 'national' security. In the past, such narrow communitarian formulations of political life have led to debilitating cycles of inter-national violence, or at the very least, long periods of institutional and cultural racism against an 'enemy within'. The greatest danger of the current discourse is that we too become terrorists; and that as we demonise, dehumanise and brutalise the enemy 'other' it becomes a war *of* terrorisms, rather than a war *on* terrorism.

In a related sense, it is impossible to construct large-scale political violence – including counter-terrorism – without undermining the healthy functioning of inclusive politics and damaging democratic values. Similar campaigns against terrorism in countries such as Northern Ireland, Italy, Germany, Spain, Israel, Argentina and others, have already discovered this to their detriment. In every case, the institutions of public order – the police, the security services and the courts – were severely damaged by abuses and mistakes; Britain is still suffering under the shame of wrongly imprisoned IRA suspects and almost daily revelations about complicity in extra-judicial killings by the security forces. In every case, the practice of democratic politics was undermined. This is because, apart from destabilising society's moral consensus, the discourse and practice of counter-terrorism inevitably leads to the delegitimisation of dissent and the

183

narrowing of the discursive space for political debate. In large part, this is because fighting the 'enemy within' requires strict social discipline, patriotism, conformity, informers, loyalty pledges and the bifurcation of national life; it requires clear lines between good and evil, between self and other, citizen and foreigner, inside and outside – all of which is the antithesis of a healthy politics. The moral taxonomy of the language of good versus evil is by definition incompatible with democratic politics because it undermines the possibility of a loyal opposition (Aune 2003: 520; see also McGreal 2003). In a sense, it is the (re)construction of the 'national security state', which as we saw during the cold war, has little tolerance for dissent, political debate or the questioning of official policy.

The corrosive effects of the discourse are already plain to see: anti-globalisation protesters, academics, post-modernists, liberals, pro-choice activists, environmentalists and gay liberationists are accused of being aligned with the evil of terrorism and of undermining the nation's struggle against terrorism (see Campbell 2002); arms trade protesters are arrested under anti-terrorism legislation; blacklists of 'disloyal' professors, university departments, journalists, writers and commentators are posted on the internet and smear campaigns are launched against them; anti-administration voices are kept away from speaking at public events or in the media; and political opponents of government policy are accused of being traitors. It may not be the second coming of McCarthyism yet, but the space for debate and dissent is narrowing perceptibly and there is a definite chill in the body politic. No longer is criticism welcomed or debate encouraged; instead, political participation is redefined as 'pulling together', democracy is remade as 'unity of purpose'. There is a real danger that the 'war on terrorism' is expanding to become a 'war on dissent' or a 'war on politics'. Such a war, of course, can only result in the eventual death of participatory democracy, not in the destruction of terrorism.

A third danger is that the discursive straightjacket of the 'war on terrorism' prevents clear and creative thinking about alternative strategies and approaches; instead, it institutionalises an approach which has already proved to be counter-productive and damaging to the very institutions and values America and its allies are purportedly trying to protect. There is a genuine risk that the moral absolutism of the discourse induces political amnesia about the failures and lessons from other counter-terrorist campaigns (see Campbell 2002). For example, a clear lesson from other campaigns is that terrorism can never be defeated by military force or coercion alone; it only eases when political compromise takes place on the issues that instigated it. There are one or two exceptions to this: the Argentine military defeated a left-wing insurgency through a ruthless policy of murder, disappearance, torture and hurling hundreds of people out of helicopters over shark-infested waters. But this is perhaps the only such example, and in any case, it is a price far too high to pay. At the very least, the discourse is actually misconceiving and misunderstanding the nature of the threat and the strategies required to deal with it – it is poor 'threat assessment' and poor 'mission definition', to use military parlance. By deliberately obfuscating the underlying history and context of terrorism, the actual nature and causes of terrorism and the real motivations and aims of the terrorists (who are most certainly not sacrificing their lives in suicidal attacks simply for the sake of 'evil'), the search for more effective and long-term policy solutions is cauterised. By insisting on a false ahistoricity – it is a 'new' war, unlike any other – the possibility of learning relevant lessons from the past is obliterated.

Given the intellectual cul-de-sac of the 'war on terrorism', it is not surprising that the Bush administration's present policies are actually making terrorism worse and are intensifying those global conditions that encourage, nurture and sustain endemic violence. There is not the space here to fully explain the effects of current counter-terrorism policies on international relations and global violence; besides, many excellent books have already been written on this subject (see Boggs 2003; Burbach and Clarke 2002; Callinicos 2003; Chomsky 2002; El Fadl 2002; Mahajan 2002, 2003; Sardar and Davies 2002; Scraton 2002). It will suffice to summarise a few rather obvious points. First, the launch of a global 'war on terrorism' has played directly into the hands of the terrorists by giving them the recognition and attention they so desperately sought; it dignifies their struggle (they are fighting a 'war' against a superpower), rewards their persistence (despite being only a small group of individuals, they have indelibly altered the world's most powerful countries and the conduct of international relations) and therefore encourages them to continue with similar actions. As a consequence, it seems clear that the 'war on terrorism' is already entrenching an ever-deepening cycle of violence and counter-violence similar to that which has already occurred at a micro-level in Israel, Chechnya, Kashmir, Colombia and Spain (to name a few), where neither side can win decisively but no party is willing to abandon the military option. Second, in strategic terms, there are good reasons for thinking that American actions in Afghanistan and Iraq have created a whole new generation of terrorists and made terrorism an even greater international problem by scattering terrorist networks across many more countries and further decentralising their operations. There is also little doubt that these two wars have turned many moderate Muslims towards the extremist camp, fuelling anti-Americanism and providing potential terrorists with an even bigger sea in which to swim; they have also provided a new focus for terrorist activity and new zones of lawlessness and chaos where terrorists can operate more freely.

Other direct consequences of the 'war on terrorism' which are also likely to increase terrorism in the future include: the damage sustained to the institutions of international order and global governance, such as the United Nations and the International Criminal Court (ICC); the undermining of the accepted laws of war through the doctrine of pre-emptive (preventive) strikes against states harbouring terrorists and through the failure to uphold the Geneva Conventions regarding prisoners of war; the further destabilisation of regions where internal conflicts have now been subsumed under the mantle of the 'war on terrorism', such as Israel, Chechnya, Colombia, Kashmir and the Philippines; the support and aid provided to dictatorships willing to join the 'war on terrorism'; the misguided and poorly conceived support for Israel's recent policies; the continuation and expansion of American military bases into sensitive regions; the new arms race to develop national missile defence and new generation nuclear weapons; the diversion of resources from development aid and nation-building to military aid for allies; and the pursuit of oil politics and geo-strategic objectives in the Middle East and Caspian basin under the cover of national security. Every one of these policies increases the likelihood of future anti-American 'blowback', mounting regional violence and the intensification of global insecurity and injustice – the very conditions which breed hopelessness and the resort to terror in the first place. At the very least, these policies are obstacles to effective counter-terrorism. In one sense then, the 'war on terrorism' is already being lost; terrorists are far from being defeated and the world is no safer than it was before September 11, 2001.

Obviously, these observations raise something of a puzzle: why would the American government persist with an approach to counter-terrorism and a set of policies that is proving to be both ineffective and highly damaging to domestic political life? Surely these officials are not so ignorant or wilfully blind to such basic errors? There are a number of possible answers to this question, and in combination they go some way towards an explanation. In the first instance, it may be a case of bureaucratic lassitude and institutional inertia; the CIA, the FBI, and all other counter-terrorism bodies in the federal structure have always thought about terrorism in these terms, and have responded to the threat in similar ways for many decades. It is actually extremely common for large bureaucracies to become trapped in a single overarching view of the world and over-committed to set patterns of operation which have always worked in the past – Weber's so-called 'iron law of bureaucracy' or so-called 'groupthink'. Second, as some authors have noted, American foreign policy displays predictable patterns, and the response to certain kinds of national security crises is virtually reflexive (see Campbell 1998, 2002). That is, the American government has taken its cues about how to respond to certain situations from its own past responses; dominant modes of behaviour have become solidified as experiences accumulate. These policy modes are informed and reinforced, as we have seen, by deeply embedded political and cultural narratives and myths – the myth of the redemptive power of violence, the narratives of American exceptionalism and the notion of the good war. In other words, there are discursive continuities that determine the trajectory of future policies: the Bush (third) 'war on terrorism' is following a similar pattern to Clinton's (second) 'war on terrorism', which followed a similar course to Reagan's (first) 'war on terrorism'. More generally, the 'war on terrorism' will be constructed in a similar mode to the 'war on drugs' and the war against communism.

Aside from these aspects of institutional and ideological continuity, there are also more prosaic reasons for persisting with the present approach. The simple fact is that the 'war on terrorism', as it is currently constructed, benefits a great many powerful actors; there are vested interests in its continuation. Most obviously, the political elite in Washington can exercise a great deal more power, and can discipline opponents and justify a great many more actions, than would have been possible in the absence of a 'war on terrorism'. Many observers have also argued that the ongoing implementation of the neoconservative political agenda, seen most plainly in the Project for the New American Century, has largely been possible only under the cover of the 'war on terrorism' (see Boggs 2003; Callinicos 2003; El Fadl 2002; Mahajan 2002, 2003). In addition to the Washington power brokers, there are also a great many vested interests among the key institutions of government; the Pentagon, the CIA, the FBI, the Department of Homeland Security, the Department of Justice, and countless other security and law-enforcement agencies, have all seen their funding, power and prestige rise since the 'war on terrorism' was declared. It is clearly in the interests of all these agencies to sustain it as long as possible. Related to this, there are a great many corporations who are benefiting directly from increased government (and private) spending on counter-terrorism: all the defence contractors and military suppliers (such as Boeing, Raytheon, Lockheed Martin and Northrop Grumman); the pharmaceutical companies providing vaccines and decontamination equipment to the emergency services; private security companies working in Iraq; and some of the energy corporations. These industries all have powerful lobbyists in Washington. They contribute to presidential election campaigns and some of them, like Halliburton, are actually linked to members of the current administration. In sum, there are a powerful set of interlocking corporate and political interests in the current form that the 'war on terrorism' is taking.

Final thoughts

It is an example of the powerful and ubiquitous character of the discourse of the 'war on terrorism' that I find it necessary to reiterate that my purpose in writing this book was not to justify or excuse the terrorist attacks of September 11, 2001; or to oppose the wars against Afghanistan and Iraq simply because they were prosecuted by America; or to suggest that we should give in to terrorist demands; or that we should do nothing to fight terrorist violence. Nothing could be further from the truth. My primary aspiration was actually to engage in the search for effective counter-terrorism policies which would result in increased security and at the same time safeguard the democratic values we treasure. Following the WTC and Pentagon attacks, I was concerned that without a reasoned, reflective and wide-ranging political debate, the temptation would be simply to react with massive counter-violence (as America has previously), and that this would lead to even greater levels of terrorist activity, personal insecurity and global instability. I was concerned that the historical lessons of dealing with previous terrorist threats would be ignored, and that more creative and long-term solutions would be sidelined.

Unfortunately, this exact scenario has come to pass: the 'war on terrorism' – the *response* to the initial attacks – has made the situation far worse. Mistakes have been made because insufficient thought, study and debate was undertaken, and the opportunity to engage in a fundamental restructuring of international relations which might have prevented further atrocities has been squandered. In large part, it was (and still is) the nature of the political discourse that has prevented the consideration of alternative paradigms and approaches to counter-terrorism; the inbuilt logic of the language, and the privileging of only certain kinds of knowledge, has circumvented the kind of in-depth, rigorous and informed debate that a complex political challenge such as terrorism requires. It is my fear that unless we break out of the stultifying confines of the discourse, more effective policies will continue to prove elusive; unless or until both politicians and the wider public learn to speak and think in a language outside of the official rhetoric, we are condemned to live under an endless spiral of terrorist violence and state counter-violence. In a sense, the only hope of ever winning the 'war on terrorism' lies in ceasing to invest in its bankrupt philosophy, or speak in its morally corrosive language.

Beyond this self-interested concern for greater security however, there is another reason for opposing the language of counter-terrorism: it is damaging to our moral values and to our political life, and in the process, people are being violated, abused and killed. We are implicated in this monstrosity if we sit back and do nothing. As David Campbell expressed it, 'to live ethically, we must think and act politically' (Campbell 1998: 519). For this reason alone, I believe we have an ethical duty to resist the discourse, to deconstruct it at every opportunity and continually to interrogate the exercise of power. Importantly, the observation that large-scale political violence is a discursive construction is more than simply ontological; if a campaign of violence like the 'war on terrorism' can be socially and politically constructed, it can also be deconstructed. And, as I have demonstrated in this book, the discourse of counter-terrorism is vulnerable and full of instabilities; it contains contradictions, moral hypocrisies, deliberate deceptions, fabrications and misconceptions which can be exploited. Counter-hegemonic struggle and intellectual and ethical self-determination – for both individuals and society – is, I believe, possible. Alternative narratives are waiting to be discovered in independent study, in the alternative media, in the protest community, in sections of the church and the academy, in the voices of the developing world, in the countries where terrorism has been fought for decades already and in genuine debate and dialogue – if only we have the moral courage to act now. In the words of the protest community, 'another world is possible', but only if we – individually and collectively – build it ourselves.

Appendix:
official texts

Explanatory note: A number of important speeches and interviews are reproduced here, although some are abridged for reasons of space and relevance. Readers are encouraged to study them in their entirety in order to appreciate fully the kinds of discursive strategies and rhetorical forms that are employed in a single text.

Remarks by President George W. Bush after two planes crash into the World Trade Center, Emma Booker Elementary School, Sarasota, Florida, September 11, 2001

Ladies and gentlemen, this is a difficult moment for America. I, unfortunately, will be going back to Washington after my remarks. Secretary Rod Paige and the Lt. Governor will take the podium and discuss education. I do want to thank the folks here at Booker Elementary School for their hospitality.

Today we've had a national tragedy. Two airplanes have crashed into the World Trade Center in an apparent terrorist attack on our country. I have spoken to the Vice President, to the Governor of New York, to the Director of the FBI, and have ordered that the full resources of the federal government go to help the victims and their families, and to conduct a full-scale investigation to hunt down and to find those folks who committed this act.

Terrorism against our nation will not stand. And now if you would join me in a moment of silence. May God bless the victims, their families, and America. Thank you very much.

Statement by President George W. Bush, address to the nation, The Oval Office, September 11, 2001

Good evening. Today, our fellow citizens, our way of life, our very freedom came under attack in a series of deliberate and deadly terrorist acts. The victims were in airplanes, or in their offices; secretaries, businessmen and women, military and federal workers; moms and dads, friends and neighbors. Thousands of lives were suddenly ended by evil, despicable acts of terror.

The pictures of airplanes flying into buildings, fires burning, huge structures collapsing, have filled us with disbelief, terrible sadness, and a quiet, unyielding anger. These acts of mass murder were intended to frighten our nation into chaos and retreat. But they have failed; our country is strong.

A great people has been moved to defend a great nation. Terrorist attacks can shake the foundations of our biggest buildings, but they cannot touch the foundation of America. These acts shattered steel, but they cannot dent the steel of American resolve.

America was targeted for attack because we're the brightest beacon for freedom and opportunity in the world. And no one will keep that light from shining.

Today, our nation saw evil, the very worst of human nature. And we responded with the best of America – with the daring of our rescue workers, with the caring for strangers and neighbors who came to give blood and help in any way they could.

Immediately following the first attack, I implemented our government's emergency response plans. Our military is powerful, and it's prepared. Our emergency teams are working in New York City and Washington, D.C. to help with local rescue efforts.

Our first priority is to get help to those who have been injured, and to take every precaution to protect our citizens at home and around the world from further attacks.

The functions of our government continue without interruption. Federal agencies in Washington which had to be evacuated today are reopening for essential personnel tonight, and will be open for business tomorrow. Our financial institutions remain strong, and the American economy will be open for business, as well.

The search is underway for those who are behind these evil acts. I've directed the full resources of our intelligence and law enforcement communities to find those responsible and to bring them to justice. We will make no distinction between the terrorists who committed these acts and those who harbor them.

I appreciate so very much the members of Congress who have joined me in strongly condemning these attacks. And on behalf of the American people, I thank the many world leaders who have called to offer their condolences and assistance.

America and our friends and allies join with all those who want peace and security in the world, and we stand together to win the war against terrorism. Tonight, I ask for your prayers for all those who grieve, for the children whose worlds have been shattered, for all whose sense of safety and security has been threatened. And I pray they will be comforted by a power greater than any of us, spoken through the ages in Psalm 23: 'Even though I walk through the valley of the shadow of death, I fear no evil, for You are with me.'

This is a day when all Americans from every walk of life unite in our resolve for justice and peace. America has stood down enemies before, and we will do so this time. None of us will ever forget this day. Yet, we go forward to defend freedom and all that is good and just in our world.

Thank you. Good night, and God bless America.

President George W. Bush, address to a Joint Session of Congress and the American people, September 20, 2001

Mr Speaker, Mr President Pro Tempore, members of Congress, and fellow Americans:

In the normal course of events, Presidents come to this chamber to report on the state of the Union. Tonight, no such report is needed. It has already been delivered by the American people.

We have seen it in the courage of passengers, who rushed terrorists to save others on the ground – passengers like an exceptional man named Todd Beamer. And would you please help me to welcome his wife, Lisa Beamer, here tonight. [Applause.]

We have seen the state of our Union in the endurance of rescuers, working past exhaustion. We have seen the unfurling of flags, the lighting of candles, the giving of blood, the saying of prayers – in English, Hebrew, and Arabic. We have seen the decency of a loving and giving people who have made the grief of strangers their own.

My fellow citizens, for the last nine days, the entire world has seen for itself the state of our Union – and it is strong. [Applause.]

Tonight we are a country awakened to danger and called to defend freedom. Our grief has turned to anger, and anger to resolution. Whether we bring our enemies to justice, or bring justice to our enemies, justice will be done. [Applause.]

I thank the Congress for its leadership at such an important time. All of America was touched on the evening of the tragedy to see Republicans and Democrats joined together on the steps of this Capitol, singing 'God Bless America.' And you did more than sing; you acted, by delivering $40 billion to rebuild our communities and meet the needs of our military.

Speaker Hastert, Minority Leader Gephardt, Majority Leader Daschle and Senator Lott, I thank you for your friendship, for your leadership and for your service to our country. [Applause.]

And on behalf of the American people, I thank the world for its outpouring of support. America will never forget the sounds of our National Anthem playing at Buckingham Palace, on the streets of Paris, and at Berlin's Brandenburg Gate.

We will not forget South Korean children gathering to pray outside our embassy in Seoul, or the prayers of sympathy offered at a mosque in Cairo. We will not forget moments of silence and days of mourning in Australia and Africa and Latin America.

Nor will we forget the citizens of 80 other nations who died with our own: dozens of Pakistanis; more than 130 Israelis; more than 250 citizens of India; men and women from El Salvador, Iran, Mexico and Japan; and hundreds of British citizens. America has no truer friend than Great Britain. [Applause.] Once again, we are joined together in a great cause – so honored the British Prime Minister has crossed an ocean to show his unity of purpose with America. Thank you for coming, friend. [Applause.]

On September the 11th, enemies of freedom committed an act of war against our country. Americans have known wars – but for the past 136 years, they have been wars on foreign soil, except for one Sunday in 1941. Americans have known the casualties of war – but not at the center of a great city on a peaceful morning. Americans have known surprise attacks – but never before on thousands of civilians. All of this was brought upon us in a single day – and night fell on a different world, a world where freedom itself is under attack.

Americans have many questions tonight. Americans are asking: Who attacked our country? The evidence we have gathered all points to a collection of loosely affiliated terrorist organizations known as al Qaeda. They are the same murderers indicted for bombing American embassies in Tanzania and Kenya, and responsible for bombing the USS Cole.

Al Qaeda is to terror what the mafia is to crime. But its goal is not making money; its goal is remaking the world – and imposing its radical beliefs on people everywhere.

The terrorists practice a fringe form of Islamic extremism that has been rejected by Muslim scholars and the vast majority of Muslim clerics – a fringe movement that perverts the peaceful teachings of Islam. The terrorists' directive commands them to kill Christians and Jews, to kill all Americans, and make no distinction among military and civilians, including women and children.

This group and its leader – a person named Osama bin Laden – are linked to many other organizations in different countries, including the Egyptian Islamic Jihad and the Islamic Movement of Uzbekistan. There are thousands of these terrorists in more than 60 countries. They are recruited from their own nations and neighborhoods and brought to camps in places like Afghanistan, where they are trained in the tactics of terror. They are sent back to their homes or sent to hide in countries around the world to plot evil and destruction.

The leadership of al Qaeda has great influence in Afghanistan and supports the Taliban regime in controlling most of that country. In Afghanistan, we see al Qaeda's vision for the world.

Afghanistan's people have been brutalized – many are starving and many have fled. Women are not allowed to attend school. You can be jailed for owning a television. Religion can be practiced only as their leaders dictate. A man can be jailed in Afghanistan if his beard is not long enough.

The United States respects the people of Afghanistan – after all, we are currently its largest source of humanitarian aid – but we condemn the Taliban regime. [Applause.] It is not only repressing its own people, it is threatening people everywhere by sponsoring and sheltering and supplying terrorists. By aiding and abetting murder, the Taliban regime is committing murder.

And tonight, the United States of America makes the following demands on the Taliban: Deliver to United States authorities all the leaders of al Qaeda who hide in your land. [Applause.] Release all foreign nationals, including American citizens, you have unjustly imprisoned. Protect foreign journalists, diplomats and aid workers in your country. Close immediately and permanently every terrorist training camp in Afghanistan, and hand over every terrorist, and every person in their support structure, to appropriate authorities. [Applause.] Give the United States full access to terrorist training camps, so we can make sure they are no longer operating.

These demands are not open to negotiation or discussion. [Applause.] The Taliban must act, and act immediately. They will hand over the terrorists, or they will share in their fate.

I also want to speak tonight directly to Muslims throughout the world. We respect your faith. It's practiced freely by many millions of Americans, and by millions more in countries that America counts as friends. Its teachings are good and peaceful, and those who commit evil in the name of Allah blaspheme the name of Allah. [Applause.]

The terrorists are traitors to their own faith, trying, in effect, to hijack Islam itself. The enemy of America is not our many Muslim friends; it is not our many Arab friends. Our enemy is a radical network of terrorists, and every government that supports them. [Applause.]

Our war on terror begins with al Qaeda, but it does not end there. It will not end until every terrorist group of global reach has been found, stopped and defeated. [Applause.]

Americans are asking, why do they hate us? They hate what we see right here in this chamber – a democratically elected government. Their leaders are self-appointed. They hate our freedoms – our freedom of religion, our freedom of speech, our freedom to vote and assemble and disagree with each other.

They want to overthrow existing governments in many Muslim countries, such as Egypt, Saudi Arabia, and Jordan. They want to drive Israel out of the Middle East. They want to drive Christians and Jews out of vast regions of Asia and Africa.

These terrorists kill not merely to end lives, but to disrupt and end a way of life. With every atrocity, they hope that America grows fearful, retreating from the world and forsaking our friends. They stand against us, because we stand in their way.

We are not deceived by their pretenses to piety. We have seen their kind before. They are the heirs of all the murderous ideologies of the 20th century. By sacrificing human life to serve their radical visions – by abandoning every value except the will to power – they follow in the path of fascism, and Nazism, and totalitarianism. And they will follow that path all the way, to where it ends: in history's unmarked grave of discarded lies. [Applause.]

Americans are asking: How will we fight and win this war? We will direct every resource at our command – every means of diplomacy, every tool of intelligence, every instrument of law enforcement, every financial influence, and every necessary weapon of war – to the disruption and to the defeat of the global terror network.

This war will not be like the war against Iraq a decade ago, with a decisive liberation of territory and a swift conclusion. It will not look like the air war above Kosovo two years ago, where no ground troops were used and not a single American was lost in combat.

Our response involves far more than instant retaliation and isolated strikes. Americans should not expect one battle, but a lengthy campaign, unlike any other we have ever seen. It may include dramatic strikes, visible on TV, and covert operations, secret even in success. We will starve terrorists of funding, turn them one against another, drive them from place to place, until there is no refuge or no rest. And we will pursue nations that provide aid or safe haven to terrorism. Every nation, in every region, now has a decision to make. Either you are with us, or you are with the terrorists. [Applause.] From this day forward, any nation that continues to harbor or support terrorism will be regarded by the United States as a hostile regime.

Our nation has been put on notice: We are not immune from attack. We will take defensive measures against terrorism to protect Americans. Today, dozens of federal departments and agencies, as well as state and local governments, have responsibilities affecting homeland security. These efforts must be coordinated at the highest level. So tonight I announce the creation of a Cabinet-level position reporting directly to me – the Office of Homeland Security.

And tonight I also announce a distinguished American to lead this effort, to strengthen American security: a military veteran, an effective governor, a true patriot, a

194

trusted friend – Pennsylvania's Tom Ridge. [Applause.] He will lead, oversee and coordinate a comprehensive national strategy to safeguard our country against terrorism, and respond to any attacks that may come.

These measures are essential. But the only way to defeat terrorism as a threat to our way of life is to stop it, eliminate it, and destroy it where it grows. [Applause.]

Many will be involved in this effort, from FBI agents to intelligence operatives to the reservists we have called to active duty. All deserve our thanks, and all have our prayers. And tonight, a few miles from the damaged Pentagon, I have a message for our military: Be ready. I've called the Armed Forces to alert, and there is a reason. The hour is coming when America will act, and you will make us proud. [Applause.]

This is not, however, just America's fight. And what is at stake is not just America's freedom. This is the world's fight. This is civilization's fight. This is the fight of all who believe in progress and pluralism, tolerance and freedom.

We ask every nation to join us. We will ask, and we will need, the help of police forces, intelligence services, and banking systems around the world. The United States is grateful that many nations and many international organizations have already responded – with sympathy and with support. Nations from Latin America, to Asia, to Africa, to Europe, to the Islamic world. Perhaps the NATO Charter reflects best the attitude of the world: An attack on one is an attack on all.

The civilized world is rallying to America's side. They understand that if this terror goes unpunished, their own cities, their own citizens may be next. Terror, unanswered, can not only bring down buildings, it can threaten the stability of legitimate governments. And you know what – we're not going to allow it. [Applause.]

Americans are asking: What is expected of us? I ask you to live your lives, and hug your children. I know many citizens have fears tonight, and I ask you to be calm and resolute, even in the face of a continuing threat.

I ask you to uphold the values of America, and remember why so many have come here. We are in a fight for our principles, and our first responsibility is to live by them. No one should be singled out for unfair treatment or unkind words because of their ethnic background or religious faith. [Applause.]

I ask you to continue to support the victims of this tragedy with your contributions. Those who want to give can go to a central source of information, libertyunites.org, to find the names of groups providing direct help in New York, Pennsylvania, and Virginia.

The thousands of FBI agents who are now at work in this investigation may need your cooperation, and I ask you to give it.

I ask for your patience, with the delays and inconveniences that may accompany tighter security; and for your patience in what will be a long struggle.

I ask your continued participation and confidence in the American economy. Terrorists attacked a symbol of American prosperity. They did not touch its source. America is successful because of the hard work, and creativity, and enterprise of our people. These were the true strengths of our economy before September 11th, and they are our strengths today. [Applause.]

And, finally, please continue praying for the victims of terror and their families, for those in uniform, and for our great country. Prayer has comforted us in sorrow, and will help strengthen us for the journey ahead.

Tonight I thank my fellow Americans for what you have already done and for what you will do. And ladies and gentlemen of the Congress, I thank you, their representatives, for what you have already done and for what we will do together.

Tonight, we face new and sudden national challenges. We will come together to improve air safety, to dramatically expand the number of air marshals on domestic flights, and take new measures to prevent hijacking. We will come together to promote stability and keep our airlines flying, with direct assistance during this emergency. [Applause.]

We will come together to give law enforcement the additional tools it needs to track down terror here at home. [Applause.] We will come together to strengthen our intelligence capabilities to know the plans of terrorists before they act, and find them before they strike. [Applause.]

We will come together to take active steps that strengthen America's economy, and put our people back to work.

Tonight we welcome two leaders who embody the extraordinary spirit of all New Yorkers: Governor George Pataki, and Mayor Rudolph Giuliani. [Applause.] As a symbol of America's resolve, my administration will work with Congress, and these two leaders, to show the world that we will rebuild New York City. [Applause.]

After all that has just passed – all the lives taken, and all the possibilities and hopes that died with them – it is natural to wonder if America's future is one of fear. Some speak of an age of terror. I know there are struggles ahead, and dangers to face. But this country will define our times, not be defined by them. As long as the United States of America is determined and strong, this will not be an age of terror; this will be an age of liberty, here and across the world. [Applause.]

Great harm has been done to us. We have suffered great loss. And in our grief and anger we have found our mission and our moment. Freedom and fear are at war. The advance of human freedom – the great achievement of our time, and the great hope of every time – now depends on us. Our nation – this generation – will lift a dark threat of violence from our people and our future. We will rally the world to this cause by our efforts, by our courage. We will not tire, we will not falter, and we will not fail. [Applause.]

It is my hope that in the months and years ahead, life will return almost to normal. We'll go back to our lives and routines, and that is good. Even grief recedes with time and grace. But our resolve must not pass. Each of us will remember what happened that day, and to whom it happened. We'll remember the moment the news came – where we were and what we were doing. Some will remember an image of a fire, or a story of rescue. Some will carry memories of a face and a voice gone forever.

And I will carry this: It is the police shield of a man named George Howard, who died at the World Trade Center trying to save others. It was given to me by his mom, Arlene, as a proud memorial to her son. This is my reminder of lives that ended, and a task that does not end. [Applause.]

I will not forget this wound to our country or those who inflicted it. I will not yield; I will not rest; I will not relent in waging this struggle for freedom and security for the American people.

The course of this conflict is not known, yet its outcome is certain. Freedom and fear, justice and cruelty, have always been at war, and we know that God is not neutral between them. [Applause.]

Fellow citizens, we'll meet violence with patient justice – assured of the rightness of our cause, and confident of the victories to come. In all that lies before us, may God grant us wisdom, and may He watch over the United States of America.

Thank you. [Applause.]

Memorial service in remembrance of those lost on September 11th, remarks prepared for delivery by Secretary of Defense Donald H. Rumsfeld, The Pentagon, Arlington, VA, October 11, 2001

We are gathered here because of what happened here on September 11th. Events that bring to mind tragedy – but also our gratitude to those who came to assist that day and afterwards, those we saw at the Pentagon site every day – the guards, police, fire and rescue workers, the Defense Protective service, hospitals, Red Cross, family center professionals and volunteers and many others. And yet our reason for being here today is something else. We are gathered here to remember, to console and to pray. To remember comrades and colleagues, friends and family members – those lost to us on September 11th. We remember them as heroes. And we are right to do so. They died because – in words of justification offered by their attackers – they were Americans. They died, then, because of how they lived – as free men and women, proud of their freedom, proud of their country and proud of their country's cause – the cause of human freedom. And they died for another reason - the simple fact they worked here in this building – the Pentagon. It is seen as a place of power, the locus of command for what has been called the greatest accumulation of military might in history. And yet a might used far differently than the long course of history has usually known.

In the last century, this building existed to oppose two totalitarian regimes that sought to oppress and to rule other nations. And it is no exaggeration of historical judgment to say that without this building, and those who worked here, those two regimes would not have been stopped or thwarted in their oppression of countless millions. But just as those regimes sought to rule and oppress, others in this century seek to do the same by corrupting a noble religion. Our President has been right to see the similarity – and to say that the fault, the evil is the same. It is the will to power, the urge to dominion over others, to the point of oppressing them, even to taking thousands of innocent lives – or more. And that this oppression makes the terrorist a believer – not in the theology of God, but the theology of self – and in the whispered words of temptation: 'Ye shall be as Gods.' In targeting this place, then, and those who worked here, the attackers, the evildoers correctly sensed that the opposite of all they were, and stood for, resided here.

Those who worked here – those who on September 11 died here – whether civilians or in uniform, side by side they sought not to rule, but to serve. They sought not to oppress, but to liberate. They worked not to take lives, but to protect them. And they tried not to preempt God, but see to it His creatures lived as He intended – in the light and dignity of human freedom. Our first task then is to remember the fallen as they were – as they would have wanted to be remembered – living in freedom, blessed by it, proud of it and willing – like so many others before them, and like so many today, to die for it. And to remember them as believers in the heroic ideal for which this nation stands and for which this building exists – the ideal of service to country and to others. Beyond all this, their deaths remind us of a new kind of evil, the evil of a threat and menace to which this nation and the world has now fully awakened, because of them. In causing this awakening, then, the terrorists have assured their own destruction. And those we mourn today have, in the moment of their death, assured their own triumph over hate and fear. For out of this act of terror – and the awakening it brings – here and across the globe – will surely come a victory over terrorism. A victory that one day may save millions from the harm of weapons of mass destruction. And this victory – their victory – we pledge today.

But if we gather here to remember them – we are also here to console those who shared their lives, those who loved them. And yet, the irony is that those whom we have come to console have given us the best of all consolations, by reminding us not only of the meaning of the deaths, but of the lives of their loved ones. 'He was a hero long before the eleventh of September,' said a friend of one of those we have lost – 'a hero every single day, a hero to his family, to his friends and to his professional peers.' A veteran of the Gulf War – hardworking, who showed up at the Pentagon at 3:30 in the morning, and then headed home in the afternoon to be with his children – all of whom he loved dearly, but one of whom he gave very special care, because she needs very special care and love.

About him and those who served with him, his wife said: 'It's not just when a plane hits their building. They are heroes every day.' 'Heroes every day.' We are here to affirm that. And to do this on behalf of America. And also to say to those who mourn, who have lost loved ones: Know that the heart of America is here today, and that it speaks to each one of you words of sympathy, consolation, compassion and love. All the love that the heart of America – and a great heart it is – can muster. Watching and listening today, Americans everywhere are saying: I wish I could be there to tell them how sorry we are, how much we grieve for them. And to tell them too, how thankful we are for those they loved, and that we will remember them, and recall always the meaning of their deaths and their lives. A Marine chaplain, in trying to explain why there could be no human explanation for a tragedy such as this, said once: 'You would think it would break the heart of God.' We stand today in the midst of tragedy – the mystery of tragedy. Yet a mystery that is part of that larger awe and wonder that causes us to bow our heads in faith and say of those we mourn, those we have lost, the words of scripture: 'Lord now let Thy servants go in peace, Thy word has been fulfilled.' To the families and friends of our fallen colleagues and comrades we extend today our deepest sympathy and condolences – and those of the American people. We pray that God will give some share of the peace that now belongs to those we lost, to those who knew and loved them in this life. But as we grieve together we are also thankful – thankful for their lives, thankful for the time we had with them. And proud too – as proud as they were – that they lived their lives as Americans. We are mindful too – and resolute that their deaths, like their lives, shall have meaning. And that the birthright of human freedom – a birthright that was theirs as Americans and for which they died – will always be ours and our children's. And through our efforts and example, one day, the birthright of every man, woman, and child on earth.

Attorney General John Ashcroft, prepared remarks for the US Mayors Conference, October 25, 2001

For more than two hundred years, Attorneys General have called on the men and women of justice to be faithful stewards of the law. Rarely in history has an Attorney General asked America's prosecutors and law enforcement officers to do what they are asked to do today: to be both defenders of justice and defenders of the people; to devote their talents and energies to the urgent task of saving lives ahead of losing cases. On September 11, the wheel of history turned and the world will never be the same. A turning point was reached, as well, in the administration of justice. The fight against terrorism is now the first and overriding priority of the Department of Justice. But our war against terrorism is not merely or primarily a criminal justice endeavor – our battle is the defense of our nation and its citizens.

The men and women of justice and law enforcement are called on to combat a terrorist threat that is both immediate and vast; a threat that resides here, at home, but whose supporters, patrons and sympathizers form a multinational network of evil. The attacks of September 11 were acts of terrorism against America orchestrated and carried out by individuals living within our borders. Today's terrorists enjoy the benefits of our free society even as they commit themselves to our destruction. They live in our communities – plotting, planning and waiting to kill Americans again. They have crossed the Rubicon of terror with the use of biological agents. We cannot explicitly link the recent terrorist attacks to the September 11 hijackers. Yet, terrorists – people who were either involved with, associated with or are seeking to take advantage of the September 11 attacks – are now poisoning our communities with Anthrax. Forty years ago, another Attorney General was confronted with a different enemy within our borders. Robert F. Kennedy came to the Department of Justice at a time when organized crime was threatening the very foundations of the republic. Mobsters controlled one of the nation's largest labor unions. Racketeers murdered, bribed and extorted with impunity in many of the nation's largest cities. Then, as now, the enemy that America faced was described bluntly – and correctly – as a conspiracy of evil. Then, as now, the enemy was well-financed, expertly organized and international in scope. Then, as now, its operations were hidden under a code of deadly silence.

As Attorney General, Robert Kennedy launched an extraordinary campaign against organized crime. Under his leadership, the mission and momentum of the Department of Justice were directed toward one overarching goal: to identify, disrupt and dismantle the organized-crime enemy within. A new spirit of cooperation was forged, both among federal agencies and between state and federal law enforcement. Prosecutors were action oriented – pursuing cases rather than waiting for the cases to come to them. Investigators focused on function, not form – they focused on doing what was necessary to get the job done rather than what was dictated by the organizational chart. Attorney General Kennedy made no apologies for using all of the available resources in the law to disrupt and dismantle organized crime networks. Very often, prosecutors were aggressive, using obscure statutes to arrest and detain suspected mobsters. One racketeer and his father were indicted for lying on a federal home loan application. A former gunman for the Capone mob was brought to court on a violation of the Migratory Bird Act. Agents found 563 game birds in his freezer – a mere 539 birds over the limit. There are obvious differences, of course, between the network of organized crime America faced in 1961 and the network of terror we face today. Today, many more innocent lives have been lost. Many more innocent lives continue to be threatened. But these differences serve only to call us more urgently to action. The American people face a serious, immediate and ongoing threat from terrorism. At this moment, American service men and women are risking their lives to battle the enemy overseas. It falls to the men and women of justice and law enforcement to engage terrorism at home. History's judgment will be harsh – and the people's judgment will be sure – if we fail to use every available resource to prevent future terrorist attacks. Robert Kennedy's Justice Department, it is said, would arrest mobsters for 'spitting on the sidewalk' if it would help in the battle against organized crime. It has been and will be the policy of this Department of Justice to use the same aggressive arrest and detention tactics in the war on terror.

Let the terrorists among us be warned: If you overstay your visa – even by one day – we will arrest you. If you violate a local law, you will be put in jail and kept in custody as long as possible. We will use every available statute. We will seek every prosecutorial advantage. We will use all our weapons within the law and under the Constitution to protect life and enhance security for America. In the war on terror, this Department of Justice will arrest and detain any suspected terrorist who has violated the law. Our single objective is to prevent terrorist attacks by taking suspected terrorists off the street. If suspects are found not to have links to terrorism or not to have violated the law, they are released. But terrorists who are in violation of the law will be convicted, in some cases deported, and in all cases prevented from doing further harm to Americans. Within days of the September 11 attacks, we launched this anti-terrorism offensive to prevent new attacks on our homeland. To date, our anti-terrorism offensive has arrested or detained nearly 1,000 individuals as part of the September 11 terrorism investigation. Those who violated the law remain in custody. Taking suspected terrorists in violation of the law off the streets and keeping them locked up is our clear strategy to prevent terrorism within our borders. Today, the Department of Justice is positioned to launch a new offensive against terrorism. Due to extraordinary bi-partisan and bi-cameral cooperation in the Congress, law enforcement will have new weapons in the war on terrorism. Yesterday, by an overwhelming margin, the House passed the Anti-terrorism Act of 2001. Hours from now, the Senate is poised to follow suit.

The president is expected to sign this legislation on Friday. The hour that it becomes law, I will issue guidance to each of our 94 US Attorney's Offices and 56 FBI field offices directing them to begin immediately implementing this sweeping legislation. I will issue directives requiring law enforcement to make use of new powers in intelligence gathering, criminal procedure and immigration violations. A new era in America's fight against terrorism, made tragically necessary by the attacks of September 11, is about to begin. The legislation embodies two overarching principles: The first principle is airtight surveillance of terrorists. Upon the president's signature, I will direct investigators and prosecutors to begin immediately seeking court orders to intercept communications related to an expanded list of crimes under the legislation. Communications regarding terrorist offenses such as the use of biological or chemical agents, financing acts of terrorism or materially supporting terrorism will be subject to interception by law enforcement. Agents will be directed to take advantage of new, technologically neutral standards for intelligence gathering. So-called 'roving' wiretaps, that allow taps of multiple phones a suspect may use, are being added as an important weapon in our war against terror.

Investigators will be directed to pursue aggressively terrorists on the internet. New authority in the legislation permits the use of devices that capture senders and receivers addresses associated with communications on the internet. Law enforcement will begin immediately to seek search warrants to obtain unopened voice-mail stored on a computer – just as they traditionally have used search warrants to obtain unopened email. They will also begin to use new subpoena power to obtain payment information such as credit card or bank account numbers of suspected terrorists on the internet. The second principle enshrined in the legislation is speed in tracking down and intercepting terrorists. As soon as possible, law enforcement will begin to employ new tools that ease administrative burdens and delays in apprehending terrorists. Investigators are now able to use a single court order to trace a communication even when it travels outside the judicial district in which the order was issued. The scope of search warrants for unopened e-mail and other evidence is now also nationwide.

The new tools for law enforcement in the war against terrorism are the products of hundreds of hours of consultation and careful consideration by the administration, members of Congress, and state and local officials. They are careful, balanced, and long overdue improvements in our capacity to prevent terrorism. The federal government cannot fight this reign of terror alone. Every American must help us defend our nation against this enemy. Every state, every county, every municipality must join together to form a common defense against terrorism. The law enforcement campaign that will commence in earnest when the legislation is signed into law will be many years in duration. Some will ask whether a civilized nation – a nation of law and not of men – can use the law to defend itself from barbarians and remain civilized. Our answer, unequivocally, is 'yes.' Yes, we will defend civilization. And yes, we will preserve the rule of law because it makes us civilized.

The men and women of justice and law enforcement have been asked to shoulder a great burden for the safety and security of the American people. We will, as we have in the past, never waiver in our faith and loyalty to the Constitution and never tire in our defense of the rights it enshrines. Years after he left the office of Attorney General, an observer of Robert Kennedy wrote that RFK brought these assets to his successful campaign against organized crime: 'A constructive anger. An intimate knowledge of his subject. A talented team of prosecutors. And, finally, a partner in the White House.' Today, as we embark on this campaign against terrorism, we are blessed with a similar set of advantages. Our anger, too, is constructive. Our knowledge is growing. Our team is talented. And our leadership in the White House is unparalleled.

George W. Bush has done more – much more – than declare war on terrorism. George W. Bush is fighting a war on terrorism. Under his leadership, we have pledged ourselves to victory. Terrorists live in the shadows, under the cover of darkness. We will shine the light of justice on them. Americans alive today and yet to be born and freedom-loving people everywhere will have new reason to hope because our enemies now have new reason to fear. Thank you.

**The President's State of the Union Address, Washington, DC,
January 29, 2002 – abridged**

Thank you very much. Mr Speaker, Vice President Cheney, members of Congress, distinguished guests, fellow citizens: As we gather tonight, our nation is at war, our economy is in recession, and the civilized world faces unprecedented dangers. Yet the state of our Union has never been stronger. [Applause.] We last met in an hour of shock and suffering. In four short months, our nation has comforted the victims, begun to rebuild New York and the Pentagon, rallied a great coalition, captured, arrested, and rid the world of thousands of terrorists, destroyed Afghanistan's terrorist training camps, saved a people from starvation, and freed a country from brutal oppression. [Applause.]

The American flag flies again over our embassy in Kabul. Terrorists who once occupied Afghanistan now occupy cells at Guantanamo Bay. [Applause.] And terrorist leaders who urged followers to sacrifice their lives are running for their own. [Applause.] America and Afghanistan are now allies against terror. We'll be partners in rebuilding that country. And this evening we welcome the distinguished interim leader of a liberated Afghanistan: Chairman Hamid Karzai. [Applause.] The last time we met in this chamber, the mothers and daughters of Afghanistan were captives in their own homes, forbidden from working or going to school. Today women are free, and are part of Afghanistan's new government. And we welcome the new Minister of Women's Affairs, Doctor Sima Samar. [Applause.]

Our progress is a tribute to the spirit of the Afghan people, to the resolve of our coalition, and to the might of the United States military. [Applause.] When I called our troops into action, I did so with complete confidence in their courage and skill. And tonight, thanks to them, we are winning the war on terror. [Applause.] The men and women of our Armed Forces have delivered a message now clear to every enemy of the United States: Even 7,000 miles away, across oceans and continents, on mountaintops and in caves – you will not escape the justice of this nation. [Applause.] For many Americans, these four months have brought sorrow, and pain that will never completely go away. Every day a retired firefighter returns to Ground Zero, to feel closer to his two sons who died there. At a memorial in New York, a little boy left his football with a note for his lost father: Dear Daddy, please take this to heaven. I don't want to play football until I can play with you again some day. Last month, at the grave of her husband, Michael, a CIA officer and Marine who died in Mazur-e-Sharif, Shannon Spann said these words of farewell: 'Semper Fi, my love.' Shannon is with us tonight. [Applause.] Shannon, I assure you and all who have lost a loved one that our cause is just, and our country will never forget the debt we owe Michael and all who gave their lives for freedom.

Our cause is just, and it continues. Our discoveries in Afghanistan confirmed our worst fears, and showed us the true scope of the task ahead. We have seen the depth of our enemies' hatred in videos, where they laugh about the loss of innocent life. And the depth of their hatred is equaled by the madness of the destruction they design. We have found diagrams of American nuclear power plants and public water facilities, detailed instructions for making chemical weapons, surveillance maps of American cities, and thorough descriptions of landmarks in America and throughout the world. What we have found in Afghanistan confirms that, far from ending there, our war against terror is only beginning. Most of the 19 men who hijacked planes on September the 11th were trained in Afghanistan's camps, and so were tens of thousands of others. Thousands of dangerous killers, schooled in the methods of murder, often supported by outlaw regimes, are now spread throughout the world like ticking time bombs, set to go off without warning. Thanks to the work of our law enforcement officials and coalition partners, hundreds of terrorists have been arrested. Yet, tens of thousands of trained terrorists are still at large. These enemies view the entire world as a battlefield, and we must pursue them wherever they are. [Applause.] So long as training camps operate, so long as nations harbor terrorists, freedom is at risk. And America and our allies must not, and will not, allow it. [Applause.]

Our nation will continue to be steadfast and patient and persistent in the pursuit of two great objectives. First, we will shut down terrorist camps, disrupt terrorist plans, and bring terrorists to justice. And, second, we must prevent the terrorists and regimes who seek chemical, biological or nuclear weapons from threatening the United States and the world. [Applause.] Our military has put the terror training camps of Afghanistan out of business, yet camps still exist in at least a dozen countries. A terrorist underworld – including groups like Hamas, Hezbollah, Islamic Jihad, Jaish-i-Mohammed – operates in remote jungles and deserts, and hides in the centers of large cities. While the most visible military action is in Afghanistan, America is acting elsewhere. We now have troops in the Philippines, helping to train that country's armed forces to go after terrorist cells that have executed an American, and still hold hostages. Our soldiers, working with the Bosnian government, seized terrorists who were plotting to bomb our embassy. Our Navy is patrolling the coast of Africa to block the shipment of weapons and the establishment of terrorist camps in Somalia.

My hope is that all nations will heed our call, and eliminate the terrorist parasites who threaten their countries and our own. Many nations are acting forcefully. Pakistan is now cracking down on terror, and I admire the strong leadership of President Musharraf. [Applause.] But some governments will be timid in the face of terror. And make no mistake about it: If they do not act, America will. [Applause.] Our second goal is to prevent regimes that sponsor terror from threatening America or our friends and allies with weapons of mass destruction. Some of these regimes have been pretty quiet since September the 11th. But we know their true nature. North Korea is a regime arming with missiles and weapons of mass destruction, while starving its citizens. Iran aggressively pursues these weapons and exports terror, while an unelected few repress the Iranian people's hope for freedom. Iraq continues to flaunt its hostility toward America and to support terror. The Iraqi regime has plotted to develop anthrax, and nerve gas, and nuclear weapons for over a decade. This is a regime that has already used poison gas to murder thousands of its own citizens – leaving the bodies of mothers huddled over their dead children. This is a regime that agreed to international inspections – then kicked out the inspectors. This is a regime that has something to hide from the civilized world.

States like these, and their terrorist allies, constitute an axis of evil, arming to threaten the peace of the world. By seeking weapons of mass destruction, these regimes pose a grave and growing danger. They could provide these arms to terrorists, giving them the means to match their hatred. They could attack our allies or attempt to blackmail the United States. In any of these cases, the price of indifference would be catastrophic. We will work closely with our coalition to deny terrorists and their state sponsors the materials, technology, and expertise to make and deliver weapons of mass destruction. We will develop and deploy effective missile defenses to protect America and our allies from sudden attack. [Applause.] And all nations should know: America will do what is necessary to ensure our nation's security. We'll be deliberate, yet time is not on our side. I will not wait on events, while dangers gather. I will not stand by, as peril draws closer and closer. The United States of America will not permit the world's most dangerous regimes to threaten us with the world's most destructive weapons. [Applause.]

Our war on terror is well begun, but it is only begun. This campaign may not be finished on our watch – yet it must be and it will be waged on our watch. We can't stop short. If we stop now – leaving terror camps intact and terror states unchecked – our sense of security would be false and temporary. History has called America and our allies to action, and it is both our responsibility and our privilege to fight freedom's fight. [Applause.] Our first priority must always be the security of our nation, and that will be reflected in the budget I send to Congress. My budget supports three great goals for America: We will win this war; we'll protect our homeland; and we will revive our economy. September the 11th brought out the best in America, and the best in this Congress. And I join the American people in applauding your unity and resolve. [Applause.] Now Americans deserve to have this same spirit directed toward addressing problems here at home. I'm a proud member of my party – yet as we act to win the war, protect our people, and create jobs in America, we must act, first and foremost, not as Republicans, not as Democrats, but as Americans. [Applause.]

[...]

I ask you to join me on these important domestic issues in the same spirit of cooperation we've applied to our war against terrorism. [Applause.] During these last few months, I've been humbled and privileged to see the true character of this country in a time of testing. Our enemies believed America was weak and materialistic, that we would splinter in fear and selfishness. They were as wrong as they are evil. [Applause.] The American people have responded magnificently, with courage and compassion, strength and resolve. As I have met the heroes, hugged the families, and looked into the tired faces of rescuers, I have stood in awe of the American people.

And I hope you will join me – I hope you will join me in expressing thanks to one American for the strength and calm and comfort she brings to our nation in crisis, our First Lady, Laura Bush. [Applause.] None of us would ever wish the evil that was done on September the 11th. Yet after America was attacked, it was as if our entire country looked into a mirror and saw our better selves. We were reminded that we are citizens, with obligations to each other, to our country, and to history. We began to think less of the goods we can accumulate, and more about the good we can do. For too long our culture has said, 'If it feels good, do it.' Now America is embracing a new ethic and a new creed: 'Let's roll.' [Applause.] In the sacrifice of soldiers, the fierce brotherhood of firefighters, and the bravery and generosity of ordinary citizens, we have glimpsed what a new culture of responsibility could look like. We want to be a nation that serves goals larger than self. We've been offered a unique opportunity, and we must not let this moment pass. [Applause.]

My call tonight is for every American to commit at least two years – 4,000 hours over the rest of your lifetime – to the service of your neighbors and your nation. [Applause.] Many are already serving, and I thank you. If you aren't sure how to help, I've got a good place to start. To sustain and extend the best that has emerged in America, I invite you to join the new USA Freedom Corps. The Freedom Corps will focus on three areas of need: responding in case of crisis at home; rebuilding our communities; and extending American compassion throughout the world. One purpose of the USA Freedom Corps will be homeland security. America needs retired doctors and nurses who can be mobilized in major emergencies; volunteers to help police and fire departments; transportation and utility workers well-trained in spotting danger. Our country also needs citizens working to rebuild our communities. We need mentors to love children, especially children whose parents are in prison. And we need more talented teachers in troubled schools. USA Freedom Corps will expand and improve the good efforts of AmeriCorps and Senior Corps to recruit more than 200,000 new volunteers. And America needs citizens to extend the compassion of our country to every part of the world. So we will renew the promise of the Peace Corps, double its volunteers over the next five years – [Applause] – and ask it to join a new effort to encourage development and education and opportunity in the Islamic world. [Applause.]

This time of adversity offers a unique moment of opportunity – a moment we must seize to change our culture. Through the gathering momentum of millions of acts of service and decency and kindness, I know we can overcome evil with greater good. [Applause.] And we have a great opportunity during this time of war to lead the world toward the values that will bring lasting peace. All fathers and mothers, in all societies, want their children to be educated, and live free from poverty and violence. No people on Earth yearn to be oppressed, or aspire to servitude, or eagerly await the midnight knock of the secret police. If anyone doubts this, let them look to Afghanistan, where the Islamic 'street' greeted the fall of tyranny with song and celebration. Let the skeptics look to Islam's own rich history, with its centuries of learning, and tolerance and progress. America will lead by defending liberty and justice because they are right and true and unchanging for all people everywhere. [Applause.] No nation owns these aspirations, and no nation is exempt from them. We have no intention of imposing our culture. But America will always stand firm for the non-negotiable demands of human dignity: the rule of law; limits on the power of the state; respect for women; private property; free speech; equal justice; and religious tolerance. [Applause.] America will take the side of brave men and women who advocate these values around the world, including the Islamic world, because we have a greater objective than eliminating threats and containing resentment. We seek a just and peaceful world beyond the war on terror.

In this moment of opportunity, a common danger is erasing old rivalries. America is working with Russia and China and India, in ways we have never before, to achieve peace and prosperity. In every region, free markets and free trade and free societies are proving their power to lift lives. Together with friends and allies from Europe to Asia, and Africa to Latin America, we will demonstrate that the forces of terror cannot stop the momentum of freedom. [Applause.] The last time I spoke here, I expressed the hope that life would return to normal. In some ways, it has. In others, it never will. Those of us who have lived through these challenging times have been changed by them. We've come to know truths that we will never question: evil is real, and it must be opposed. [Applause.] Beyond all differences of race or creed, we are one country, mourning together and facing danger together. Deep in the American character, there is honor, and it is stronger than cynicism. And many have discovered again that even in tragedy – especially in tragedy – God is near. [Applause.] In a single instant, we realized that this will be a decisive decade in the history of liberty, that we've been called to a unique role in human events. Rarely has the world faced a choice more clear or consequential.

Our enemies send other people's children on missions of suicide and murder. They embrace tyranny and death as a cause and a creed. We stand for a different choice, made long ago, on the day of our founding. We affirm it again today. We choose freedom and the dignity of every life. [Applause.] Steadfast in our purpose, we now press on. We have known freedom's price. We have shown freedom's power. And in this great conflict, my fellow Americans, we will see freedom's victory. Thank you all. May God bless. [Applause.]

Deputy Secretary of Defense Paul Wolfowitz,
Interview with Greta Van Susteren, Fox News Channel, July 9, 2002

Van Susteren: As President Bush tackles the CEOs terrorizing your 401(k) accounts, he's also vowing to tackle Saddam Hussein and Osama bin Laden. Earlier, I spoke to Deputy Secretary of Defense Paul Wolfowitz and asked him about the state of al-Qaida today.

Wolfowitz: Today is roughly just a couple days more than nine months since we started Operation Enduring Freedom, and we've accomplished a lot in that period of time. But, people should understand this is an organization that has burrowed in all over the world. We estimate some 60 countries that have or have had Al-Qaida presence. Afghanistan is only one of them. And I think sometimes people make the mistake of thinking that al-Qaida is like a snake, and that if you can just find the head and cut it off, it would be harmless. And it's absolutely the wrong analogy. What I think is the better way to understand it: it's like an infection that has taken over a healthy body, and you've got to fight all of the various different sources of infection. From that point of view, I think we've made a great deal of progress. But if we let up the pressure, it will come back, and you see all kinds of signs that they continue to try to regroup and reorganize, and we've got to keep them on the run.

Van Susteren: Any clue – the 60 countries is one indication – any clue the number of people who are part of al-Qaida? Can you quantify it, or is that impossible?

Wolfowitz: You can come up with numbers, but in some ways they're misleading because – take September 11th, for example, there were four or five people who were the key people who were the pilots and who knew they were on a suicide mission. From what we can tell, most of the others, the 14 or 15 kind of mules that were sent in at the last minute, from what bin Laden said in that weird tape that he was recorded on, he took some pleasure in the fact that they didn't even know they were on a suicide mission. So, the number of people that are really key to this organization is probably much smaller than the number in the hundreds of people who have some loose affiliation.

Van Susteren: Any ability to sort of quantify, I mean, how many people are in the know, the important members of al-Qaida, the numbers of those people?

Wolfowitz: Well, we do try to get our hands around what seems like the top ones on the list, and there are, in fact, wanted posters out on the major ones. And, from what one can tell – I really hesitate here, not only because they're classified, but because we're talking about an organization about which a lot is not known. I think we're talking about in the dozens of key people, not in the hundreds. On the other hand, until we've nearly eliminated their ability to organize, eliminated their sanctuaries, you have to assume that if you get rid of some of the top people others will replace them.

Van Susteren: You said it's not a snake where you can cut off the head and the whole thing dies. But, if bin Laden is killed and/or captured, and Al-Zubari, his number two, is killed or captured, does that change the dynamics of the organization so much that that puts us significantly ahead of the game?

Wolfowitz: I think every time you get one of these top, any of them, but every time you get one of these top people, I think it has a big payoff. Abu Zubaydah, for example, who was – it's not a hierarchical structure, but we said he's probably the number three in the organization, he was captured. And, by the way, he would not have been captured except because we drove him out of Afghanistan through the success of our military operation there, he was captured in a neighboring country. He has now given us information that has led to some other people, including this man, Padilla, the American citizen who was arrested in Chicago. Every time you catch one, especially if you can get them to reveal some information, or you can get some information out of their computers that leads you to others – we got a videotape out of an al-Qaida safe house in Afghanistan. It revealed a plot underway in Singapore. The Singaporeans picked up the whole group, that led them to other people in the Philippines, in Malaysia and Indonesia. It's chasing down a network, and you get one node in the network and it leads you to other nodes.

Van Susteren: You know, it's so enormously complicated, it's so large, and the president has said, this is going to be a long war. We're looking into the future, how will we know when the war is over? Is there a way to tell?

Wolfowitz: Well, I think we will know, but it's not going to be because there's a great surrender ceremony on the deck of the Missouri. There are many things that are unusual about this war, one of the things that's most unusual is, on the one hand, in terms of the number of Americans killed directly, in terms of the threat to the United States, in terms of the ongoing threat of the potential of chemical and biological weapons, this is, in some respects, as big as any war we've fought. And, at the same time, it's against an enemy that hides, an enemy that is in important ways invisible.

Van Susteren: But if you –

Wolfowitz: And victory is going to be measured by what doesn't happen as opposed to what does happen. When Americans can go to malls and shopping centers and not have to worry about being hit by terrorists, and we don't think that on any moment there might be a suicidal airplane attack, then we'll know that we've dealt with it. I think there will be lots of indications that this network is gone, but the indications are that it's weakened, but it's still very much there.

Van Susteren: Stand by, sir, we're going to take a short break.

Wolfowitz: OK.

Van Susteren: We'll be right back.

Van Susteren: Welcome back. I want to focus on Iraq. Is there a plan? I know that I've heard that there is a concept for the United States to go into Iraq. Do we take it one step further and call it a plan?

Wolfowitz: We get into semantics here. There are obviously a lot of serious discussions going on because the president has said very clearly, as a country, we face a very serious problem. In certain ways, September 11th is a wake-up call. We've had problems. They've been out there. Terrorism has been an evil aspect of international relations for a long time. But September 11th reminded us just how dangerous terrorism is in this new era when terrorists have access to weapons of mass destruction, and there could be much worse things than – as bad as it was – than airplanes loaded with 300,000 pounds of jet fuel. What the president talked about in the State of the Union message was countries, and Iraq is one of them, that have weapons of mass destruction, that is chemical, biological, and possibly nuclear weapons, that are working on getting more of those weapons, that have, as a matter of national policy been supporting terrorists, and are hostile to the United States. That's a deadly mixture that we can't continue living with indefinitely.

Van Susteren: Does he have a delivery system to get those deadly weapons here to the United States?

Wolfowitz: Well, one delivery system are terrorists, and we learned that on September 11th. You don't have to have a long-range missile necessarily to deliver a deadly weapon, especially if it's powdered anthrax, for example. That doesn't need a long-range missile.

Van Susteren: What would it take to go into Iraq? Do we need support of the Kurds?

Wolfowitz: You know, what the president has done is lay out a plan. And he's got a lot of smart people working and figuring out what kind of solution there would be. But I think one thing that's very important in understanding this whole problem, and in a sense you could say there's a certain generalization here, every regime that I know of that supports terrorism as a matter of national policy also terrorizes their own people. That was true of the Taliban, and that's why when we succeeded in removing the Taliban in Afghanistan, we received such a welcome from the Afghan people. I think it's nothing compared to what the Iraqi people will say and do when they're rid of Saddam Hussein. That includes the Kurds, but it's much more than just the Kurds. The Shi'a in the south, who are the majority, roughly 60 percent of the population, have been brutally repressed by Saddam's regime for decades now. But even the Sunni Arabs who are sort of the core of the regime are, for the most part, terrified, repressed people. And I believe when there's a new regime in Iraq, and hopefully one that really speaks to the democratic possibilities of what is one of the most talented populations in the Arab world, you're going to see a great, huge national sigh of relief.

Van Susteren: You know, you hear or read so much that the United States in order to be successful against Iraq must have support, must have support of European nations as well as Arab countries. Do we really need that, or could we do it alone?

Wolfowitz: Well, the more support you have, the better it is. There's no question about it. But, one of the things that gives the United States a great ability to protect our own interests and help other people is there is an awful lot we can do without other people helping us. And what you find, I think, frequently, is, if you go to people and say, we desperately have to have your help, they may decide they don't want to give it to you. If you go to people and say, we have to take certain actions that are in our national interest, and we would appreciate having you with us, but we're going to go anyway, you find a lot more people coming along. I was with Secretary Cheney, it's 11 years ago now this coming August, when he went to Saudi Arabia right after Iraq invaded Kuwait. And he didn't go there simply asking for their help. He went there saying, here is what the United States is planning to do, and of course we'd like you with us. I think we got a positive reaction because we went there in a leadership role, not in a pleading role.

Van Susteren: You've had a long career in public service. You mentioned your service with now Vice President Cheney. You talk about your job, when you got your job, I mean, I assume you didn't realize what you were signing up for in terms of September 11th. What's the most gratifying part about it?

Wolfowitz: The sense that if you do your job right, you can help protect this country, and help make the world a better place.

President George W. Bush, remarks to the nation on the anniversary of 9/11, Ellis Island, New York, September 11, 2002

Good evening. A long year has passed since enemies attacked our country. We've seen the images so many times they are seared on our souls, and remembering the horror, reliving the anguish, re-imagining the terror, is hard – and painful.

For those who lost loved ones, it's been a year of sorrow, of empty places, of newborn children who will never know their fathers here on earth. For members of our military, it's been a year of sacrifice and service far from home. For all Americans, it has been a year of adjustment, of coming to terms with the difficult knowledge that our nation has determined enemies, and that we are not invulnerable to their attacks.

Yet, in the events that have challenged us, we have also seen the character that will deliver us. We have seen the greatness of America in airline passengers who defied their hijackers and ran a plane into the ground to spare the lives of others. We've seen the greatness of America in rescuers who rushed up flights of stairs toward peril. And we continue to see the greatness of America in the care and compassion our citizens show to each other. September 11, 2001 will always be a fixed point in the life of America. The loss of so many lives left us to examine our own. Each of us was reminded that we are here only for a time, and these counted days should be filled with things that last and matter: love for our families, love for our neighbors, and for our country; gratitude for life and to the Giver of life.

We resolved a year ago to honor every last person lost. We owe them remembrance and we owe them more. We owe them, and their children, and our own, the most enduring monument we can build: a world of liberty and security made possible by the way America leads, and by the way Americans lead our lives.

The attack on our nation was also an attack on the ideals that make us a nation. Our deepest national conviction is that every life is precious, because every life is the gift of a Creator who intended us to live in liberty and equality. More than anything else, this separates us from the enemy we fight. We value every life; our enemies value none – not even the innocent, not even their own. And we seek the freedom and opportunity that give meaning and value to life.

There is a line in our time, and in every time, between those who believe all men are created equal, and those who believe that some men and women and children are expendable in the pursuit of power. There is a line in our time, and in every time, between the defenders of human liberty and those who seek to master the minds and souls of others. Our generation has now heard history's call, and we will answer it.

America has entered a great struggle that tests our strength, and even more our resolve. Our nation is patient and steadfast. We continue to pursue the terrorists in cities and camps and caves across the earth. We are joined by a great coalition of nations to rid the world of terror. And we will not allow any terrorist or tyrant to threaten civilization with weapons of mass murder. Now and in the future, Americans will live as free people, not in fear, and never at the mercy of any foreign plot or power.

This nation has defeated tyrants and liberated death camps, raised this lamp of liberty to every captive land. We have no intention of ignoring or appeasing history's latest gang of fanatics trying to murder their way to power. They are discovering, as others before them, the resolve of a great country and a great democracy. In the ruins of two towers, under a flag unfurled at the Pentagon, at the funerals of the lost, we have made a sacred promise to ourselves and to the world: we will not relent until justice is done and our nation is secure. What our enemies have begun, we will finish.

I believe there is a reason that history has matched this nation with this time. America strives to be tolerant and just. We respect the faith of Islam, even as we fight those whose actions defile that faith. We fight, not to impose our will, but to defend ourselves and extend the blessings of freedom.

We cannot know all that lies ahead. Yet, we do know that God had placed us together in this moment, to grieve together, to stand together, to serve each other and our country. And the duty we have been given – defending America and our freedom – is also a privilege we share.

We're prepared for this journey. And our prayer tonight is that God will see us through, and keep us worthy.

Tomorrow is September the 12th. A milestone is passed, and a mission goes on. Be confident. Our country is strong. And our cause is even larger than our country. Ours is the cause of human dignity; freedom guided by conscience and guarded by peace. This ideal of America is the hope of all mankind. That hope drew millions to this harbor. That hope still lights our way. And the light shines in the darkness. And the darkness will not overcome it. May God bless America.

The President's State of the Union Address, Washington, DC, January 20, 2004 – abridged

Mr Speaker, Vice President Cheney, members of Congress, distinguished guests, and fellow citizens:

America this evening is a nation called to great responsibilities. And we are rising to meet them.

As we gather tonight, hundreds of thousands of American servicemen and women are deployed across the world in the war on terror. By bringing hope to the oppressed, and delivering justice to the violent, they are making America more secure. [Applause.]

Each day, law enforcement personnel and intelligence officers are tracking terrorist threats; analysts are examining airline passenger lists; the men and women of our new Homeland Security Department are patrolling our coasts and borders. And their vigilance is protecting America. [Applause.]

Americans are proving once again to be the hardest working people in the world. The American economy is growing stronger. The tax relief you passed is working. [Applause.]

Tonight, members of Congress can take pride in the great works of compassion and reform that skeptics had thought impossible. You're raising the standards for our public schools, and you are giving our senior citizens prescription drug coverage under Medicare. [Applause.]

We have faced serious challenges together, and now we face a choice: We can go forward with confidence and resolve, or we can turn back to the dangerous illusion that terrorists are not plotting and outlaw regimes are no threat to us. We can press on with economic growth, and reforms in education and Medicare, or we can turn back to old policies and old divisions.

We've not come all this way – through tragedy, and trial and war – only to falter and leave our work unfinished. Americans are rising to the tasks of history, and they expect the same from us. In their efforts, their enterprise, and their character, the American people are showing that the state of our union is confident and strong. [Applause.]

Our greatest responsibility is the active defense of the American people. Twenty-eight months have passed since September 11th, 2001 – over two years without an attack on American soil. And it is tempting to believe that the danger is behind us. That hope is understandable, comforting – and false. The killing has continued in Bali, Jakarta, Casablanca, Riyadh, Mombasa, Jerusalem, Istanbul, and Baghdad. The terrorists continue to plot against America and the civilized world. And by our will and courage, this danger will be defeated. [Applause.]

Inside the United States, where the war began, we must continue to give our homeland security and law enforcement personnel every tool they need to defend us. And one of those essential tools is the Patriot Act, which allows federal law enforcement to better share information, to track terrorists, to disrupt their cells, and to seize their assets. For years, we have used similar provisions to catch embezzlers and drug traffickers. If these methods are good for hunting criminals, they are even more important for hunting terrorists. [Applause.] Key provisions of the Patriot Act are set to expire next year. [Applause.] The terrorist threat will not expire on that schedule. [Applause.] Our law enforcement needs this vital legislation to protect our citizens. You need to renew the Patriot Act. [Applause.]

America is on the offensive against the terrorists who started this war. Last March, Khalid Shaikh Mohammed, a mastermind of September the 11th, awoke to find himself in the custody of U.S. and Pakistani authorities. Last August the 11th brought the capture of the terrorist Hambali, who was a key player in the attack in Indonesia that killed over 200 people. We're tracking al Qaeda around the world, and nearly two-thirds of their known leaders have now been captured or killed. Thousands of very skilled and determined military personnel are on the manhunt, going after the remaining killers who hide in cities and caves, and one by one, we will bring these terrorists to justice. [Applause.]

As part of the offensive against terror, we are also confronting the regimes that harbor and support terrorists, and could supply them with nuclear, chemical or biological weapons. The United States and our allies are determined: We refuse to live in the shadow of this ultimate danger. [Applause.]

The first to see our determination were the Taliban, who made Afghanistan the primary training base of al Qaeda killers. As of this month, that country has a new constitution, guaranteeing free elections and full participation by women. Businesses are opening, health care centers are being established, and the boys and girls of Afghanistan are back in school. With the help from the new Afghan army, our coalition is leading aggressive raids against the surviving members of the Taliban and al Qaeda. The men and women of Afghanistan are building a nation that is free and proud and fighting terror – and America is honored to be their friend. [Applause.]

Since we last met in this chamber, combat forces of the United States, Great Britain, Australia, Poland and other countries enforced the demands of the United Nations, ended the rule of Saddam Hussein, and the people of Iraq are free. [Applause.] Having broken the Ba'athist regime, we face a remnant of violent Saddam supporters. Men who ran away from our troops in battle are now dispersed and attack from the shadows. These killers, joined by foreign terrorists, are a serious, continuing danger. Yet we're making progress against them. The once all-powerful ruler of Iraq was found in a hole, and now sits in a prison cell. [Applause.] Of the top 55 officials of the former regime, we have captured or killed 45. Our forces are on the offensive, leading over 1,600 patrols a day and conducting an average of 180 raids a week. We are dealing with these thugs in Iraq, just as surely as we dealt with Saddam Hussein's evil regime. [Applause.]

The work of building a new Iraq is hard, and it is right. And America has always been willing to do what it takes for what is right. Last January, Iraq's only law was the whim of one brutal man. Today our coalition is working with the Iraqi Governing Council to draft a basic law, with a bill of rights. We're working with Iraqis and the United Nations to prepare for a transition to full Iraqi sovereignty by the end of June.

As democracy takes hold in Iraq, the enemies of freedom will do all in their power to spread violence and fear. They are trying to shake the will of our country and our friends, but the United States of America will never be intimidated by thugs and assassins. [Applause.] The killers will fail, and the Iraqi people will live in freedom. [Applause.]

Month by month, Iraqis are assuming more responsibility for their own security and their own future. And tonight we are honored to welcome one of Iraq's most respected leaders: the current President of the Iraqi Governing Council, Adnan Pachachi. Sir, America stands with you and the Iraqi people as you build a free and peaceful nation. [Applause.]

212

Because of American leadership and resolve, the world is changing for the better. Last month, the leader of Libya voluntarily pledged to disclose and dismantle all of his regime's weapons of mass destruction programs, including a uranium enrichment project for nuclear weapons. Colonel Qadhafi correctly judged that his country would be better off and far more secure without weapons of mass murder. [Applause.]

Nine months of intense negotiations involving the United States and Great Britain succeeded with Libya, while 12 years of diplomacy with Iraq did not. And one reason is clear: For diplomacy to be effective, words must be credible, and no one can now doubt the word of America. [Applause.]

Different threats require different strategies. Along with nations in the region, we're insisting that North Korea eliminate its nuclear program. America and the international community are demanding that Iran meet its commitments and not develop nuclear weapons. America is committed to keeping the world's most dangerous weapons out of the hands of the most dangerous regimes. [Applause.]

When I came to this rostrum on September the 20th, 2001, I brought the police shield of a fallen officer, my reminder of lives that ended, and a task that does not end. I gave to you and to all Americans my complete commitment to securing our country and defeating our enemies. And this pledge, given by one, has been kept by many.

You in the Congress have provided the resources for our defense, and cast the difficult votes of war and peace. Our closest allies have been unwavering. America's intelligence personnel and diplomats have been skilled and tireless. And the men and women of the American military – they have taken the hardest duty. We've seen their skill and their courage in armored charges and midnight raids, and lonely hours on faithful watch. We have seen the joy when they return, and felt the sorrow when one is lost. I've had the honor of meeting our servicemen and women at many posts, from the deck of a carrier in the Pacific to a mess hall in Baghdad.

Many of our troops are listening tonight. And I want you and your families to know: America is proud of you. And my administration, and this Congress, will give you the resources you need to fight and win the war on terror. [Applause.]

I know that some people question if America is really in a war at all. They view terrorism more as a crime, a problem to be solved mainly with law enforcement and indictments. After the World Trade Center was first attacked in 1993, some of the guilty were indicted and tried and convicted, and sent to prison. But the matter was not settled. The terrorists were still training and plotting in other nations, and drawing up more ambitious plans. After the chaos and carnage of September the 11th, it is not enough to serve our enemies with legal papers. The terrorists and their supporters declared war on the United States, and war is what they got. [Applause.]

Some in this chamber, and in our country, did not support the liberation of Iraq. Objections to war often come from principled motives. But let us be candid about the consequences of leaving Saddam Hussein in power. We're seeking all the facts. Already, the Kay Report identified dozens of weapons of mass destruction-related program activities and significant amounts of equipment that Iraq concealed from the United Nations. Had we failed to act, the dictator's weapons of mass destruction programs would continue to this day. Had we failed to act, Security Council resolutions on Iraq would have been revealed as empty threats, weakening the United Nations and encouraging defiance by dictators around the world. Iraq's torture chambers would still be filled with victims, terrified and innocent. The killing fields of Iraq – where hundreds of thousands of men and women and children vanished into the sands – would still be known only to the killers. For all who love freedom and peace, the world without Saddam Hussein's regime is a better and safer place. [Applause.]

Some critics have said our duties in Iraq must be internationalized. This particular criticism is hard to explain to our partners in Britain, Australia, Japan, South Korea, the Philippines, Thailand, Italy, Spain, Poland, Denmark, Hungary, Bulgaria, Ukraine, Romania, the Netherlands – [Applause] – Norway, El Salvador, and the 17 other countries that have committed troops to Iraq. [Applause.] As we debate at home, we must never ignore the vital contributions of our international partners, or dismiss their sacrifices.

From the beginning, America has sought international support for our operations in Afghanistan and Iraq, and we have gained much support. There is a difference, however, between leading a coalition of many nations, and submitting to the objections of a few. America will never seek a permission slip to defend the security of our country. [Applause.]

We also hear doubts that democracy is a realistic goal for the greater Middle East, where freedom is rare. Yet it is mistaken, and condescending, to assume that whole cultures and great religions are incompatible with liberty and self-government. I believe that God has planted in every human heart the desire to live in freedom. And even when that desire is crushed by tyranny for decades, it will rise again. [Applause.]

As long as the Middle East remains a place of tyranny and despair and anger, it will continue to produce men and movements that threaten the safety of America and our friends. So America is pursuing a forward strategy of freedom in the greater Middle East. We will challenge the enemies of reform, confront the allies of terror, and expect a higher standard from our friend. To cut through the barriers of hateful propaganda, the Voice of America and other broadcast services are expanding their programming in Arabic and Persian – and soon, a new television service will begin providing reliable news and information across the region. I will send you a proposal to double the budget of the National Endowment for Democracy, and to focus its new work on the development of free elections, and free markets, free press, and free labor unions in the Middle East. And above all, we will finish the historic work of democracy in Afghanistan and Iraq, so those nations can light the way for others, and help transform a troubled part of the world. [Applause.]

America is a nation with a mission, and that mission comes from our most basic beliefs. We have no desire to dominate, no ambitions of empire. Our aim is a democratic peace – a peace founded upon the dignity and rights of every man and woman. America acts in this cause with friends and allies at our side, yet we understand our special calling: This great republic will lead the cause of freedom. [Applause.]

[...]

For all Americans, the last three years have brought tests we did not ask for, and achievements shared by all. By our actions, we have shown what kind of nation we are. In grief, we have found the grace to go on. In challenge, we rediscovered the courage and daring of a free people. In victory, we have shown the noble aims and good heart of America. And having come this far, we sense that we live in a time set apart.

I've been witness to the character of the people of America, who have shown calm in times of danger, compassion for one another, and toughness for the long haul. All of us have been partners in a great enterprise. And even some of the youngest understand that we are living in historic times. Last month a girl in Lincoln, Rhode Island, sent me a letter.

214

It began, 'Dear George W. Bush. If there's anything you know, I, Ashley Pearson, age 10, can do to help anyone, please send me a letter and tell me what I can do to save our country.' She added this P.S.: 'If you can send a letter to the troops, please put, "Ashley Pearson believes in you."' [Applause.]

Tonight, Ashley, your message to our troops has just been conveyed. And, yes, you have some duties yourself. Study hard in school, listen to your mom or dad, help someone in need, and when you and your friends see a man or woman in uniform, say, 'thank you.' [Applause.] And, Ashley, while you do your part, all of us here in this great chamber will do our best to keep you and the rest of America safe and free. [Applause.]

My fellow citizens, we now move forward, with confidence and faith. Our nation is strong and steadfast. The cause we serve is right, because it is the cause of all mankind. The momentum of freedom in our world is unmistakable – and it is not carried forward by our power alone. We can trust in that greater power who guides the unfolding of the years. And in all that is to come, we can know that His purposes are just and true.

May God continue to bless America. [Applause.]

References

Books and articles

Anderson, B., 1983. *Imagined Communities*, London: Verso.

Aune, J., 2003. 'The argument from evil in the rhetoric of reaction', *Rhetoric & Public Affairs*, 6(3): 518–22.

Barker, J., 2002. *The No-Nonsense Guide to Terrorism*, Oxford: New Internationalist Publications.

Bergen, P., 2001. *Holy War Inc.: Inside the Secret World of Osama bin Laden*, London: Weidenfeld & Nicolson.

Betts, R., 2002. 'The soft underbelly of American primacy: Tactical advantages of terror', *Political Science Quarterly*, 117(1): 19–36.

Boggs, C., 2003. 'Introduction: Empire and globalization', in C. Boggs, ed., *Masters of War: Militarism and Blowback in the Era of American Empire*, New York and London: Routledge.

Bowman, G., 1994. 'Xenophobia, fantasy and the nation: The logic of ethnic violence in former Yugoslavia', in V. Goddard, J. Llobera and C. Shore, eds, *Anthropology of Europe: Identity and Boundaries in Conflict*, available online at www.ukc.ac.uk/anthropology/staff/glenn/Goldsmit.html, accessed May 10, 2002.

Burbach, R. and B. Clarke, eds, 2002. *September 11 and the U.S. War: Beyond the Curtain of Smoke*, San Francisco: City Lights Books.

Callinicos, A., 2003. *The New Mandarins of American Power*, Cambridge: Polity Press.

Campbell, D., 1998. *Writing Security: United States Foreign Policy and the Politics of Identity*, revised edition, Manchester: Manchester University Press.

Campbell, D., 2002. 'Time is broken: The return of the past in the response to September 11', *Theory & Event*, 5(4).

Card, C., 2003. 'Forum: questions regarding a war on terrorism', *Hypatia*, 18(1): 164–9.

Carruthers, S., 2000. *The Media at War: Communication and Conflict in the Twentieth Century*, London: Macmillan.

Carter, A., J. Deutch and P. Zelikow, 1998. 'Catastrophic terrorism', *Foreign Affairs*, 77(6): 80–94.

Chomsky, N., 2001. *9/11*, New York: Seven Seals Press.

References

Chomsky, N., 2002. 'Who are the global terrorists?', in K. Booth and T. Dunne, eds, *Worlds in Collision: Terror and the Future of Global Order*, New York: Palgrave Macmillan.

Chomsky, N., 2003. 'The war on terrorism', *Perspectives on Evil and Human Wickedness*, 1(2): 8–11.

Cloud, D., 2003. 'Introduction: Evil in the agora', *Rhetoric & Public Affairs*, 6(3): 509–10.

Cole, D., 2003. *Enemy Aliens: Double Standards and Constitutional Freedoms in the War on Terrorism*, New York and London: The New Press.

Collins, J. and R. Glover, eds, 2002. *Collateral Language: A User's Guide to America's New War*, New York: New York University Press.

Corrado, R., 1981. 'A critique of the mental disorder perspective of political terrorism', *International Journal of Law and Psychiatry*, 4(3–4): 293–309.

Crenshaw, M., 1981. 'The causes of terrorism', *Comparative Politics*, 13: 379–99.

Crenshaw, M., 1992. 'How terrorists think: What psychology can contribute to understanding terrorism', in L. Howard, ed., *Terrorism: Roots, Impact, Responses*, London: Praeger.

Crenshaw, M., ed., 1995. *Terrorism in Context*, University Park, PA: Pennsylvania State University Press.

Der Derian, J., 2002a. '*In terrorem*: Before and after 9/11', in K. Booth and T. Dunne, eds, *Worlds in Vollision: Terror and the Future of Global Order*, New York: Palgrave Macmillan.

Der Derian, J., 2002b. 'The war of networks', *Theory & Event*, 5(4).

El Fadl, K., 2002. 'Introduction', in K. El Fadl, ed., *Shattered Illusions: Analyzing the War on Terrorism*, Bristol: Amal Press.

Elshtain, J. 2002. 'How to fight a just war', in K. Booth and T. Dunne, eds, *Worlds in Collision: Terror and the Future of Global Order*, New York: Palgrave Macmillan.

Enloe, C., 2002. 'Masculinity as a foreign policy issue', in S. Hawthorne and B. Winter, eds, *September 11, 2001: Feminist Perspectives*, Melbourne: Spinifex Press.

Evans, M., 2004. 'Idealists rush to join MI5's army of spies', *The Times* (London), March 2, 2004.

Fairclough, N. 1992. *Discourse and Social Change*, Cambridge: Polity Press.

Fairclough, N., 1995. *Media Discourse*, London: Edward Arnold.

Falk, R., 2001. 'Defining a just war', *The Nation*, October 29, 2001.

Falk, R. 2002. 'Testing patriotism and citizenship in the global terror war', in K. Booth and T. Dunne, eds, *Worlds in Collision: Terror and the Future of Global Order*, New York: Palgrave Macmillan.

Falkenrath, R. 2001. *America's Achilles' Heel: Nuclear, Biological and Chemical Terrorism and Covert Attack*, 4th edition, London: MIT Press.

Foucault, M., 1977. *Discipline and Punishment: The Birth of the Prison*, New York: Vintage.

Freedman, L., ed., 2002. *Superterrorism: Policy Responses*, Oxford: Blackwell.

Friedman, T., 2002. *Longitudes and Attitudes: Exploring the World Before and After September 11*, London: Penguin Books.

Glassner, B., 1999. *The Culture of Fear: Why Americans are Afraid of the Wrong Things*, New York: Basic Books.

Gupta, S., 2002. *The Replication of Violence: Thoughts on International Terrorism After September 11th 2001*, London: Pluto Press.

Hanson, V., 2002. *An Autumn of War: What America Learned from September 11 and the War on Terrorism*, New York: Anchor Books.

Hariman, R., 2003. 'Speaking of evil', *Rhetoric & Public Affairs*, 6(3): 511–17.

Herman, E. and N. Chomsky, 1988. *Manufacturing Consent: The Political-Economy of the Mass Media*, New York: Pantheon.

Herold, M., 2002. '"Collateral damage"? Civilians and the U.S. air war in Afghanistan', in K. El Fadl, ed., *Shattered Illusions: Analyzing the War on Terrorism*, Bristol: Amal Press.

Hertsgaard, M., 2002. *The Eagle's Shadow: Why America Fascinates and Infuriates the World*, London: Bloomsbury.

Hiro, D., 2002. *War Without End: The Rise of Islamist Terrorism and Global Response*, London and New York: Routledge.

Hodgson, D., 2000. *Discourse, Discipline and the Subject: A Foucauldian Analysis of the UK Financial Services Industry*, Aldershot, UK: Ashgate.

Horgan, J., 2003. 'The search for the terrorist personality', in A. Silke, ed., *Terrorists, Victims and Society: Psychological Perspectives on Terrorism and its Consequences*, Chichester, UK: John Wiley & Sons.

Hough, P., 2004. *Understanding Global Security*, London and New York: Routledge.

Hughes, R., 2003. *Myths America Lives By*, Urbana and Chicago: University of Illinois Press.

Hurrell, A., 2002. '"There are no rules" (George W. Bush): International order after September 11', *International Relations*, 16(2): 185–204.

Jabri, V., 1996. *Discourses on Violence: Conflict Analysis Reconsidered*, Manchester: Manchester University Press.

Jackson, R., (forthcoming). *What Causes Intra-State Conflict? Theories and Approaches to the Causes of Internal War*, Manchester: Manchester University Press.

Jenkins, B., 1998. 'Will terrorists go nuclear? A reappraisal', in H. Kushner, ed., *The Future of Terrorism: Violence in the New Millennium*, London: Sage.

Jorgensen, M. and L. Phillips, 2002. *Discourse Analysis as Theory and Method*, London: Sage.

Kampfner, J., 2003. *Blair's Wars*. London: The Free Press.

Kaplan, A., 2003. 'Homeland insecurities: Reflections on language and space', *Radical History Review*, 85: 82–93.

Kaufman, S., 2001. *Modern Hatreds: The Symbolic Politics of Ethnic War*, London: Cornell University Press.

Kern, M., M. Just and P. Norris, 2003. 'The lessons of framing terrorism', in P. Norris, M. Kern and M. Just, eds, *Framing Terrorism: The News Media, the Government, and the Public*, New York: Routledge.

Laqueur, W., 1999. *The New Terrorism: Fanaticism and the Arms of Mass Destruction*, Oxford: Oxford University Press.

Lawler, P., 2002. 'The "good war" after September 11', *Government and Opposition*, 37(2): 151–72

Lewis, J., 2002. 'Speaking of wars …', *Television & New Media*, 3(2): 169–72.

Lewis, J., R. Maxwell and T. Miller, 2002. 'Editorial: 9-11', *Television & New Media*, 3(2): 125–31.

Lincoln, B., 2002. *Holy Terrors: Thinking About Religion after September 11*, Chicago: Chicago University Press.

Livingston, S., 1994. *The Terrorism Spectacle*, Boulder: Westview Press.

References

Llorente, M., 2002. 'Civilization versus barbarism', in J. Collins and R. Glover, eds, *Collateral Language: A User's guide to America's New War*, New York: New York University Press.

Louw, E., 2003. 'The "war against terrorism": A public relations challenge for the Pentagon', *Gazette: The International Journal for Communication Studies*, 65(3): 211–30.

Lynas, M., 2004. 'Essay: The sixth mass extinction', *New Statesman*, 23 February, 2004.

Macallister, C., 2004. 'The (re)legitimisation of state violence in Britain and the USA', in R. Jackson, ed., *(Re)constructing Cultures of Violence and Peace*, Amsterdam and New York: Rodopi.

Maxwell, R., 2002. 'Honour among patriots?', *Television & New Media*, 3(2): 239–48.

McCarthy, E., 2002. 'Justice', in J. Collins and R. Glover, eds, *Collateral Language: A User's Guide to America's New War*, New York: New York University Press.

McChesney, R., 2002. 'The zillionth time as tragedy', *Television & New Media*, 3(2): 133–7.

McDaniel, J., 2003. 'Figures of evil: A triad of rhetorical strategies for theo-politics', *Rhetoric & Public Affairs*, 6(3): 539–50.

MacDonald, D., 2002. *Balkan Holocaust? Serbian and Croatian Victim-Centred Propaganda and the War in Yugoslavia*, Manchester: Manchester University Press.

McGreal, R., 2003. 'Paradigm bait and switch', *Perspectives on Evil and Human Wickedness*, 1(2): 99–107.

Mahajan, R., 2002. *The New Crusade: America's War on Terrorism*, New York: Monthly Review Press.

Mahajan, R., 2003. *Full Spectrum Dominance: U.S. Power in Iraq and Beyond*, New York: Seven Stories Press.

Martin, G., 2003. *Understanding Terrorism: Challenges, Perspectives, and Issues*, London: Sage.

Maxwell, R., 2002. 'Honor among patriots?', *Television & New Media*, 3(2): 239–48.

Miller, D., 2002. 'Opinion polls and the misrepresentation of public opinion on the war with Afghanistan', *Television & New Media*, 3(2): 153–61.

Morris, R., 2002. 'Theses on the questions of war: History, media, terror', *Social Text* 20(3): 149–75.

Murphy, J., 2003. '"Our mission and our moment": George W. Bush and September 11', *Rhetoric and Public Affairs*, 6(4): 607–32.

Nacos, B., 2002. *Mass-Mediated Terrorism: The Central Role of the Media in Terrorism and Counterterrorism*, New York: Rowman & Littlefield.

Nacos, B., and O. Torres-Reyna, 2003. 'Framing Muslim-Americans before and after 9/11', in P. Norris, M. Kern and M. Just, eds, *Framing Terrorism: The News Media, the Government, and the Public*, New York: Routledge.

Neisser, P., 2002. 'Targets', in J. Collins and R. Glover, eds, *Collateral Language: A User's Guide to America's New War*, New York: New York University Press.

Neuffer, E., 2001. *The Key to My Neighbor's House: Seeking Justice in Bosnia and Rwanda*, London: Bloomsbury.

Norris, P., M. Kern and M. Just, 2003. 'Framing terrorism', in P. Norris, M. Kern and M. Just, eds, *Framing Terrorism: The News Media, the Government, and the Public*, New York: Routledge.

North, M., 2002. 'Dangers of the armed response at home', in P. Scraton, ed., *Beyond September 11: An Anthropology of Dissent*, London: Pluto Press.

References

Parmar, I. (forthcoming). 'Catalysing events, think tanks and American foreign policy shifts: A comparative analysis of the impacts of Pearl Harbor 1941 and September 11 2001', *Government and Opposition*.

Passavant, P. and J. Dean, 2002. 'Representation and the event', *Theory & Event*, 5(4).

Pfaff, W., 2003. 'Scaring America half to death', *International Herald Tribune*, 8 May, 2003.

Pilger, J. 2004. 'Get out now', *New Statesman*, 19 April, 2004, 10–12.

Pollard, T., 2003. 'The Hollywood war machine', in C. Boggs, ed., *Masters of War: Militarism and Blowback in the Era of American Empire*, New York and London: Routledge.

Rampton, S. and J. Stauber, 2003. *Weapons of Mass Deception: The Uses of Propaganda in Bush's War on Iraq*, London: Robinson.

Rasmussen, M., 2002. '"A parallel globalization of terror": 9-11, security and globalization', *Cooperation and Conflict*, 37(3): 323–49.

Rediehs, L., 2002. 'Evil', in J. Collins and R. Glover, eds, *Collateral Language: A User's Guide to America's New War*, New York: New York University Press.

Religion News Service, 2002. 'Christian ethicists: Afghan war is just', *Christianity Today*, 46(3): 23.

Rosenberg, E., 2003. *A Date Which Will Live: Pearl Harbor in American Memory*, Durham and London: Duke University Press.

Rubenstein, R., 1987. *Alchemists of Revolution: Terrorism in the Modern World*, New York: Basic Books.

Said, E. 1978. *Orientalism*, New York: Pantheon Books.

Salter, M., 2002. *Barbarians and Civilization in International Relations*, London: Pluto Press.

Sardar, Z. and M. Davies, 2002. *Why do People Hate America?*, Cambridge: Icon Books.

Schechter, D., 2003. *Media Wars: News at a Time of Terror*, Lanham: Rowman & Littlefield.

Schweitzer, G., 1999. *Superterrorism: Assassins, Mobsters, and Weapons of Mass Destruction*, London: Plenum Press.

Scraton, P., ed., 2002. *Beyond September 11: An Anthology of Dissent*, London: Pluto Press.

Shpiro, S., 2002. 'Conflict media strategies and the politics of counter-terrorism', *Politics*, 22(2): 76–85.

Silberstein, S., 2002. *War of Words: Language, Politics and 9/11*, London: Routledge.

Silke, A., 1998. 'Cheshire-cat logic: the recurring theme of terrorist abnormality in psychological research', *Psychology, Crime and Law*, 4: 51–69.

Singh, N. 2003. 'Cold war redux: on the "new totalitarianism"', *Radical History Review*, Issue 85: 171–81.

Snow, N. 2003. *Information War: American Propaganda, Free Speech and Opinion Control Since 9-11*, New York: Seven Stories Press.

Solomon, N., 2002. 'Media war without end', in R. Burbach and B. Clarke, eds, *September 11 and the U.S. War: Beyond the Curtain of Smoke*, San Francisco: City Lights Books.

Solomon, N., 2003. 'Mass media: Aiding and abetting militarism', in C. Boggs, ed., *Masters of War: Militarism and Blowback in the Era of American Empire*, New York and London: Routledge.

Sprinzak, E., 1998. 'The great superterrorism scare', *Foreign Policy*, Fall, 112: 110–24.

Sterling, C., 1981. *The Terror Network: The Secret War of International Terrorism*, New York: Holt, Rinehart, and Winston.

Stern, J., 1999. *The Ultimate Terrorists*, London: Harvard University Press.

Stoddard, E. and G. Cornwell, 2002. 'Unity', in J. Collins and R. Glover, eds, *Collateral Language: A User's Guide to America's New War*, New York: New York University Press.

Thomas, P., 2002. 'Legislative responses to terrorism', in P. Scraton, ed., *Beyond September 11: An Anthology of Dissent*, London: Pluto Press.

Tickner, J., 2002. 'Feminist perspectives on 9/11', *International Studies Perspectives*, 3: 333–50.

Tilly, C. 1985. 'War making and state making as organised crime', in P. Evans, D. Rueschemeyer and T. Skocpol, eds, *Bringing the State Back In*, Cambridge: Cambridge University Press.

Townshend, C., 2002. *Terrorism: A Very Short Introduction*, Oxford: Oxford University Press.

Troyer, L., 2002. 'The calling of counterterrorism', *Theory & Event*, 5(4).

Van Ham, P., 2003. 'War, lies, and videotape: Public diplomacy and the USA's war on terrorism', *Security Dialogue*, 34(4): 427–44.

Walzer, M. 1992. *Just and Unjust Wars: A Moral Argument with Historical Illustrations*, 2nd edition, New York: Basic Books.

Wendt, A., 1992. 'Anarchy is what states make of it', *International Organization*, 46: 391–425.

Wheeler, N. 2002. 'Dying for "enduring freedom": Accepting responsibility for civilian casualties in the war against terrorism', *International Relations*, 16(2): 205–25.

Wight, M., 1978. *Power Politics*, edited by H. Bull and C. Holbraad, Leicester: Leicester University Press.

Wills, D., 2003. *The First War on Terrorism: Counter-Terrorism Policy During the Reagan Administration*, Lanham: Rowman & Littlefield.

Wilmer, F., 2002. *The Social Construction of Man, the State, and War: Identity, Conflict, and Violence in the Former Yugoslavia*, New York and London: Routledge.

Woodward, B., 2002. *Bush at War*, London and New York: Pocket Books.

Yallop, D., 1993. *To the Ends of the Earth: The Hunt for the Jackal*, London: Jonathan Cape.

Younge, G. 'Now dissent is "immoral"', *Guardian*, 2 June, 2003.

Zulaika, J., 2003. 'The self-fulfilling prophesies of counterterrorism', *Radical History Review*, 85 (Winter 2003): 191–9.

Zulaika, J. and W. Douglass, 1996. *Terror and Taboo: The Follies, Fables, and Faces of Terrorism*, New York and London: Routledge.

Speeches and documents cited

Note: All American administration speeches on terrorism are available online at http://usinfo.state.gov/topical/pol/terror/

Amnesty International, 2004. *Amnesty International Report 2004*, available online at http://web.amnesty.org/report2004/index-eng

Antiwar.com, a division of the Randolph Bourne Institute. Available online at www.antiwar.com/casualties

Ashcroft, John, Attorney General, Testimony to House Committee on the Judiciary, September 24, 2001.

References

Ashcroft, John, Attorney General, Prepared Remarks for the US Mayors Conference, October 25, 2001.

Ashcroft, John, Attorney General, News Conference with Immigration and Naturalization Service Commissioner James Ziglar and Steve McGraw, Newly Appointed Director Foreign Terrorist Tracking Task Force, Department of Justice Conference Center, October 31, 2001.

Ashcroft, John, Attorney General, News Conference Announcing Responsible Cooperation Program, Department of Justice Conference Room, November 29, 2001.

Baker, Howard H. Jr., U.S. Ambassador, Japanese Observance Ceremony for Victims of Terrorism in the US, September 23, 2001, Tokyo.

Black, Cofer, Spokesman Coordinator for Counterterrorism, US Department of State, Press Conference for 2002 Annual Report 'Patterns of Global Terrorism', Washington, DC, April 30, 2003.

Blair, Dennis, Admiral, Commander-in-Chief of the US Pacific Command, 'Taking Back Our World from Osama bin Laden', Released by the Office of the US Commander-in-Chief, Pacific Command (CINCPAC), October, 23, 2001.

Bush, George W., Remarks by the President to Journalists, Emma Booker Elementary School, Sarasota, Florida, September 11, 2001a.

Bush, George W., Statement by the President in His Address to the Nation, September 11, 2001b.

Bush, George W., President's Remarks at National Day of Prayer and Remembrance, the National Cathedral, Washington, DC, September 14, 2001.

Bush, George W., President, Secretary of State Colin Powell, and Attorney General John Ashcroft, Remarks at Camp David, September 15, 2001.

Bush, George W., President, Remarks by the President at Islamic Center of Washington, DC, September 17, 2001.

Bush, George W., Address to a Joint Session of Congress and the American People, September 20, 2001.

Bush, George W., Statement by the President on Military Strikes in Afghanistan, The Treaty Room, White House, October 7, 2001.

Bush, George W., Press Conference, The East Room, Washington, DC, October 11, 2001.

Bush, George W., Remarks by the President to the CEO Summit, Pudong Shangri-La Hotel, Shanghai, People's Republic of China, October 20, 2001.

Bush, George W., Remarks by the President to Employees of the Dixie Printing Company, Dixie Printing Company, Glen Burnie, Maryland, The White House, Office of the Press Secretary, October 24, 2001.

Bush, George W., Radio Address of the President to the Nation, October 27, 2001.

Bush, George W., Radio Address by the President to the Nation, November 24, 2001.

Bush, George W., Presidential Remarks to US Attorneys Conference, Dwight David Eisenhower Office Building, November 29, 2001.

Bush, George W., The President's State of the Union Address, January 29, 2002.

Bush, George W., The President's Remarks to the Nation on the Anniversary of September 11, 2001, Ellis Island, New York, September 11, 2002.

Bush, George W., Remarks by the President at the 2002 Graduation Exercise of the United States Military Academy, West Point, New York, June 1, 2002.

References

Bush, George W., Remarks by the President at the Signing of HR 5005, The Homeland Security Act of 2002, The East Room, Washington, DC, November 25, 2002.

Bush, George W., Remarks to the Employees of United Defense Industries Ground Systems Division, United Defense Industries, Santa Clara, California, May 2, 2003.

Bush, George W., Remarks in Commencement Address To United States Coast Guard Academy, Nitchman Field, New London, Connecticut, May 21, 2003.

Bush, George W., Remarks to the People of Poland, Wawel Royal Castle, Krakow, Poland, May 31, 2003.

Cheney, Dick, Vice-President, Remarks to the American Society of News Editors, The Fairmont Hotel, New Orleans, April 9, 2003.

Cheney, Dick, Vice President, Remarks to the Heritage Foundation, The Ronald Reagan Building, Washington, DC. May 1, 2003.

Dam, Kenneth W., Deputy US Treasury Secretary, 'Money That Kills: The Financial Front of the War On Terrorism', News From The Office Of Public Affairs, October 22, 2001.

Grossman, Marc, Interview of Under Secretary of State, Digital Video Conference October 19, 2001 Washington, DC A trans-Atlantic digital interview with London-based journalists of Arab newspapers.

Hartung, W., 2003. 'The hidden costs of war', A Report Commissioned by Howard S. Brembeck and the Fourth Freedom Forum, 14 February 2003, URL: www.fourthfreedom.org/php/t-si-index.php?hinc=Hartung_report.hinc, accessed 29 August, 2003.

Institute for American Values, 2002. What We're Fighting For: A Letter from America, available at www.americanvalues.org/html/wwff.html

IraqBodyCount.com Open Community, available online at www.iraqbodycount.com/forum

Iraq Coalition Casualty Count, available online at www.icasualties.org/oif

Kerry, John, Senator (D), Speech on National Security', Georgetown University, Washington, January 23, 2003, available online at: www.gwu.edu/~action/2004/issues/kerr012303spfp.html

Kerry, John, Senator (D), 'Making America Secure Again: Setting the Right Course for Foreign Policy', An Address to the Council on Foreign Relations, New York, December 3, 2003, available online at www.gwu.edu/~action/2004/issues/kerr120303spfp.html.

Kerry, John, Senator (D), 'Fighting a Comprehensive War on Terrorism', Remarks by Senator John Kerry at the Ronald W. Burkle Center for International Relations, University of California at Los Angeles, February 27, 2004, available online at www.johnkerry.com/pressroom/speeches/spc_2004_0227.html

Land, R., 2001. 'Draining the swamp of terrorists', available online at www.christianity.com/partner/Article_Display_Page/0,,PTID314166|CHID596454|CIID1552430,00.html

Lantos, Tom, (Representative, Democrat, California), Statement on Fighting Terrorism, 10 October, 2001.

Melshen, Paul, Marine Colonel, Address to Inter-Governmental Authority on Development (IGAD) conference, June 27, 2003.

Powell, Colin L., Secretary of State, Interview on NBC's Meet The Press, September 23, 2001.

Powell, Colin L., Remarks by the Secretary of State to the National Foreign Policy Conference for Leaders of Nongovernmental Organisations (NGO), Loy Henderson Conference Room, U.S. Department of State, Washington, DC, October 26, 2001.

Powell, Colin L., Secretary of State, Interview on CBS's Face the Nation with Bob Schieffer, October 21, 2001.

Powell, Colin L., Secretary of State, Release of the 2002 'Patterns of Global Terrorism' Annual Report, US Department of State, Washington, DC, April 30, 2003.

Rice, Condoleeza, National Security Advisor, Interview by Al Jazeera Television, October 15, 2001.

Rice, Condoleeza, National Security Advisor, Foreign Press Center Briefing, The Washington Foreign Press Center, Washington, DC, May 14, 2003.

Robertson, Pat, 'The roots of terrorism and a strategy for victory', Address to the Economic Club of Detroit, March 25, 2002, available online at www.patrobertson.com/Speeches/TerrorismEconomicClub.asp

Rumsfeld, Donald H., Secretary of Defense, with Chairman of the Joint Chiefs of Staff Gen. Henry H. Shelton, Assistant Secretary of Defense (Public Affairs) Victoria Clarke, and Assistant Secretary of Defense (Force Management Policy) Charles S. Abell, News Briefing, Department of Defense, September 27, 2001.

Rumsfeld, Donald H., Secretary of Defense, and Joint Chiefs of Staff, Gen. Richard Myers, Briefing on Enduring Freedom, The Pentagon, October 7, 2001.

Rumsfeld, Donald H., Secretary of Defense, and Joint Chiefs of Staff, Gen. Richard Myers, Press Briefing, The Pentagon, October 8, 2001.

Rumsfeld, Donald H., Secretary of Defense, Remarks at a Memorial Service in Remembrance of Those Lost on September 11th, The Pentagon, Arlington, VA Thursday, October 11, 2001

Rumsfeld, Donald H., Secretary of Defense, Interview with Al Jazeera Television, October 16, 2001

Rumsfeld, Donald H., Secretary of Defense, Interview with editorial board of USA Today, News Transcript from the United States Department of Defense, October 24, 2001.

Rumsfeld, Donald H., Secretary of Defense, Interview with Wolf Blitzer, CNN, October 28, 2001.

Wolfowitz, Paul, Deputy Secretary of Defense, Prepared Testimony: 'Building a Military for the 21st Century', to the Senate Armed Services Committee, October 4, 2001.

Index

Abu Ghraib 5, 37, 62, 75, 89, 91, 157
  see also interrogation; Iraqi prisoner abuse
    scandal; prisoners; torture
academic institutions 6, 20, 23, 105, 164,
    172–5, 177, 184, 188
act of war 5, 31, 38–40, 42–3, 53, 122,
    125, 156, 176
  see also Twin Towers
ACTA *see* American Council of Trustees and
    Alumni
Afghanistan 3, 9–16 *passim*, 36, 43, 50, 58,
    73–5, 78–84 *passim*, 89–90, 93, 109,
    118, 123, 125, 127, 130–7 *passim*,
    141, 146–7, 151, 155, 157–9, 162,
    168, 170–1, 174, 180, 185, 187
  see also Operation Enduring Freedom;
    Taliban
African embassy bombings 16
al Qaeda 11, 37, 43, 50–8 *passim*, 75,
    97–8, 102, 105, 109, 111, 128–30,
    158, 163, 172, 174–5
Albright, Madeline 144, 146
Algeria 37, 93
alien 5, 61, 70–5, 90, 108
  invasion movies 71
  terrorists 71–2, 74
  see also enemy aliens; foreign terrorists
Alien Enemy Bureau 71
alternative counter-terrorism strategies 6,
    40, 140–1, 184, 188
alternative discourses 19–20, 37, 105, 153,
    159, 161, 168
alternative narratives 27, 51, 56, 58, 154,
    159, 161, 188
alternative readings 31, 54–5
American Council of Trustees and Alumni
    175
American exceptionalism 35, 142, 144,
    154, 186
  see also God's chosen nation;
    indispensable nation; nature's nation
American foreign policy 2–5, 31, 37, 54–6,
    76, 108, 123, 158, 162–3, 167, 170,
    186

American hegemony 52, 58
American military 12, 15–16, 37, 43, 47,
    55, 58, 108, 135, 183, 186
American political discourse 68, 83–4, 154
American political life 2, 20, 84, 114, 122,
    142, 177
Amnesty International 13, 89
analogies 40–1, 47, 51, 58, 158
Anderson, Benedict 61
  see also imagined community
animals 5, 48–9, 73, 75
  see also inhuman terrorists
Annan, Secretary General Kofi 12
anti-Americanism 13, 186
anti-globalisation 19, 23, 55, 83
anti-modern 53, 55–6
Argentina 131, 183–4
assassination 9, 14, 29, 33, 40, 95, 123,
    130, 146, 180, 182
  see also covert operations
asylum seekers 13, 182
axis of evil 44, 46, 68, 106, 146–7

Baghram 73
  see also Afghanistan; Guantanamo Bay
barbarism 2, 5, 21, 31, 38, 41, 47–59
    passim, 62, 66, 73, 90, 140, 142,
    154–5, 160, 176–7
  see also new barbarians; savage
Bergen, Peter 56
bifurcation 86, 88, 184
bin Laden, Osama 19, 56, 65–6, 129–30,
    138, 141, 144, 157, 168, 170
  see also al Qaeda
binary structure of language 21, 48, 62–3,
    72, 82, 146, 149
biological weapons 22, 96, 101–2, 104–7,
    161, 173, 177
Blair, Tony 91, 164, 172
Blunkett, David 111
Britain 10, 16, 37, 41, 91–3, 116–18, 131,
    163, 180, 183
Bush doctrine 11, 126